Couples on the Couch

Couples on the Couch provides a clear guide to applying the Tavistock model of couple psychotherapy in clinical psychoanalytic practice, offering a compelling sampling of ideas about couple relationships and couple psychotherapy from a broadly relational psychoanalytic perspective. The book provides an in-depth perspective to understanding intimate relationships and the complexities of working in this domain. The chapters and their accompanying discussion also offer a fertile resource of material for readers who have not previously had exposure to the theory and technique of psychoanalytic psychotherapy, as well as offering an expanded and more rigorous approach to those who are already familiar with the Tavistock model. The chapters cover key topics, including: unconscious beliefs, forms of couple relating, sex and aging, and draw upon the work of Klein, Winnicott and Bion, as well as attachment and object relations theory.

The majority of the contributors are affiliated with the Tavistock Centre for Couple Relations (TCCR) in London or The Psychoanalytic Couple Psychotherapy Group (PCPG) in Berkeley, California, and make fundamental use of the theoretical model that has been developed at TCCR since the 1940s. *Couples on the Couch* provides an introduction to the TCCR approach to couple psychotherapy and exposure to the depth and breadth of this framework. Each of the chapters contains in-depth theoretical and clinical case material, presented in tandem with formal discussion, demonstrating how theory may be applied in a variety of clinical encounters and, by doing so, deepening the theoretical understanding of the difficulties that beset couples and the challenges posed to those who work with them. The book provides an in-depth perspective to understanding intimate relationships and the complexities of working in this domain.

Couples on the Couch will be of great interest to couple psychotherapists and counselors, marriage and family therapists, psychoanalysts, as well as graduate and postgraduate students in psychology, marriage and family therapy, or those in psychoanalytic training programs.

Shelley Nathans, Ph.D. is on the faculty at California Pacific Medical Center, Psychoanalytic Couple Psychotherapy Group, and the Psychoanalytic Institute of Northern California. She has authored papers on infidelity and projective identification in couples, and is the director and producer of the film *Robert Wallerstein: 65 Years at the Center of Psychoanalysis*. She is in private practice in San Francisco and Oakland.

Milton Schaefer, Ph.D. is a psychoanalyst in private practice in San Francisco. He is on the faculty at the San Francisco Center for Psychoanalysis where he has taught Relational Theory and Couples Therapy and is a faculty member of the Psychoanalytic Couples Psychotherapy Group. He has presented and published on high conflict divorce, ethical issues, and psychoanalysis and art.

RELATIONAL PERSPECTIVES BOOK SERIES

LEWIS ARON & ADRIENNE HARRIS
Series Co-Editors
STEVEN KUCHUCK & EYAL ROZMARIN
Associate Editors

The Relational Perspectives Book Series (RPBS) publishes books that grow out of or contribute to the relational tradition in contemporary psychoanalysis. The term *relational psychoanalysis* was first used by Greenberg and Mitchell[1] to bridge the traditions of interpersonal relations, as developed within interpersonal psychoanalysis, and object relations, as developed within contemporary British theory. But, under the seminal work of the late Stephen A. Mitchell, the term *relational psychoanalysis* grew and began to accrue to itself many other influences and developments. Various tributaries – interpersonal psychoanalysis, object relations theory, self psychology, empirical infancy research, and elements of contemporary Freudian and Kleinian thought – flow into this tradition, which understands relational configurations between self and others, both real and fantasied, as the primary subject of psychoanalytic investigation.

We refer to the relational tradition, rather than to a relational school, to highlight that we are identifying a trend, a tendency within contemporary psychoanalysis, not a more formally organized or coherent school or system of beliefs. Our use of the term *relational* signifies a dimension of theory and practice that has become salient across the wide spectrum of contemporary psychoanalysis. Now under the editorial supervision of Lewis Aron and Adrienne Harris, with the assistance of Associate Editors Steven Kuchuck and Eyal Rozmarin, the Relational Perspectives Book Series originated in 1990 under the editorial eye of the late Stephen A. Mitchell. Mitchell was the most prolific and influential of the originators of the relational tradition. Committed to dialogue among psychoanalysts, he abhorred the authoritarianism that dictated adherence to a rigid set of beliefs or technical restrictions. He championed open discussion, comparative and integrative approaches, and promoted new voices across the generations.

Included in the Relational Perspectives Book Series are authors and works that come from within the relational tradition, extend and develop that tradition, as well as works that critique relational approaches or compare and contrast it with alternative points of view. The series includes our most distinguished senior psychoanalysts, along with younger contributors who bring fresh vision. A full list of titles in this series is available at www.routledge.com/series/LEARPBS.

1 Greenberg, J. & Mitchell, S. (1983). *Object relations in psychoanalytic theory.* Cambridge, MA: Harvard University Press.

Couples on the Couch

Psychoanalytic Couple Psychotherapy and the Tavistock Model

Edited by Shelley Nathans
and Milton Schaefer

Routledge
Taylor & Francis Group
LONDON AND NEW YORK

First published 2017
by Routledge
2 Park Square, Milton Park, Abingdon, Oxon OX14 4RN

and by Routledge
711 Third Avenue, New York, NY 10017

Routledge is an imprint of the Taylor & Francis Group, an informa business

© 2017 selection and editorial matter, Shelley Nathans and Milton Schaefer; individual chapters, the contributors

The right of the editors to be identified as the author of the editorial matter, and of the authors for their individual chapters, has been asserted in accordance with sections 77 and 78 of the Copyright, Designs and Patents Act 1988.

All rights reserved. No part of this book may be reprinted or reproduced or utilized in any form or by any electronic, mechanical, or other means, now known or hereafter invented, including photocopying and recording, or in any information storage or retrieval system, without permission in writing from the publishers.

Trademark notice: Product or corporate names may be trademarks or registered trademarks, and are used only for identification and explanation without intent to infringe.

British Library Cataloguing in Publication Data
A catalogue record for this book is available from the British Library

Library of Congress Cataloging in Publication Data
Names: Nathans, Shelley, editor | Schaefer, Milton, editor.
Title: Couples on the couch : psychoanalytic couple psychotherapy and the Tavistock model / edited by Shelley Nathans and Milton Schaefer.
Other titles: Relational perspectives book series ; v. 87.
Description: Abingdon, Oxon ; New York, NY : Routledge, 2018. | Series: Relational perspectives book series ; 87 | Includes bibliographical references and index.
Identifiers: LCCN 2017002453 (print) | LCCN 2017005699 (ebook) | ISBN 9781138242258 (hardback : alk. paper) | ISBN 9781138242265 (pbk. : alk. paper) | ISBN 9781315278810 (ebk) | ISBN 9781315278810 (Master) | ISBN 9781315278803 (Web PDF) | ISBN 9781315278797 (ePub) | ISBN 9781315278780 (Mobipocket)
Subjects: | MESH: Couples Therapy | Psychoanalytic Therapy
Classification: LCC RC488.5 (print) | LCC RC488.5 (ebook) | NLM WM 430.5.M3 | DDC 616.89/1562–dc23
LC record available at https://lccn.loc.gov/2017002453

ISBN: 978-1-138-24225-8 (hbk)
ISBN: 978-1-138-24226-5 (pbk)
ISBN: 978-1-315-27881-0 (ebk)

Typeset in Times New Roman
by Wearset Ltd, Boldon, Tyne and Wear

For our loving husbands, Sam Gerson and Scott Plakun.

"We are never so defenseless against suffering as when we love."
Sigmund Freud

Contents

Notes on contributors	ix
Preface	xiv
Acknowledgments	xxii

1 Introduction: core concepts of the Tavistock couple psychotherapy model 1
SHELLEY NATHANS

2 Couples on the couch: working psychoanalytically with couple relationships 30
STANLEY RUSZCZYNSKI

3 Discussion of "Couples on the couch: working psychoanalytically with couple relationships" 48
RACHEL COOKE

4 Unconscious beliefs about being a couple 62
MARY MORGAN

5 Discussion of "Unconscious beliefs about being a couple": beliefs about a couple and beliefs about the other 82
MILTON SCHAEFER

6 The Macbeths in the consulting room 90
JAMES V. FISHER

7	Discussion of "The Macbeths in the consulting room" SHELLEY NATHANS	113
8	Psychotic and depressive processes in couple functioning FRANCIS GRIER	123
9	Discussion of "Psychotic and depressive processes in couple functioning" JULIE FRIEND	142
10	Romantic bonds, binds, and ruptures: couples on the brink VIRGINIA GOLDNER	154
11	Discussion of "Romantic bonds, binds, and ruptures: couples on the brink" RACHAEL PELTZ	180
12	How was it for you? Attachment, sexuality and mirroring in couple relationships CHRISTOPHER CLULOW	193
13	Discussion of "How was it for you? Attachment, sexuality and mirroring in couple relationships" LEORA BENIOFF	213
14	Growing old together in mind and body ANDREW BALFOUR	221
15	Discussion of "Growing old together in mind and body" LESLYE RUSSELL	245
	Index	254

Contributors

Andrew Balfour qualified in clinical psychology at University College London and went on to train and work as an adult psychoanalytic psychotherapist at the Tavistock & Portman NHS Trust. He subsequently trained as a couple psychotherapist at Tavistock Relationships (formerly Tavistock Centre for Couple Relationships) where for 10 years he was Clinical Director, and he is now Chief Executive there. He has a research interest in the area of dementia care and has written and taught widely both in Britain and abroad. He is the co-editor, with Mary Morgan and Christopher Vincent, of *How Couple Relationships Shape our World: Clinical Practice, Research and Policy Perspectives* (Karnac, 2012).

Leora Benioff, Ph.D. is in private practice as a psychologist and psychoanalyst in Berkeley and San Francisco. She has completed the Tavistock Centre for Couple Relations Advanced Training in Psychoanalytic Couples Therapy and is a founding member and faculty of the Psychoanalytic Couple Psychotherapy Group. She is a member and faculty of the San Francisco Center for Psychoanalysis and also teaches at the Access Institute.

Christopher Clulow is a Senior Fellow of Tavistock Relationships, London. He has published extensively on marriage, partnerships, parenthood and couple psychotherapy, most recently from an attachment perspective. His two edited books in this area are *Adult Attachment and Couple Psychotherapy: The "Secure Base" in Practice and Research* (2001, Brunner-Routledge) and *Attachment, Sex and Couple Psychotherapy: Psychoanalytic Perspectives* (2009, Karnac). His most recent co-authored book, *Couple Therapy for Depression: A Clinician's Guide to Integrative Practice*, was published by Oxford

University Press in 2014. He is a Fellow of the Centre for Social Policy, Dartington, a member of the editorial board of *Couple and Family Psychoanalysis* and an international editorial consultant for *Sexual and Relationship Therapy*. He maintains a private clinical and training practice from his home in St Albans, UK.

Rachel Cooke PsyD is a clinical psychologist in private practice in Oakland and San Francisco. She is a founding member of the Psychoanalytic Couple Psychotherapy Group (PCPG) of the San Francisco Bay Area. She has completed the Tavistock Relationships Advanced Training in Psychoanalytic Psychotherapy with Couples. She teaches Psychoanalytic Couple Therapy for PCPG, Access Institute in San Francisco and taught previously for the Northern California Society of Psychoanalytic Psychology (NCSPP), an affiliate of Section 39.

James V. Fisher (1937–2012) was a psychoanalyst, couple psychotherapist and a senior staff member at the Tavistock Marital Studies Institute (now known as Tavistock Relationships). He was the author of *The Uninvited Guest: Emerging from Narcissism towards Marriage* (Karnac, 1999) and co-editor, with S. Ruszczynski, of *Intrusiveness and Intimacy in the Couple* (Karnac, 1995). His many other publications include "The Emotional Experience of K," published in *The International Journal of Psychoanalysis* (2006).

Julie Friend, LCSW, BCD is the Program Chair of the Psychoanalytic Couple Psychotherapy Group's training program in psychoanalytic couple psychotherapy. She has served on the teaching and/or supervisory faculty at Contemporary Psychoanalytic Couple Psychotherapy of New York, California Pacific Medical Center, Access Institute, The Psychotherapy Institute and the San Francisco Center for Psychoanalysis. Her most recent paper, "Love as Creative Illusion and Its Place in Psychoanalytic Couple Psychotherapy," was published in *Couple and Family Psychoanalysis* in 2013. She has a private practice including individuals, couples and consultation in Berkeley, California.

Virginia Goldner, Ph.D. is the Founding Editor of the journal *Studies in Gender and Sexuality* and an Associate Editor of *Psychoanalytic Dialogues*. She is on the faculty of the NYU Post-doctoral Program in Psychoanalysis and Psychotherapy, the Stephen A. Mitchell Center for Relational Psychoanalysis and the doctoral program in clinical psychology at CUNY. Virginia has received awards for her Distinguished Contributions to psychoanalysis by Division 39 of the APA, and to family therapy by the American Family Therapy Academy. She is the co-editor of two books, *Gender in Psychoanalytic Space*, with Muriel Dimen (Other Press, 2002) and *Predatory Priests, Silenced Victims*, with Mary Gail Frawley O'Dea (Routledge, 2007), and is at work on a collection of her major papers, to be published in 2017.

Francis Grier is a Training Analyst and Supervisor of the British Psychoanalytical Society and a member of the Society of Couple Psychoanalytic Psychotherapists. He edited *Brief Encounters with Couples: Some Analytical Perspectives* (2001, Karnac) and *Oedipus and the Couple* (2005, Karnac). His other publications include "Lively and Deathly Intercourse" in *Sex, Attachment and Couple Psychotherapy: Psychoanalytic Perspectives*, ed. C. Clulow (2009, Karnac), "Thoughts on Rigoletto" in *The International Journal of Psychoanalysis* in 2011, and "La Traviata and Oedipus" in 2015. He contributed a chapter entitled "The Hidden Traumas of the Young Boarding School Child as Seen Through the Lens of Adult Couple Therapy" for *Enduring Trauma through the Life-Cycle*, eds. E. McGinley and A. Varchevker.

Mary Morgan is a psychoanalyst, Fellow of the British Psychoanalytic Society, Reader in Couple Psychoanalysis and Consultant Couple Psychotherapist at Tavistock Relations, London. She is a member of the IPA's Committee on Couple and Family Psychoanalysis and on the Board of the International Association for Couple and Family Psychoanalysis. She teaches internationally and has published many papers about working analytically with couples. She is on the editorial board of the journals *Couple & Family Psychoanalysis* and *Interatzioni*.

Shelley Nathans, Ph.D. is on the faculty of the California Pacific Medical Center and The Psychoanalytic Institute of Northern California. She is a founding member of the Psychoanalytic Couple Psychotherapy Group training program. She has completed the Tavistock Center for Couple Relations Advanced Training in Psychoanalytic Psychotherapy with Couples and is on the International Advisory Board for *Psychoanalytic Couple and Family Psychoanalysis*. Her most recent publications include "Whose Disgust is it Anyway?: Projection and Projective Identification in the Couple Relationship" in *Psychoanalytic*

Dialogues (2016) and "Infidelity as Manic Defense" in *Couple and Family Psychoanalysis* (2012). She is the director and producer of the film *Robert Wallerstein: 65 Years at the Center of Psychoanalysis*. She is in private practice in both San Francisco and Oakland, California.

Rachael Peltz, Ph.D. is a faculty member at PINC, NCSPP and Access Institute, supervising and personal analyst at PINC and past President of Section 9, Division 39, APA. She has published in *Psychoanalytic Dialogues*, *fort da*, *Rivista di Psicoanalisi* and *Psychoanalysis, Class and Politics: Encounters in the Clinical Setting*, among others. She maintains a private practice for adults, adolescents, couples and families in Berkeley.

Leslye Russell practices psychoanalytic psychotherapy for individuals and couples. She is interested in the intersection of the arts and psychoanalysis. Recent publications and conference papers include *The Flaneur and the Analysand (fort da*, Spring, 2004*), Group Mindedness* (Supervisors Symposium, The Psychotherapy Institute, 2007), *The Necessity of Astonishment* (International Association of Relational Psychoanalysis and Psychotherapy, Conference, 2008*), Freud's Theory and Trollope's Depiction of Moral Masochism (fort da*, Fall 2013), and *Ethics in Context: Psychoanalysis and Modernism* (presented at The Psychotherapy Institute, Berkeley, 2013.

Stanley Ruszczynski is an individual and couple psychoanalytic psychotherapist and a psychoanalyst. He is a Consultant Adult Psychotherapist and for over 11 years (2005–2016) was the Clinical Director of the Portman Clinic (Tavistock and Portman NHS Foundation Trust, London), an NHS outpatient clinic offering psychoanalytic treatment to patients disturbed by their criminality, violence or damaging sexual behaviors. He is a past Deputy Director of TCCR. He has edited and co-edited a number of books, including with James Fisher, *Intrusiveness and Delinquency* (Karnac 1995) and the last, co-edited with David Morgan, being *Lectures in Violence, Perversion and Delinquency* (Karnac Books, 2007). He is the author of many journal articles and book chapters, teaches and offers organizational consultancy in the UK and abroad, and has a private clinical practice.

Milton Schaefer, Ph.D. is a psychologist and psychoanalyst in private practice in San Francisco, where he sees adults and couples. He is on the faculty of the San Francisco Center of Psychoanalysis where he has taught classes on Psychoanalytic Couple Psychotherapy and the American Relational School. Dr. Schaefer has presented and published on children's adjustment in high conflict divorcing families, ethical issues and the interface of psychoanalysis and the arts. He is a founding member of the Psychoanalytic Couples Psychotherapy Group and supervises and teaches in numerous Bay Area venues.

Preface

Shelley Nathans and Milton Schaefer

The chapters in this book and their accompanying discussions offer a compelling sampling of ideas about couple relationships and couple psychotherapy from a psychoanalytic point of view. The authors of these chapters, with one exception, are affiliated with the Tavistock Centre for Couple Relations (TCCR)[1] in London and rely heavily on the theoretical model that has been developed there since the 1940s. This book provides an introduction to the TCCR approach to couple psychotherapy and exposure to the depth and breadth of this framework. Each of the chapters in this book contains in-depth theoretical and clinical case material and is presented in tandem with a formal discussion. This selection of chapters and the accompanying discussions provide an opportunity for those who are unfamiliar with these concepts to become acquainted with this approach. Additionally, those who wish to deepen their understanding of the Tavistock model will find a trove of material to enhance their knowledge.

All of these chapters and discussions were originally presented at the Annual Psychoanalytic Couple Psychotherapy lecture series in the San Francisco Bay Area between 2008 and 2014, sponsored by the Psychoanalytic Couple Psychotherapy Group (PCPG) and the Northern California Society for Psychoanalytic Psychology (NCSPP). This annual conference brings renowned scholars from the TCCR in London to San Francisco. Each year, a visiting scholar from the TCCR is invited to write and present an original chapter that is formally discussed by a local psychoanalytic couple psychotherapist. This lecture series has become a highly respected fixture in the educational offerings for couple psychotherapists and psychoanalysts in Northern California and beyond, and has become a nexus of thought and training for working with couples from a psychoanalytic perspective. This has also led to the development of an intensive, multiyear post-graduate training program in psychoanalytic couple psychotherapy, offered in Berkeley, California by the PCPG.

The majority of chapters in this collection were authored by clinicians affiliated with PCPG and TCCR and were previously published in our local psychoanalytic journal *fort da*. The chapter by Virginia Goldner appeared in *Psychoanalytic Dialogues* (2014) and Francis Grier's chapter was previously published in an edited book (2013).

We have arranged the chapters and their companion discussions to provide coherence, rather than in the chronological order in which they were presented. The book begins with an introduction by Shelley Nathans that describes psychoanalytic couple psychotherapy, outlines the history, theoretical basis and development of the Tavistock psychoanalytic couple psychotherapy model, and discusses some of these key concepts and their relevance to working psychoanalytically with couples. The subsequent chapters demonstrate how theory may be applied in a variety of clinical encounters and deepen the theoretical understanding of the difficulties that beset couples and the challenges posed to those who work with them.

In "Couples on the couch" (Chapter 2), Stanley Ruszczynski presents a detailed description of the application of psychoanalytic theory to working with couples. The author discusses the core theoretical and technical concepts that underlie and distinguish psychoanalytic couple psychotherapy. He argues that the psychoanalytic couple psychotherapy model relies on a stance that focuses on the conscious and the unconscious, as well as the intra-psychic and interpersonal nature of the couple relationship, all of which is created through the transference–countertransference interaction between the partners. In addition, the concepts of the shared unconscious, unconscious partner choice, projective identification and triangular space are discussed with regard to understanding couples. He then describes the qualities of narcissistic relating and contrasts this with the more mature form of relating associated with depressive position capacities.

In Chapter 3, Rachel Cooke places Stanley Ruszczynski's chapter in the broader context of his other writings, showing how they all share a focus on the negotiation of difference in couple relationships. She proposes ways that the couple therapist can facilitate healthier, less narcissistic forms of relating. Dr. Cooke explores the developmental roots and impediments to the sense of separateness and how it impacts the development of empathy in couple relationships. She concludes her discussion with thoughts about the diagnostic and mutative aspects of the therapist's positive, empathetic response to the couple.

In her chapter "Unconscious beliefs about being a couple" (Chapter 4), Mary Morgan elaborates the ways that a couple's unconscious beliefs about the other and the relationship are central to the therapist's understanding of couple difficulties. She describes how individuals often mistake their beliefs about the relationship and their partner as facts, and she links this to the problem of the partner's lack of curiosity about their spouse. These unconscious beliefs are often strongly defended against by keeping out any new information, resulting in the types of relationships characterized by spirals of frustration and stagnation that often present in our consulting rooms. Using case examples, she explores two prevalent unconscious beliefs: that the relationship is dangerous, and that a relationship requires the perfect attunement of the partners. Morgan makes the point that the affective tone in the room and the therapist's attention to her own countertransference reactions play a central part in both the diagnosis and the effective treatment of a couple's unconscious beliefs.

In Chapter 5, Milton Schaefer's discussion of Mary Morgan's chapter connects her view of unconscious beliefs about a couple to her seminal ideas about "the creative couple" and "projective gridlock", highlighting both the positive and the pathological forms of couple relating. He posits that unconscious beliefs are not just pathognomonic but serve as essential models for being a couple. He contrasts religion with cults as respective positive and negative models illustrative of how beliefs function in the individual, in couples and in society. The author uses Morgan's case examples to contrast the Tavistock and American Relational views of enactment and the role they play in couple psychotherapy, while emphasizing the therapist's ability to maintain and model curiosity.

Using the couple dynamics at the center of Shakespeare's play and an elegant theoretical argument that mines both Freud and Bion, James Fisher in Chapter 6, "The Macbeths in the Consulting Room," addresses the problem of working with deep disturbance in couples through the lens of the "proleptic imagination." This is a concept borrowed from the field of rhetoric that refers to the representation of the future as if it has already occurred or existed – a state of mind that obliterates the distinction between the imagined and the real. As applied to couples, this can create a problematic form of relating that relies on certainty as opposed to curiosity and can escalate destructive dynamics rather than facilitate communication. Fisher argues that this conceptualization has technical implications in working psychoanalytically with couples. He stresses the importance of the therapist's capacity to listen to the partners' projections as communications and advocates shifting away from the use of interpretations directed toward each of the partners in attempts to get them to reclaim their split-off projections.

In her response to James Fisher's chapter, Shelley Nathans (Chapter 7) describes in vibrant detail the ways that his concept of "the proleptic imagination" – where a couple takes their fantasies about the future as concrete reality – manifest in the day-to-day experience of working with couples. She illustrates how this concept can help the therapist track the often dizzying oscillations that one encounters in the work. The author sheds light on how Dr. Fisher adopts a more Bionian point of view, whereby projections are seen as more communicative than evacuative of unwanted parts of the self, and how this results in Fisher's view that interpretations addressing the couple's use of projective identification are not particularly helpful. Taking issue with this, Dr. Nathans points out the ubiquitous nature of such projections and argues for a more inclusive and flexible interpretive therapeutic stance.

In Chapter 8, "Psychotic and depressive processes in couple functioning," Francis Grier describes a couple operating in the near psychotic, paranoid-schizoid level. He discusses how this gets played out in the arenas of idealization and the passage of time. He argues that these types of couples often defensively cling to the idea that they should function as a single, almost undifferentiated unit and can experience an overwhelming sense of blame and betrayal when this unrealistic ideal is not met. The author shows how idealization can function both as a hideout to protect the partner's sense of dependency and vulnerability, but also to contain destructive aspects of the self that are resistant to change and development. There is an unreal sense of time and a denial of the need to change in the face of the couple's changing circumstances – for example, with the arrival of children. He also takes up the perplexing problem of what happens when one party in the couple is more able to develop than the other and the varying ways this gets played out in the transference. In two extended case examples, he illustrates how couples triumphantly force a continual re-enactment of a fantasized past in present time. Grier then describes the ways in which couple psychotherapy can facilitate a movement to a more mature, differentiated state of mind where there is less need for projection and blame, a greater boundary between each individual, between the couple and others, and an enhanced realistic sense of a combined purpose that is shared.

Drawing on ideas regarding the unconscious choice of a partner, in Chapter 9 Julie Friend extends Grier's thinking about the role and fate of idealization in the couple. She shows how a couple's asymmetric development can lead one party to feel that there is "breach of contract" between the couple, with accompanying feelings of hurt and abandonment. Friend cautions against using pathologizing terminology that may foreclose the therapist's empathic stance and she suggests clinical interventions that can facilitate the couple having a more realistic conception of time. The author's close reading of the clinical material also highlights how Grier's interpretive focus on the transference can promote change in one of the partners, but at the same time, may lead to enactments of the couple's underlying problematic dynamic.

In "Romantic bonds, binds, and ruptures: couples on the brink" (Chapter 10), Virginia Goldner discusses the complexities of working with couples on the brink of disillusion and argues that adult romantic partners are bonded with the same monumentality, and for the same hard-wired reasons, as are mothers and babies. Consequently, romantic loss, injury and deadlock can be understood as instances of what trauma theorists now call "relational trauma" or "small t trauma". By interweaving dynamic systems, attachment and neuropsychological theories, she explains the primitive mental processes and relentless enactments common to couple psychotherapy treatments. Goldner views couples as enacting an unconscious symmetry whereby they are looking for a "relational home" and seeking to gain mastery over the unresolved traumas of the other's non-recognition.

In her commentary on Virginia Goldner's chapter, Rachael Peltz (Chapter 11) reminds the reader that a couple's desire to be fully known is matched by its impossibility and that it is this search for recognition and the ensuing disappointment that fuels the repetitive recriminations one sees in couples in trouble. Drawing connections between Bion's ideas about the dynamic unconscious and field and systems theory, the author lays out the ways in which couples look to each other, and to the therapist, to process and contain unacceptable parts of themselves. In the maelstrom of projected part-objects it is the therapist's reverie – as part of the field – that can serve as a guidepost to making interventions that both hold and uncover what is most poignant and unspoken.

Christopher Clulow's chapter, "How was it for you? Attachment, sexuality and mirroring in couple relationships" (Chapter 12), tackles the frequent presenting problem of couples with difficulties in sexual desire. He draws on Winnicott's ideas about mirroring, as well as attachment theory, to understand and treat these frequently intractable problems. Clulow proposes that sexual feelings are only discovered through one's relationships with others, that desire has to do with absence and longing, and that sexuality must be negotiated in a field of disappointment and loss. The author uses finely detailed examples from Frederic Fonteyne's 1999 film, *Une Liaison Pornographic*, as an illustration of the ways couples navigate sex and attachment in their attempts to delineate the realities of their relationships. Clulow highlights and distinguishes the ways that difficulties with attachment in infancy and childhood can lead to a later deadening of desire. This can include neglectful or overly intrusive mirroring of the infant's first displays of sensuality, leading to an insecure base of attachment and subsequent sexual problems in adulthood. In such cases, attachment and sexuality become intertwined so that sexual arousal sparks anxiety, disappointment and fears of rejection. Clulow argues that insecure and anxious attachments are related to a person's use of psychic equivalence producing a confusion between internal psychic states and external realities. Finally, he shows how the attachment concepts of contingency and marking can be used as effective therapeutic tools to establish a sense of safety in the session and help the couple move beyond their shared defensive stance.

In Chapter 13, Leora Benioff responds and expands on the chapter by Christopher Clulow and notes that even individuals with no history or indication of attachment issues can exhibit symptoms of low sexual desire. She draws upon LaPlanche, Stein, Benjamin and Mitchell to explore how the fundamental unknowability of the other, coupled with the unruliness, excess and mystery of sexuality, can lead to a defensive stifling of sexual desire. She argues for conceptualizing difficulties in desire not only through the lens of attachment theory, but also through the acknowledgment of the extremely private and self-contained nature of sexual experience.

We close this collection with an eye on endings. The final chapter and penultimate chapter of the book is "Growing old together in mind and body," by Andrew Balfour. The author relies on neo-Kleinian ideas, including the capacity for mourning, to poignantly explore the themes arising in clinical work with some elderly couples. He asks, "How can we be aware of transience in a way that enhances our capacity to live, rather than filling us with despair or distancing us from immersing ourselves in life while we have it?" Balfour employs a developmental model in which the anxieties and defenses of the individual's early life are seen as effecting subsequent developmental challenges and determinate of the capacity for coping with the experience of growing older. He emphasizes how aging entails a return to the body and the reemergence of the anxieties associated with early somatic experience. Balfour describes the couple's experience of illness, especially dementia, and reminds us that the threat or actuality of cognitive fragmentation and physical decline may foster a claustrophobic experience of being trapped within a damaged object. The case examples in this chapter vividly describe these clinical phenomena and illustrate the application of a psychoanalytic model to understanding the elderly couple.

In Leslye Russell's response to Andrew Balfour (Chapter 15), the author applies Ogden's concept of the "autistic-contiguous position" to understand how the world of the elderly can seem to shrink, forcing the psyche back to the sensorium where concrete experience and the routine patterns of daily life attain primacy. Drawing upon Meltzer's concept of the aesthetic conflict, she highlights the psychological parallel between the infant's experience of dependency on the mother and the elderly person's dependency on the caregiver. Russell, following Winnicott, usefully reminds us that dependency and caretaking are complex and can include hateful, destructive aspects that the aging couple must negotiate. She posits that these challenges can be a liability and limitation for the couple, but that they may also provide the possibility of renewed connection and intimacy if the couple can accept the ensuing losses associated with aging. With her sensitivity to the psychic demands imposed on the elderly couple, she provides an inspirational framework for all of us as we face the final stages of life.

We are confident that *Couples on the Couch: Psychoanalytic Couple Psychotherapy and the Tavistock Model* provides an in-depth approach to understanding intimate relationships and the complexities of working in this domain. It offers a fertile trove of material for readers who have not previously had exposure to the theory and technique of psychoanalytic couple psychotherapy, as well as offering an expanded and rigorous approach to those who are already familiar with the Tavistock model of working with couples.

Note

1 In 2016, the Tavistock Centre for Couple Relationships changed its name to Tavistock Relationships (TR). For the sake of consistency, we continue to refer to it as TCCR.

Acknowledgments

It is not possible to produce a book of such theoretical complexity and depth without the help and guidance of others. We are deeply grateful to the authors who have allowed us to include their work in *Couples on the Couch: Psychoanalytic Couple Psychotherapy and the Tavistock Model* and to the many other colleagues who have supported this project.

The Annual Psychoanalytic Couple Psychotherapy Lecture and the papers and discussions reproduced in this book are the result of many years of organizational work and collaboration with our colleagues in the Psychoanalytic Couple Psychotherapy Group (PCPG): Leora Benioff, Rachel Cooke, Julie Friend, the late Yael Lieberman-Goldblatt, Peter Klein and Sandra Seidlitz. We are fortunate to have had the benefit of participating in such a rich and creative working group and we sincerely thank them for their contributions and years of friendship and collaboration.

PCPG has worked with The Northern California Society for Psychoanalytic Psychology (NCSPP) for the past 10 years to co-sponsor the Annual Psychoanalytic Couple Psychotherapy Lecture and we are grateful to all of those who have been on the Education Committee and helped with producing these events. In particular, we would like to thank Michele McGuiness, Bear Korngold, Jennifer Fitch, Annice Ormiston-Fulwiler, Susana Bernat and Garrett Howard for their organizational support and many hours of work on the annual lecture.

We would also like to thank the Editorial Board of the psychoanalytic journal *fort da*, for previously publishing the majority of the papers in this book and for their commitment to the psychoanalytic couple psychotherapy lecture series. We are particularly grateful to Alan Kubler, Patricia Marra and Peter Silen for their support.

A number of colleagues have been helpful in various ways during the long process of editing this book. Stanley Ruszczynski graciously gave us the title. Thank you to Robin Deutsch, Eileen Keller, Elizabeth Biggert, Dena Sorbo, Gary Grossman, Marilyn Kanter, Joyce Lindenbaum, Molly Ludlam, Lisa Buchberg and Beth Roosa for their support. We are especially grateful to Julie Friend, Mary Morgan, David Hewison and Stanley Ruszczynski for their close reading and commentaries on the introductory chapter. We are also grateful to the members of the Semi-Baked writing group (Richard Almond, Terry Becker, Joe Caston, Daphne de Marneffe, Eric Hesse, Diane Elise, Sam Gerson, Peter Goldberg, Mary Main, Deborah Melman, Harvey Peskin, Tzipora Peskin, Carolyn Wilson and Mitch Wilson) for their support and helpful feedback on some of the early material for this book.

This book would never have come to fruition without our colleagues at the Tavistock Centre for Couple Relationships (TCCR). We are indebted to them for their innovative ideas, dedicated and creative teaching, clinical acumen and support for our endeavors over the last 20 plus years. We thank the TCCR faculty with whom we have had the pleasure and privilege to learn from and work with: Susanah Abse, Andrew Balfour, Christopher Clulow, Lynn Cudmore, Francis Grier, David Hewison, Stanley Ruszczynski and the late James Fisher. We are especially grateful to Mary Morgan for her teaching, consultation, encouragement, wisdom and friendship. Special thanks to our editors, Adrienne Harris and Lew Aron, Emma Critchley at Wearset, and to our editors at Routledge, Charles Bath and Kate Hawes.

Finally, thank you to the members of our dear families: Mara Gerson, Nina Gerson, Sam Gerson and Scott Plakun.

Permissions acknowledgments

Every effort has been made to contact copyright holders for their permission to reprint selections of this book. The publishers would be grateful to hear from any copyright holder who is not here rightfully acknowledged and will undertake to rectify any errors or omissions in future editions of this book.

Excerpts from DANCING FISH AND AMMONITES: A MEMOIR by Penelope Lively, copyright © 2013 by Penelope Lively. Used by permission of Viking Books, an imprint of Penguin Publishing Group, a division of Penguin Random House LLC.

Excerpt from "Hands," by Elaine Feinstein in *Talking to the Dead* by Elaine Feinstein (2007). Permission for use kindly granted by Carcanet Press, Ltd.

Excerpts from "The Plain Sense of Things" from THE COLLECTED POEMS OF WALLACE STEVENS by Wallace Stevens, copyright © 1954 by Wallace Stevens and copyright renewed 1982 by Holly Stevens. Used by permission of Alfred A. Knopf, an imprint of the Knopf Doubleday Publishing Group, a division of Penguin Random House LLC. All rights reserved.

Excerpts from "The Desire to Be Gisella" from WRITING IN THE DARK: ESSAYS ON LITERATURE AND POLITICS by David Grossman © 2008 by David Grossman. Reprinted by permission of Farrar, Straus and Giroux, LLC and by The Deborah Harris Agency.

Excerpt from "Misery and Splendour" from HUMAN WISHES by ROBERT HASS. Copyright © 1989 by Robert Hass. Reprinted by permission of HarperCollins Publishers.

Excerpts from "The Cocktail Party" and "East Coker" from THE COMPLETE POEMS AND PLAYS, 1909–1962 by T.S. Eliot. Copyright © 1950 by T.S. Eliot, renewed 1978 by Esme Valerie Eliot. Used by permission of Houghton Mifflin Harcourt Publishing Company and Faber and Faber, Ltd. All rights reserved.

Chapter 10, Romantic Bonds, Binds, and Ruptures: Couples on the Brink, by Virginia Goldner, was previously published in *Psychoanalytic Dialogues: The International Journal of Relational Perspectives* 24 (4): 402–418 and is reprinted with permission of Taylor & Francis, LLC, (www.tandfonline.com).

The following chapters were previously published in *fort da:* The Journal of The Northern California Society for Psychoanalytic Psychology and are reprinted with the kind permission of the journal:

Chapter 2 first published as "Couples on the Couch: Working Psychoanalytically with Couple Relationships" by Stanley Ruszczynski, *fort da*, XX (2) Fall, 2014 pp. 8–25.

Chapter 3 first published as "Discussion of 'Couples on the Couch: Working Psychoanalytically with Couple Relationships'" by Rachel Cooke, *fort da*, XX (2) Fall, 2014 pp. 26–28.

Chapter 4 first published as "Unconscious Beliefs about Being a Couple" by Mary Morgan, *fort da*, XVI (1) Spring, 2010 pp. 36–55.

Chapter 5 first published as "Discussion of 'Unconscious Beliefs about Being a Couple'" by Milton Schaefer, *fort da*, XVI (1) Spring, 2010 pp. 56–63.

Chapter 6 first published as "Macbeth in the Consulting Room: Proleptic Imagination" by James V. Fisher, *fort da*, XV (2) Fall, 2009 pp. 33–55.

Chapter 7 first published as "Discussion of 'Macbeth in the Consulting Room: Proleptic Imagination'" by Shelley Nathans, *fort da*, XV (2) Fall, 2009 pp. 56–65.

Chapter 8 first published as "Psychotic and Depressive Processes in Couple Functioning" by Francis Grier, *fort da*, XVII (1) Spring, 2011 pp. 11–29. Chapter 8 also featured as a book chapter under the same title in *Living on the Border: Psychotic Processes in the Individual, the Couple, and the Group*, edited by David Bell and Aleksandra Novakovic (published by Karnac Books in 2013), and is reprinted with the kind permission of Karnac Books.

Chapter 9 first published as "Discussion of 'Psychotic and Depressive Processes in Couple Functioning'" by Julie Friend, *fort da*, XVII (1) Spring, 2011 pp. 30–41.

Chapter 11 has been extensively rewritten from "The Blaze that Burns": The Field of the Couple by Rachael Peltz, *fort da*, XIX (2) Fall, 2013 pp. 8–20.

Chapter 12 first published as "How Was It For You? Attachment, Mirroring, and the Psychotherapeutic Process with Couples Presenting Sexual Problems" by Christopher Clulow, *fort da*, XVIII (2) Fall, 2012 pp. 9–28.

Chapter 13 first published as "Discussion of 'How Was It For You? Attachment, Mirroring, and the Psychotherapeutic Process with Couples'" by Leora Benioff, *fort da*, XVIII (2) Fall, 2012 pp. 29–37.

Chapter 14 first published as "Growing Old Together in Mind and Body" by Andrew Balfour, *fort da*, XXI (2) Fall, 2015 pp. 53–76.

Chapter 15 first published as "Response to Andrew Balfour's 'Growing Old Together in Mind and Body'" by Leslye Russell, *fort da*, XXI (2) Fall, 2015 pp. 77–85.

Chapter 1

Introduction
Core concepts of the Tavistock couple psychotherapy model

Shelley Nathans

This chapter provides the reader with an introduction to the key psychoanalytic concepts that are fundamental to psychoanalytic couple psychotherapy and highlight those that are the cornerstones of the Tavistock Centre for Couple Relationships (TCCR) model. This approach is rooted in psychoanalytic theory and technique and facilitates in-depth work with couples that is dynamic, capacious and creative.

There is an unquestionable demand for couple psychotherapy services in the United States and although there is a surfeit of techniques and couple treatment modalities, few formal training opportunities in psychoanalytic couple psychotherapy exist in the United States.[1] Some American psychoanalytic institutes offer elective courses in couple psychotherapy, but therapeutic work with couples has not been developed within the psychoanalytic training paradigm. As a result, many psychoanalysts and psychoanalytically oriented psychotherapists have not had the benefit of a rigorous training in couple psychotherapy and are left without access to a coherent psychoanalytic model to support their clinical work with couples.

A brief history of the Tavistock Centre for Couple Relationships

In contrast, clinicians in England have had access to high-quality education in psychoanalytic couple psychotherapy for many years because couple psychotherapy has been regarded as a distinct discipline with its own specific training, literature and identity (Clulow, 2009). The development of this professional identity has fundamental psychoanalytic roots that can be traced to its origin and association with the Tavistock Clinic and the Tavistock Institute of Human Relations. From their inceptions, these institutions incorporated psychoanalytic thinking to better understand and address the pressing social issues of the public, including the mental health of children, families and couples.

The awareness of the detrimental psychological impact of World War II on couples and families led to the establishment of the Family Discussion Bureau in 1948 (now called the Tavistock Centre for Couple Relationships[2]). This constituted the first formalized attempt to apply psychoanalytic concepts to the understanding and treatment of marital difficulties. Born out of a desire to address the needs of couples and families in distress, most particularly following the traumas of the war, the founders turned to psychoanalysis to deepen their understanding of the emotional pressures inherent in relationships (Ruszczynski, 1993). Using the ideas of Freud and Jung, and in consultation with psychoanalysts at the Tavistock Institute, such as Michael Balint, they developed an application of psychoanalysis to treating couples. The family welfare workers on staff were trained to attend to the unconscious dynamics in couple relationships and to the impact of transferences and countertransferences on treatment outcomes (Dicks, 1967).

In addition to the work of Freud and Jung, the model was influenced by the research and clinical endeavors of others working at the Tavistock, such as John Bowlby (1969, 1973), whose infant observation studies emphasized the issues of separation and loss. This research had a significant impact on the model for treating war victims and on the understanding of the importance of attachment between children and their parents, as well as between adults in intimate relationships.

Due to the high demand for services following the war, a group psychotherapy model was developed. This led to the application of psychoanalytic ideas to the understanding of groups – a specialty for which the Tavistock has earned an international reputation. Isabel Menzies Lyth, a founder of the Family Discussion Bureau, formulated a highly influential theory of the unconscious forces that shape organizational life (Menzies, 1949). Wilfred Bion (1961) began his work on the unconscious phenomena that shape the behavior of groups at the Tavistock and his understanding of group dynamics and mental functioning is clearly evident in the Tavistock model of couple relationships.

The early model was also influenced by a number of other important psychoanalysts who were affiliated with the Tavistock, including Enid and Michael Balint, Elizabeth Bott Spillius and Henry Dicks. Dicks' seminal book, *Marital Tensions* (1967), integrating the ideas of W.E. Fairbairn and Melanie Klein, offered the first comprehensive theoretical and clinical application of psychoanalytic theory to couple relationships and served as an organizing text for analytic family therapy (Sander, 1993).

Today, the TCCR is internationally respected for its clinical rigor and scholarly contributions, for its training programs, for research on couple dynamics and couple psychotherapy, and for its numerous publications. The faculty of TCCR have authored or edited a number of influential books over the past two decades, and taken collectively, they provide a broad exposure to this theory (Ruszczynski, 1993; Ruszczynski & Fisher, 1995; Fisher, 1999; Grier, 2001, 2005; Ludlam & Nyberg, 2007; Clulow, 2001, 2009; Balfour, Morgan & Vincent, 2012). Despite these many contributions, this model is not widely known outside of the United Kingdom and, as such, what follows is an introduction to its historical development and contemporary practice.

Theoretical origins of the Tavistock couple psychotherapy model

The Tavistock theoretical model has evolved from its original Freudian foundation to a model that draws deeply from the work of Klein (1928, 1945, 1946), Fairbairn (1952, 1963), Bion (1961, 1962a, 1962b), Winnicott (1947a, 1947b, 1956, 1965) and Meltzer (1967, 1992). It is also extremely influenced by the contemporary British object relations theorists such as Britton (1989), Steiner (1993), Feldman (1989), Joseph (1989) and Rosenfeld (1964, 1983). In recent years, attachment theory and mentalization theory have had increasing influences on both the clinical and the research work at TCCR (e.g., Abse, 2013b; Clulow, 2001, 2009; Ludlam & Nyberg, 2007).

Henry Dicks (1967), an early member of the Tavistock Institute, developed the idea that couple interactions were largely based on unconscious, ambivalent relations to earlier love objects contained within each partners' inner world. He maintained that these interactions could be understood using analytic concepts and techniques. Dicks combined Fairbairn's object relations theory with Kleinian theory to construct a model for working with couples (Ludlam, 2014). He observed that it was possible for one partner to perceive the other partner not as "other" but rather as a reflection of some other person or as part of another person. He stated:

> the perception of the partner as if the partner was not himself but some other person or part of a person. This coincided with dovetailing behavior by the subject in his or her own role taking – as if in relation to the spouse one had to be one's own parent, or could be a little boy or girl and not one's ordinary adult self such as with friends or at work.
>
> (Dicks, 1967)

Dicks described the utility of interpreting the persecutory nature of split off traits, weaknesses or faults that may be rejected by the self and projected into the partner, as well as the ways in which one partner may seek to find those parts of the self that are missing.

Object relations theory and couple psychotherapy

Object relations theory offers a particularly useful vantage point from which to view the couple as it can be conceptualized as attending to the juncture between the inner psychic reality and the external reality of interpersonal relationships. Fairbairn (1952), countering Freud's classical psychoanalytic model, offered the idea that individuals, from early on, are object seeking and that attachment to others continues throughout adulthood. He argued that early important relationships with primary caretakers and the qualities and experiences associated with these early relationships are carried within the individual throughout life. These experiences influence object choice and the qualities and subjective experiences of all later relationships. From an object relations perspective, the repetition compulsion can be viewed as a need to repeat painful experiences to maintain attachments to early objects. Thus, for the couple therapist, object relations theory offers a way of holding in mind the object relations field of each partner, the interpersonal dynamics between the partners and, most crucially, the ways in which both the intrapsychic and the interpersonal worlds exert mutual influence on one another.

Core principles of psychoanalytic couple psychotherapy

Psychoanalysis is not a theoretical monolith, and as there are various different psychoanalytic theories, it would be possible to use any of these models as a basis for practicing couple psychotherapy. Some common, core concepts link most of the theories contained under the psychoanalytic umbrella (Wallerstein, 1988), and these ideas can be used to distinguish psychoanalytic couple psychotherapy from other forms of couple treatment, such as systems theory (Bowen, 1978) or emotionally focused couple therapy (Johnson, 2004).

The basic principles that would characterize any psychoanalytic couple psychotherapy model are fundamentally embedded in the Tavistock model and serve as essential pillars upon which the theory and technique have evolved. The following section highlights the core ideas that are essential to understanding the psychoanalytic approach to couples.

Psychic determinism

A psychoanalytic theory of couples must rely on a psychoanalytic model of the mind. Specifically, the treatment would be influenced by one of the fundamentals of psychoanalysis – the assumption of psychic determinism. The therapist would assume that at least some portion of the interactions between the partners is derived from unconscious structures or representations in each of the individuals and that this forms a dynamic between them. There would be an assumption that these unconscious structures would press in the direction of a tendency to repeat earlier object relations and this would be experienced or enacted within the life of the couple.

The unconscious

Owing to its intensity and intimacy, the couple relationship is the closest approximation to the early parent–child experience. As such, the deepest elements of infantile and early developmental object relations tend to emerge within the adult couple and structure the dynamics between the partners, including the formation of what may be thought of as a mutual transference relationship (Ruszczynski, 1993), a shared unconscious

(Kernberg, 1995) or a relational unconscious (Gerson, 2004). Consequently, psychoanalytic couple psychotherapy presupposes and privileges the unconscious, including the unconscious of each individual partner and the shared unconscious of the couple. In contrast, other types of couple therapy are generally more concerned with conscious communication processes, attitudes and beliefs systems, roles, negotiation and conflict resolution skills, structures of the daily life of the couple, and the current events impacting the dyad. This is not to suggest that these topics should never be a part of an analytically oriented treatment. Interventions in these areas can be useful and are often key to the therapist's attempts to provide containment. In psychoanalytic couple psychotherapy, the therapeutic action is oriented to the unconscious level.

In couple psychotherapy, the focus of the treatment and the object of therapeutic action is the relationship. Therefore, a primary concern of the psychoanalytic couple therapist would be the shared unconscious of the couple: the intersection of the content of each of the partner's unconscious minds, including shared unconscious phantasies,[3] anxieties and the unconscious processes that create the dynamic relationship between them.

The frame

Similar to individual treatments, the frame provides important functions in psychoanalytic couple psychotherapy. First, the frame provides the therapist with a standard, consistent way of setting up the conditions and boundaries of the treatment. Particular patient responses to these practices are meaningful and diagnostic and can therefore be useful as information in the treatment. When the psychoanalytic couple psychotherapist is in the practice of maintaining a consistent therapeutic frame, deviations from this may be relied upon as a resource, as an entry to understanding countertransference enactments that may provide clues to otherwise inaccessible unconscious material.

Second, and perhaps most importantly, the frame forms the holding environment of the therapy, providing a reliable, structured, bounded setting within which the conflictual, chaotic and unpredictable affects and phantasies may be gathered and safely contained in order to be experienced, reflected upon and understood. Policies and practices, such as those involving scheduling, fees and the boundaries regarding the types of contact between the therapist and the couple, are fundamental aspects of the frame. In couple psychotherapy, promoting a sense of consistency and predictability is important because the conflicts in intimate relationships can be extremely volatile and invoke highly regressed states accompanied by dramatic enactments. Many couples rely on their sessions, particularly in the early phases of the treatment, as the only safe place to discuss issues that they expect to be threatening or painful. Inconsistencies and breaks in the frame potentially erode the sense of containment provided by the therapist and the therapeutic setting. In contrast, consistencies in the frame, provided over time, promote containment for the couple.

For this reason, psychoanalytic couple psychotherapy is usually, although not always, framed as an open-ended, long-term treatment. Each couple is unique and the time required for treatment will depend on the specifics of that particular couple. Psychoanalytic couple psychotherapy is similar to psychoanalysis or individual psychoanalytic psychotherapy in that there is no standard, pre-determined period for the treatment. Time is necessary for both the therapist and the couple to understand the complex unconscious processes that are creating difficulties, to work through these issues in the presence of the therapist, and for the couple to internalize these insights and capacities such that they will be better able to relate to one another outside of the therapeutic setting

Partner choice

In addition to the conscious aspects of choosing a mate, the choice of a partner has a large unconscious component. Individuals seek out a person who will receive, via projective identification, externalized parts of the self and create the opportunity for the reenactment of old, unresolved conflicts by dint of externalization. Partner choice always seems to contain a dynamic tension between, on the one hand, transference repetitions based on the experiences of one's past and, on the other hand, the hope that the new relationship will provide novel and better experiences. Put simply, when is a partner experienced as an important figure from one's past (such as a parent or sibling), versus when does the partner offer an opportunity for reworking unresolved issues with one's self and one's objects? The repetition compulsion that drives these unconscious projections tends to create a defensive experience of living with the same, familiar objects. This always stands in dynamic tension with the developmental hope and phantasy of having a better or reconstructive experience. It is precisely the dialectical relationship between the representations of these objects that creates the oscillations between defensive and developmental relating within the couple. This is one of the main points of focus in the treatment and those trained in the Tavistock model attempt to track these oscillating cycles, both within the clinical hour and across time over the course of the treatment.

Transference and countertransference

One of the hallmarks of psychoanalytic theory is the concept of the transference. A distinct advantage of couple psychotherapy is that the couple arrives with their mutual transferences intact, already matured and ripened, and the couple therapist does not have to wait for these transferences to develop. Transferences are immediately available for observation and interpretation. Moreover, in contrast to individual treatments, the couple therapy setting, by virtue of the fact that there are usually three persons in the room, potentially highlights aspects of both pre-Oedipal and Oedipal transferences.

The transferences in a couple's treatment are more numerous than in an individual treatment. There are the two individual partner transferences to one another, the two individual partner transferences to the therapist and the couple's transference to the therapist. Although the practice has greatly diminished due to practical concerns, couple psychotherapy at the Tavistock in the past routinely employed two couple therapists, increasing the number of transferences from five to nine! If we include tracking the multiple and inevitable countertransferences, this becomes an extremely complex model that requires the therapist to hold quite a lot in his or her mind.

Similar to individual psychoanalytic work, the range and variety of transference possibilities between the partners – and from each of the partners to the therapist – would be reflective of the degree and quality of pathology of the individual partners. This would also be true with regard to the range of countertransference experiences, reflecting the unconscious influences of the individual partners and the therapist.

However, in couple psychotherapy there also exists the couple's shared transference to the therapist (based on their shared unconscious) and the therapist's countertransference to the couple – a phenomenon unique to the couple psychotherapy situation.

Frequently, the couple's transference to the therapist contains a parental quality. Because they come to the therapist for help and because the therapist accepts this role, the couple can imbue the therapist with the parental qualities of nurturance, containment, knowledge or authority. On the more negative side of parental transference, the therapist may be experienced as withholding necessary supplies or bearing judgmental, critical or punitive tendencies. One possible manifestation of this type of transference is for each of the partners to direct themselves to the therapist as rivalrous siblings. They may attempt to convince the therapist/ parent that they have done nothing wrong or plead for advice, limit setting, special attention or approval. Another version of this transference scenario may develop when two hostile, warring partners approach the therapist as judge, expecting to receive a verdict on who is culpable for their problems.

Due to the triadic structure of the couple therapy setting, transferences to the therapist may also contain themes of competition and rivalry. One or both partners may feel excluded or jealous of the attention the other is receiving in the treatment. Erotic transferences to the couple therapist can also emerge. Simply by virtue of the fact that three persons are in the room together, triangulation dynamics and Oedipal themes of all sorts need to be attended to, especially sexual triangulations and rivalries.

Clearly, any of these transference paradigms will have corresponding countertransference responses, potentially containing elements of the therapist's own unconscious conflicts and vulnerabilities. Analysis of countertransference in couple work is as essential as it is in individual work because it can provide information crucial to the understanding of the projective processes of the couple. In contemporary psychoanalysis, we rely on the countertransference as a key for accessing the unconscious and its concomitant projective processes and we regard these phenomena as inevitable. The therapist may experience intense affective states, fantasies or pulls to enactments that can be disturbing and confusing. Consequently, in psychoanalytic couple psychotherapy, close attention is paid to both the transference and the countertransference in order to minimize countertransference enactments and as sources of information about the unconscious processes in the dynamics of the couple relationship. Self-examination of the therapist's feelings including anxiety, worthlessness, omnipotent certainty, hatred or erotic excitement become central to the therapeutic work with couples and are consistent with a contemporary view of countertransference. The Tavistock model emphasizes the inevitability of the therapist's countertransference during the course of the treatment and encourages careful scrutiny to minimize enactments and deepen the work, thereby viewing this as an opportunity to access and analyze the unconscious material that has been received via projective identification.

Couple formation and the development of a shared unconscious

The processes that occur in partner choice and in romantic couple formation are both conscious and unconscious. Typically, the initial idealization of the other, achieved by the unconscious projection of an idealized representational world, creates passion's foundation and results in the experience of falling in love. As time passes, the relentless press of reality erodes phantasy and idealization gives way to the complex task of integrating the full representational world of each of the partners, including good and bad, exciting and rejecting, partial and whole internal objects. This is often a critical point in the development of a relationship, when the blush of the honeymoon phase has worn off and both partners begin to struggle with the appearance of ambivalence and the loss of the idealization of the other.

Intrapsychically, several processes are at work simultaneously at this time. First, actual lived experience tends to modify and correct idealization. Each partner will, to some degree, reclaim some of his or her idealized projections, resulting in a more complex psychic experience of the other. Second, each partner will become the object of projections based on the entire self-representational field of the other, particularly the newly emerging negative components. Siegel (1992) has described the complexities of intimacy as a reorganization of the representational world that invests in the newly formed loved object psychic functions that were previously formed internally. The projected "good" self-representations endow the newly created love object as a provider and regulator of security and esteem. The projected or split off "bad" self-representations maintain these denied aspects of the self in the unconscious and form a boundary by which "the self is able to establish greater distance from the qualities it seeks to reject" (Siegel, 1992, p. 29). The projection of bad aspects of the self also results from the unique intra-psychic opportunities provided within the intimate relationship. Each individual strives to be fully known and to have previously repressed, split off or disowned aspects of the self experienced, reworked and mastered within the desired and longed for safety of the current relationship.

Kernberg (1995) has elaborated the dialectical tensions between libidinal and aggressive drives that both create and destroy the sense of attachment of the couple and coalesce in the formation of a new, unique intra-psychic shared system. The development of this shared intra-psychic life is a third complex process that is operating during the critical phase following the loss of the idealization of the new loved object. This creation of the couple, intra-psychically, is rooted in their shared sense of history and future life together, and is born out of the complex mutual object relation field of both partners. Thus, the mutual acceptance of projections forms the unconscious attachment of the couple but this may be undermined by either partner's inability to contain or accept certain projections. This shared unconscious contains the shared fantasies and defenses that function dynamically to interweave, through containment and conflict, each partner's individual fantasies, anxieties and defenses.

States of mind

Much of the training and literature developed at the TCCR has relied on the Kleinian conception of psychic positions: the paranoid-schizoid and depressive position states of mind that Klein (1928) theorized exist in each of us and shape our experiences of ourselves, of others and of the world we inhabit. More recent TCCR writers (e.g., Berg, 2012; Sehgal, 2012) have included the addition of a third, more primitive state of mind: the autistic-contiguous position (Ogden, 1989) or claustro-agoraphobic anxieties (Rey, 1994; Meltzer, 1992) and Glasser's (1979) idea of the core complex.

In this model, the individual partners of a couple, as well as the couple relationship, are thought to reflect a range of anxieties. These anxieties exist on a continuum ranging from the quite disturbed (such as fears of annihilation, engulfment or abandonment), to more depressive anxieties (such as conflicts about aggression, inhibitions or Oedipal guilt regarding separation or competition).

These different states of mind are not only associated with qualitatively different anxieties, they are also associated with different sorts of defenses. For example, couples functioning from a more paranoid-schizoid state of mind will tend to rely on immature forms of idealization, blaming, splitting, projection, denial and projective identification in their relating. These types of relationships are often described in the TCCR literature as narcissistic in their relating (e.g., Ruszczynski, 1995), because one or both of the partners will have difficulty relating to the other as a separate person, a person with different needs, feelings and experiences. These differences may be experienced as intolerable and there may be enormous pressure to always be in agreement, resulting in an illusory and unsustainable state of merger, or a constant battle between two people who feel dominated by one another's needs.

In contrast, couples functioning with more depressive position capacities will be more likely to integrate good and bad experiences, as opposed to relying on splitting. They will have a greater capacity to relate with concern for one another, to tolerate separation and loss, and have a greater capacity for mourning and ambivalence. They will be more able to tolerate difference and be curious about the differences between them, as opposed to feeling threatened or resorting to blame. Finally, the depressive position will promote greater psychic flexibility for the couple such that they will be able to tolerate the fluctuating changes and the slings and arrows that occur over time during the couple's life together, resulting in a shared life of creativity and genuine intimacy.

In reality, these states are not binary and exist within all couples. All couples, even high-functioning ones, relate to one another in more regressed ways at times. A primary goal of couple psychotherapy in this model would be to increase the couple's awareness of the unconscious dynamics that contribute to these patterns and to help them move away from narcissistic to more mature forms of relating, from paranoid/schizoid states toward more depressive position functioning.

Bion: container/contained

Bion's concept of container/contained (1962a, 1962b) is fundamental to the Tavistock model of understanding and working with the dynamics of couple relationships. In Bion's theory of the mind, thinking is dependent on two mental developments: the development of thoughts and the development of the mental apparatus to deal with thoughts. These capacities are rooted in the early parent–infant dyad and are crucial to mature psychic functioning, including the capacity to relate to the emotional experience of oneself and others.

Winnicott has bequeathed us the aphorism:

> There is no such thing as a baby ... if you set out to describe a baby, you will find you are describing a baby and someone. A baby cannot exist alone but is essentially a part of a relationship.
>
> (Winnicott, 1947a, p. 137)

Similarly, Bion argued that it takes two minds to think a thought and he located the origins of this development in the early relationship between the infant and the primary caretaker (Ogden, 2008). The infant, who possesses a limited capacity for processing intense emotional experience, projects into the mother the emotional experience that he or she is unable to process on his or her own. In what Bion (1962a) refers to as the mother's state of reverie, she does the unconscious psychological work of processing the infant's unbearable experience, metabolizing it and offering it back in a form that the infant is able to use. What is "contained" is one's lived emotional experience and the "container" consists of the process of bearing and understanding that experience. In this model, it takes two people to make sense of experience and this forms a template for all later intimate relationships. The experience of "container/contained" is gradually internalized by the infant and can be relied upon as a way to understand and modulate his or her own emotional experience. In Bion's model, this process is essential to the development of many aspects of mature psychological functioning and the capacity for thinking itself, including the development of curiosity.

Of course, there are many reasons why this process might not go well. For example, if the primary caretaker has limited psychological abilities, a history of past trauma, or has failed to internalize an experience of container/contained, then they may perceive their own infant's demands as an attack, rather than as a necessary experience of emotional dependency. Then the infant may be subject to its caregiver's emotional anxiety, withdrawal or other misattuned or unempathic responses. The parent's inability to take in the infant's projections may be perceived by the baby as disappointment, abandonment or counterattack. Instead of the expansion of the capacity for thought and emotional experience, the result is a shutting down of the child's development of intellectual and emotional curiosity about the self and the other.

All individuals hold unconscious beliefs about the nature of coupling and these unconscious beliefs, based on early experiences, significantly affect couple functioning (Morgan, this volume). The extent to which one has internalized the container/contained experience will greatly affect one's unconscious beliefs and expectations for emotional containment in couple relationships, determining both the extent to which one believes that they can expect to receive containment from their partner and their own capacity to provide it. A central question for the individual partners in a relationship is: "are my emotional experiences too dangerous and damaging to myself and to others and likely to cause abandonment, rejection, or retaliation?" Alongside this fear, each partner also holds the hope that they will be received, understood and helped by the other. In relationships that are working well, there is a sense that the partners can provide containment for one another and, additionally, that the relationship itself may be experienced as an emotional container (Colman, 1993).

Consonant with the importance of each individual to act as container/contained for the other and for the relationship to serve this containing function for the couple, many of the Tavistock writers highlight the importance of the containing function of the couple psychotherapist (Colman, 1993; Fisher, 1999; Morgan, 2001; Ruszczynski, 1993; Skrine, 2001; Vincent, 2001). Aspects of the therapeutic frame that promote reliability, consistency, clear boundaries and safety are certainly an essential part of providing containment for the couple and help to create a setting where it is possible to explore difficult material. Even more importantly, the Tavistock model emphasizes that the creation of the experience of container/contained rests on the therapist's capacity to struggle to understand the intense affects in the room and receive them as communications rather than to act them out. Colman (1993) references Winnicott's concept of the importance of the analyst surviving in the face of the patient's despair and views this as an essential aspect of containment in couple psychotherapy. Moreover, the therapist's capacity for containment of his or her own emotional experience lays the groundwork for the couple to develop this capacity through the therapy.

The "couple state of mind" and "the third"

The couple therapist's ability to metabolize and maintain the capacity to think is embodied in what Mary Morgan (2001) has termed the "couple state of mind" and is crucial to the therapist providing a sense of containment for the couple. The couple state of mind is a stance encompassing both a psychological and a therapeutic position. This refers to the capacity to be subjectively involved with both individuals and, at the same time, to be able to think about the couple – to be able to stand outside of them and observe their relationship, while being in relationship to them separately and together.

This is an extension of Bion's concept of container/contained to the relationship between the therapist and the couple and it is theoretically linked to Britton's (1989) idea of "the third position," Odgen's (2004) concept of the "analytic third" and Ruszczynski's (2005) idea of the "marital triangle." All of these conceptions of the "third" refer to an individual's capacity to participate in a dyad, while at the same time being able to stand "outside" of it, observe and think about the relationship. These capacities derive from the experience of container/contained and are essential to healthy relating.

Just as the child must develop the capacity to relate to the parental couple and not simply to each of the parents as individuals, the couple therapist must relate to each of the partners separately and together. According to Morgan (2001), this notion of the third is an essential element of the couple state of mind and is unconsciously sought in the figure of the therapist, someone who is hoped to be a figure possessing capacities for thinking and for objectivity, and one who can stand symbolically for the relationship. Over the course of a couple's psychotherapy, we would hope that the couple would increasingly internalize this function and gain the ability to observe, think and relate to one another from this "third" position. When the relationship is functioning well, the relationship itself becomes the symbolic third and can serve as a resource for the partners, including serving as a profound source of containment.

Projective identification

The concept of projective identification has become a cornerstone of object relations theory and is central to TCCR's theoretical model of couple dynamics. Stan Ruszczynski, Director of TCCR for many years and a major contributor to the psychoanalytic couple literature, including this volume, states: "It is not possible to understand this approach to the couple relationship without an appreciation of the centrality of projective identification" (1995, p. 2).

Melanie Klein (1946) first introduced the term "projective identification" to theorize the way the infant manages intense anxiety states and how this influences its object relations. Klein posited that the young infant, in the paranoid-schizoid position, is beset with intense internal persecutory anxieties that result from both frustrations in external reality and his or her own innate destructive impulses. In order to protect the self, the infant splits off the parts of the self that are seen as bad, hateful, attacking and projects them into the object. Consequently, these parts are no longer felt to be existing within oneself, but are experienced as belonging to the other, leading to an experience of the other as bad or as the cause of one's anxiety. This then becomes the basis for a particular type of aggressive object relationship. This is a defense against feelings of separateness, dependence and envy of the object. Because projective identification involves the phantasy that a part of oneself is put into the other, it is omnipotent in nature and characteristic of narcissistic phenomena.

Thus, for the couple functioning in this mode, projective identification dominates and there is a denial of separateness in their interactions. In contrast, the hallmark of a healthy relationship is the engagement of two individuals who have a strong sense of their own separateness. Therefore, many of the TCCR authors emphasize, in both theory and clinical practice, the development of the couple's capacity to tolerate difference and the curiosity about these differences (e.g., Balfour, 2005; Fisher, 1993, 1999; Morgan, 1995; Ruszczynski, 2005).

The projection of parts of oneself into the other can lead to the unconscious phantasy that essential, albeit dangerous parts of the self reside in the other, creating a suffocating and claustrophobic form of dependency. Couples who chronically relate on these terms can be particularly difficult to help as their mutual projections have an intractable nature. Morgan

(1995) has described this situation as a "projective gridlock" – when both members of the couple rely on projective identification to such an extent that there is an extreme lack of separation and an intense dependency between them.

For Klein, projective identification is chiefly a defense. But for Bion, projective identification not only serves a defensive function, but is primarily communicative. He extended projective identification from a form of splitting and defensive evacuation to a more universal and less pathological form of communication between the infant and the mother. He posited that this process is essential to the development of a person's ability to think about their own thoughts and feelings, as well as their capacity to think about the other's experience. From this point of view, the purpose of projective identification is not only to attack the object and get rid of unbearable feelings, but also to communicate something about affective experience. Through this interpersonal exchange of communicating feelings to another person through projective identification, the potential arises to have the other experience these feelings and the possibility of containment is created. Thus, projective identification may be understood to be a process that is multidimensional and multifunctional. It may serve as a defense, as a communication, as a primitive form of object relations or as a way of relating that facilitates change (Ogden, 1982).

The Oedipal situation

In contemporary Kleinian theory, the ubiquity and necessity of negotiating the complexities of the Oedipal situation are viewed as central organizing schema and this has been a seminal concept in the Tavistock model for understanding couples. Klein (1928) viewed the Oedipal situation as beginning in early infancy, when the infant turns away from one parent in frustration and moves toward the other parent, creating the initial triangle composed of the infant and two parents. In Klein's time, the primary parent was deemed to be the mother, and therefore the infant, the mother and the father constituted the triangle. Conceived in a more contemporary way, Klein's concept of the Oedipal triangle may be removed from its heterosexist bias and applied to modern families with two parents of the same sex or a single parent. Children in all types of family structures must come to terms with the anxieties and demands of the Oedipal situation through the experience of frustration, loss and the relinquishment of the phantasy of omnipotent control over the primary parent (Nathans, 2012).

For Klein, an important aspect of psychic development occurs with the child's awareness of the parental relationship (Klein, 1928). She argued that the confrontation with the parental couple involves the recognition of its existence, the perception of the sexual link between the parents and the experience of being excluded from this relationship. These elements are viewed as fundamental to the development of psychic functioning and are crucial to the achievement of depressive position capacities.

Ron Britton's paper, The Missing Link: Parental Sexuality in the Oedipus Complex (1989), has had a seminal influence on the Tavistock model (e.g., Balfour, 2005, Fisher, 1993; Grier, 2005; Morgan, 1995; Ruszczynski, 2005). Britton argued that the child's acceptance of the reality of the parental couple and tolerance of being excluded from this dyad results in a capacity for "flexible triangulation." This is associated with many of the qualities that are essential for forming healthy intimate relationships. Britton based this idea on the child's experience of being excluded from and observing the parental couple. This formative experience includes both being observed by the parental couple and observing the parental couple. In healthy development, this results in the development of a psychic structure that can be considered to be a "third position" making it possible to have the capacity to observe and be observed. For Britton, this third position is essential for thinking and is inextricably linked to the capacity to observe oneself and to think about the content of one's mind. Flexible triangulation allows for the development of an object relationship in which one has the capacity to see the other's point of view while still holding onto one's own point of view – an essential aspect of mature relating in an intimate relationship.

The creative couple

Mary Morgan (2005), using Britton's conceptualization, has written that these psychic developments are necessary in order to become a part of a couple and help sustain the individual in a relationship. She refers to this as the "internalization of a creative couple," an internal parental couple that is characteristic of a certain state of mind. She noted that:

the "creative couple" is primarily a psychic development, one in which it is possible to allow different thoughts and feelings to come together in one's mind, and for something to develop out of them. This capacity obviously has a major impact on an actual couple relationship. If one can allow this kind of mating within oneself, it becomes more likely that one can allow it to occur between oneself and one's partner.

(Morgan, 2005, p. 22)

A creative couple, for Morgan, is characterized by the capacities for individuation and intimacy, separateness and dependency, self-reflection, tolerance for being excluded and the ability to exclude, and most importantly, being able to hold onto one's own point of view without the anxiety of being swamped by one's partner's thoughts. The creative couple creates space for individuals to develop within and outside the relationship; it promotes space for reflective thinking. Morgan references Britton's (2004) idea of a post-depressive position in describing the creative couple's flexible movement between certainty and uncertainty, between regression and progression, between the paranoid-schizoid and depressive positions, and between destruction and creativity.

A creative couple has the capability to produce something outside of their relationship, to create a link between them, and to produce a symbolic third. Sometimes this third is symbolized by the creation of a child, but this need not necessarily be expressed in such a concrete representation. Any creative endeavor that the couple engages in may symbolically represent their creative capacity. Most importantly, for the creative couple, the couple's relationship is the third. Such couples feel that they have something to which they can relate, something that contains both of them, and something that provides them with a shared story.

Narcissistic forms of relating

In contrast to mature couples that rely primarily on depressive position capacities, many couples are beset by an absence of psychic space and lack sufficient separateness to achieve the flexibility associated with creative couple relating. The TCCR literature of the past 20 years reflects an increasing interest in what would be described as the forms of relating that underlie these types of disturbances, as opposed to the previous

TCCR primary focus on analyzing the shared unconscious fantasies of the couple.

This trend is exemplified in several important papers. Ruszczynski (1995) has detailed the particular qualities and dilemmas that often define couples who primarily relate narcissistically. He describes two presentations of narcissistic relating: couples who are aloof, self-sufficient and without mutual regard and those couples who are lacking sufficient separateness and function with a type of fusion. In both types of narcissistic couplings, the partners may feel dominated by the needs of their partner or they may feel ignored and neglected. They are "dominated by a psychic organization that requires agreement as the primary aspect of their relationship. Differentiation, ambivalence, or conflict appear to be totally unmanageable" (Ruszczynski, 1995, p. 15).

As described earlier, Morgan (1995) has extended this idea of narcissistic relating to introduce the term "projective gridlock," a specific form of narcissistic relating in a couple that keeps them locked into a defensive collusion that inhibits growth because the couple cannot tolerate feeling psychically separate from one another.

James Fisher, a Bion scholar and one of the foremost and most prolific contributors to the Tavistock couple literature (1995, 1999, 2007, 2008, 2009), has written extensively on the problems with narcissistic relating in couples. He focuses on issues of identity, separation and narcissistic fusion (Fisher, 1999). In an especially useful and erudite chapter, called "The Macbeths in the Consulting Room" (published in this book), he borrows a term from rhetoric, "the proleptic imagination," to describe a state of mind in which a representation of something in the future is related to as if it has already occurred or currently exists, as if the feeling of reality substitutes for reality. These states of mind, when operative in one or both of the individuals in the couple, create a form of narcissistic relating characterized by certainty and the absence of curiosity and can lead to unrelenting arguments over "the truth." In two of Fisher's papers (1993, 1999), he coined the term "false-self couple," following Winnicott's schema of the false self (Winnicott, 1956). Fisher extends Winnicott's idea to describe the object relation field of such couples and states that: "Every couple whose relating is structured on this pattern – every false-self couple – is made up of either a compliant self and a tyrannical other, or a tyrannical self and a compliant other" (Fisher, 1999, p. 46).

Serious disturbances in couple relating

A number of TCCR authors and others influenced by this model have examined the difficulties of trying to help couples whose problems result from very early psychic disturbances. Several authors have described the specific dynamics inherent in couples with a sadomasochistic form of relating (Fisher, 1999; Ruszczynski, 2005; Hewison, 2009). Abse (2013a, 2013b) has focused on the daunting technical problems of working with the instability, cycles of attacking and blaming, and fear of breakdown that often characterize difficult to treat, severely borderline couples. Several authors have attempted to understand the various aspects of perversion and perverse relating in couples (Morgan & Freedman, 2009; Rosenthal, 2009; Nicolo, 2013).

In Clulow's (2001) edited book, *Adult Attachment and Couple Psychotherapy*, attachment theory is used to examine many aspects of adult couple relating, including the link between different types of attachment and abuse. In the same volume, Vincent (2001) describes the intense and frightening countertransference experiences frequently encountered when working with the unresolved and unclassifiable states of mind in couples that have a disorganized attachment style.

Undoubtedly, couples functioning with these types of serious disturbances in their relating face greater problems when trying to separate or divorce. In recent years, a Divorce and Separation Unit was developed at the TCCR to focus attention on the vexing and tenacious difficulties of working with high conflict couples that are in the process of separation and or divorce. Shmueli (2012) and Vincent (2001), working within the TCCR model, give detailed descriptions of the unconscious and conscious psychological dilemmas that are associated with high conflict separation and divorce scenarios and they offer technical recommendations to help therapists manage and navigate these clinical challenges.

Sex and sexual problems in the couple relationship

In the seismic theoretical shift from Freud to Klein, an emphasis on psychic phantasy replaced classical drive theory and the primacy of sexuality became demoted from its central place in British psychoanalytic theory (Green, 1995). This fundamental change had a profound impact on the Kleinian, contemporary Kleinian and the middle school literature, all of which have provided the dominant theoretical paradigm by which the TCCR model has been informed. It is ironic that the TCCR, an institution devoted to the study of couple relationships for nearly 60 years, almost entirely neglected the topic of sexuality until very recently. Clulow (2009) offered a corrective with an edited collection of papers entitled *Sex, Attachment, and Couple Psychotherapy: Psychoanalytic Perspectives*. This book contains a number of important chapters that, taken together, begin to address some of the theoretical and technical issues pertaining to sex and sexuality that were previously neglected. Colman's (2009) paper in this volume, "What Do We Mean by Sex?" offers especially useful technical guidance. He advocates orienting therapeutic interpretations either toward or away from the sexual content in the clinical process based on an understanding of what the couple is unconsciously avoiding and defending against. Clulow and Boerma (2009) examine the dynamics and disorders of sexual desire using a complex model based on an integration of attachment theory with other psychoanalytic theories that emphasize the centrality of separation and merger issues. They argue that an early secure attachment provides an adult with important capacities in adult sexual relationships. These include mutuality in sexual relating and the capacity to maintain psychic separateness; capacities that rely on trust that merger will not swamp individuality. In this same volume, Hewison (2009) considers how the distinction between power and love is crucial to understanding sadomasochistic sexual relations.

A number of TCCR authors have discussed the frequently presenting problem of the "no-sex" couple. Grier (2005, 2009) analyzes this phenomenon in terms of unconscious Oedipal dynamics, linking Klein's (1928) ideas about primal scene anxieties and Bion's (1965) concept of catastrophic change to explain the defensive stance underlying this symptom. Two other papers on this topic from TCCR authors explain this same problem of "no-sex" coupling in terms of more disturbed anxieties. Berg (2012) and Sehgal (2012) employ the concepts of autistic-contiguous anxieties (Ogden, 1989), the claustro-agoraphobic narrative (Meltzer, 1992), and the core complex (Glasser, 1979) as an explanation for the lack of sexual activity in some couples. While there are distinctions between these concepts, each of these ideas locates these disturbances in the pre-paranoid-schizoid realm, where terrors about engulfment, claustrophobia, annihilation and disintegration reign, rendering the individual unable to be in an intimate relationship without fear that their identity will be threatened and potentially annihilated by the fusion with their partner.

The Tavistock model and relational psychoanalysis

Psychoanalysis in the United Kingdom and the couple psychotherapy model at the Tavistock have evolved under the influence of the Kleinian, neo-Kleinian and middle group theorists and, until recently, have remained largely unaffected by other psychoanalytic schools. Those familiar with intersubjective theory or relational psychoanalysis – theories developed beginning in the United States in the 1980s – may notice several points of overlap between these perspectives, object relations theory and the Tavistock model. These American frameworks marked a radical departure from the dominant "one-person" psychoanalysis of the time and proposed a "two-person" theory that, similar to the Tavistock model, assumes that individuals unconsciously influence one another in interactions. In addition, both relational theory and object relations theory embrace the assumption that psychic structure is not primarily an outcome of unconscious drives. Rather, they maintain that psychic structure is derived from early and formative relationships with other people who are carried throughout life and influence the quality and subjective experiences of later relationships.

Thus, both relational theory and the Tavistock model attend to the unconscious processes in which two people exert mutual influence on one another and form a shared intra-psychic system (Gerson, 2004; Kernberg, 1995; Ruszczynski, 1993). Although there are points of divergence regarding technique, such as differences regarding the self-disclosure of countertransference reactions, both of these paradigms rely on the countertransference as an important source of information that can provide access to unconscious interpersonal dynamics. In short, relational psychoanalytic theory, object relations theory and the Tavistock couple psychotherapy model share a primary focus on the intersection of two minds in interaction and these psychoanalytic traditions are applicable to the analytic couple and the patient couple.

Conclusion

The Tavistock couple psychotherapy model is rich and complex, examining the joys and travails of couple life and the dynamics of intimacy from a psychoanalytic lens. Certain core principles, derived from Freud, Fairbairn, Klein, Bion, Meltzer, Winnicott and contemporary psychoanalytic theorists, form the foundation of a deep and multi-layered approach to understanding and working with couples.

The vantage point of the unconscious can help us to understand the repetitive and rigid relationship dynamics that often underlie the difficulties that plague couples and perpetuate their struggles. The Tavistock Centre for Couple Relations has had a long and extensive history of conducting research, teaching, providing rigorous training and clinical services. This has resulted in a comprehensive model that will benefit all couple therapists, aid them in their attempts to go beyond the surface of interactions and help them in their struggles to understand, name and attempt to ameliorate the suffering that afflicts so many of the couples who seek our help.

Notes

1 Some notable exceptions include the program that the editors of this volume are affiliated with, the Psychoanalytic Couple Psychotherapy Program in Berkeley, California and the Washington Center for Psychoanalysis in Washington, DC. Programs that combine psychoanalytic and systems theory include the Couple Therapy Training Program at the Training Institute for Mental Health in New York City, the Advanced Specialization in Couple and Family Therapy at the NYU Postdoctoral Program in New York City and the Psychodynamic Couple and Family Institute of New England in Boston.
2 The Centre has been re-named several times from the original name, the Family Discussion Bureau, to the Institute of Marital Studies, to the Tavistock Institute of Marital Studies, to the Tavistock Centre for Couple Relationships (TCCR), to its current name – Tavistock Relationships. For the sake of consistency with the other chapters in this book, I refer to it as TCCR. For a detailed institutional and theoretical history of the Tavistock model of couple psychotherapy, see S. Ruszczynski, "The Institutional Context," in Ruszczynski (1993).
3 To be consistent with British psychoanalysis, I use different terms to distinguish between conscious (fantasy) and unconscious (phantasy) phenomena.

References

Abse, S. (2013a). When a Problem Shared Is a Problem.... Whose Illness is it Anyway? Questions of Technique When Working With a Borderline Couple. *Couple and Family Psychoanalysis, 3(2):* 163–177.

Abse, S. (2013b). Further Thoughts on When a Problem Shared is a Problem.... Whose Illness is it Anyway?: Questions of Technique When Working with a Borderline Couple. *Couple and Family Psychoanalysis, 3(2):* 178–187.

Balfour, A. (2005). The Couple, Their Marriage and Oedipus: Or, Problems Come in Two and Threes. In F. Grier (Ed.) *Oedipus and the Couple* (pp. 49–71). London: Karnac.

Balfour, A., Morgan, M. & Vincent, C. (Eds.) (2012). *How Couple Relationships Shape our World: Clinical Practice, Research, and Policy Perspectives.* London: Karnac.

Berg, J. (2012). "A Bad Moment with the Light." No-Sex Couples: The Role of Autistic Contiguous Anxieties. *Couple and Family Psychoanalysis, 2(1):* 33–48.

Bion, W. (1961). *Experiences in Groups and Other Papers.* London: Tavistock Publications.

Bion, W. (1962a). *Learning from Experience.* London: Heinemann. [Reprinted London: Karnac Books, 1984].

Bion, W. (1962b). A Theory of Thinking. In *Second Thoughts.* London: Heinemann. [Reprinted London: Karnac Books, 1984].

Bion, W. (1965). *Transformations.* London: Heinemann.

Bowen, M. (1978). *Family Therapy in Clinical Practice.* Lanham, MD: Jason Aronson.

Bowlby, J. (1969). *Attachment and Loss.* Vol. 1. Attachment. London: Hogarth Press.

Bowlby, J. (1973). *Attachment and Loss.* Vol. 2. Separation: Anxiety and Anger. London: Hogarth Press.

Britton, R. (1989). The Missing Link: Parental Sexuality in the Oedipus Complex. In J. Steiner (Ed.) *The Oedipus Complex Today: Clinical Implications* (pp. 83–101). London: Karnac.

Britton, R. (2004). *Belief and Imagination: Explorations in Psychoanalysis.* London and New York: Routledge.

Colman, W. (1993). Marriage as a Psychological Container. In S. Ruszczynski (Ed.) *Psychotherapy with Couples* (pp. 70–98). London: Karnac.

Colman, W. (2009). What Do We Mean by Sex? In C. Clulow (Ed.) *Sex, Attachment and Couple Psychotherapy* (pp. 25–44). London: Karnac.

Clulow, C. (Ed.) (2001). *Adult Attachment and Couple Psychotherapy: The "Secure Base" in Practice and Research.* London: Brunner-Routledge.

Clulow, C. (Ed.) (2009). *Sex, Attachment and Couple Psychotherapy: Psychoanalytic Perspectives.* London: Karnac.

Clulow, C. & Boerma, M. (2009). Dynamics and disorders of sexual desire. In C. Clulow (Ed.) *Sex, Attachment and Couple Psychotherapy: Psychoanalytic Perspectives* (pp. 75–102). London: Karnac.

Dicks, H. (1967). *Marital Tensions: Clinical Studies Toward a Psychological Theory of Interaction.* London: Karnac.

Fairbairn, W.D. (1952). *Psychoanalytic Studies of the Personality.* London: Tavistock.

Fairbairn, W.D. (1963). Synopsis of an Object-Relations Theory of the Personality. *International Journal of Psychoanalysis, 44:* 224–225.

Feldman, M. (1989). The Oedipus Complex: Manifestations in the Inner World and the Therapeutic Situation. In J. Steiner (Ed.) *The Oedipus Complex Today: Clinical Implications* (pp. 103–128). London: Karnac.

Fisher, J.V. (1993). The Impenetrable Other: Ambivalence and the Oedipal Conflict in Work with Couples. In S. Ruszczynski (Ed.) *Psychotherapy with Couples* (pp. 142–166). London: Karnac.

Fisher, J.V. (1995). Identity and Intimacy in the Couple: Three Kinds of Identification. In S. Ruszczynski & J. Fisher (Eds.) *Intrusiveness and Intimacy in the Couple* (pp. 74–106). London: Karnac.

Fisher, J.V. (1999). *The Uninvited Guest.* London: Karnac.

Fisher, J.V. (2007). The Marriage of the Macbeths. In M. Ludlam & V. Nyberg (Eds.) *Couple Attachments: Theoretical and Clinical Studies* (pp. 23–41). London: Karnac.

Fisher, J.V. (2008). The Role of Imagination in the Apprehension of Difference. *fort da, 14(1):* 17–35.

Fisher, J.V. (2009). The Macbeths in the Consulting Room. *fort da, 15:* 33–55.

Gerson, S. (2004). The Relational Unconscious: A Core Element of Intersubjectivity, Thirdness, and Clinical Process. *Psychoanalytic Quarterly, 73:* 63–98.

Glasser, M. (1979). Some Aspects of the Role of Aggression in the Perversions. In I. Rosen (Ed.) *Sexual Deviation* (2nd ed.) (pp. 278–305). Oxford: Oxford University Press.

Green, A. (1995). Has Sexuality Anything To Do With Psychoanalysis? *International Journal of Psycho-Analysis, 76:* 871–883.

Grier, F. (Ed.) (2001). *Brief Encounters with Couples: Some Analytical Perspectives.* London: Karnac.

Grier, F. (Ed.) (2005). *Oedipus and The Couple.* London: Karnac.

Grier, F. (2009). Lively and Deathly Intercourse. In C. Clulow (Ed.) *Sex, Attachment and Couple Psychotherapy: Psychoanalytic Perspectives* (pp. 45–62). London: Karnac.

Hewison, D. (2009). Power vs. Love in Sadomasochistic Couple Relationships. In C. Clulow (Ed.) *Sex, Attachment, and Couple Psychotherapy* (pp. 165–184). London: Karnac.

Johnson, S. (2004). *The Practice of Emotionally Focused Couple Therapy.* New York: Brunner-Routledge.

Joseph, B. (1989). *Psychic Equilibrium and Psychic Change: Selected Papers of Betty Joseph.* E. Bott Spillius & M. Feldman (Eds.), New Library of Psychoanalysis. London: Routledge.
Jung, C.G. (1954–1990). *The Collected Works of C.G. Jung.* New York: Routledge.
Kernberg, O. (1995). *Love Relations.* New Haven: Yale University Press.
Klein, M. (1928). Early Stages of the Oedipus Conflict. *International Journal of Psychoanalysis, 9:* 167–180. [Reprinted in *Love, Guilt and Reparation & Other Works.* London: Hogarth Press, 1975].
Klein, M. (1945). The Oedipus Complex in the Light of Early Anxieties. *International Journal of Psycho-Analysis, 26:* 11–33. [Reprinted in *The Writings of Melanie Klein, Vol. 1.* London: Hogarth Press, 1975; reprinted London: Karnac, 1992].
Klein, M. (1946). Notes on Some Schizoid Mechanisms. *International Journal of Psycho-Analysis, 27:* 99–110. [Reprinted in *The Writings of Melanie Klein. Vol. III* (pp. 1–24). London: Hogarth Press, 1975].
Ludlam, M. (2014). Sitting with Marital Tensions: The Work of Henry Dicks in Applying Fairbairn's Ideas to Couple Relationships. In G. Clarke & D. Scharff (Eds.) *Fairbairn and the Object Relations Tradition* (pp. 175–183). London: Karnac.
Ludlam, M. & Nyberg, V. (Eds.) (2007). *Couple Attachments: Theoretical and Clinical Studies.* London: Karnac.
Meltzer, D. (1967). *The Psycho-Analytical Process.* London: Heinemann.
Meltzer. D. (1992). *The Claustrum: An Investigation of Claustrophobic Phenomena.* Perthshire, Scotland: Clunie Press.
Menzies, I.E. (1949). Factors Affecting Family Breakdown in Urban Communities. Human Relations, *11(4):* 363–374. [Reprinted in I. Menzies Lyth, *Containing Anxiety in Institutions: Selected Essays.* London: Free Association Books, 1989].
Morgan, M. (1995). The Projective Gridlock: A Form of Projective Identification in Couple Relationships. In S. Ruszczynski & J. Fisher (Eds.) *Intrusiveness and Intimacy in the Couple* (pp. 33–48). London: Karnac.
Morgan, M. (2001). First Contacts: The Therapist's "Couple State of Mind" as a Factor in Containment of Couples Seen for Consultations. In F. Grier (Ed.) *Brief Encounters with Couples* (pp. 17–32). London: Karnac.
Morgan, M. (2005). On Being Able to Be a Couple: The Importance of a "Creative Couple" in Psychic Life. In F. Grier (Ed.) *Oedipus and the Couple* (pp. 9–30). London: Karnac.
Morgan, M. & Freedman, J. (2009). From Fear of Intimacy to Perversion. In C. Clulow (Ed.) *Sex, Attachment, and Couple Psychotherapy* (pp. 185–198). London: Karnac.
Nathans, S. (2012). Infidelity as Manic Defence. *Couple and Family Psychoanalysis, 2:* 165–180.
Nicolo, A.M. (2013). Couples and Perversion. *Couple and Family Psychoanalysis, 3(1):* 15–27.

Ogden. T. (1982). *Projective Identification and Psychotherapeutic Technique.* New York: Jason Aronson.
Ogden, T. (1989). On the Concept of an Autistic-Contiguous Position. *The International Journal of Psychoanalysis, 70(1):* 127–140.
Ogden, T. (2004). The Analytic Third: Implications for Psychoanalytic Theory and Technique. *Psychoanalytic Quarterly, 73:* 167–195.
Ogden. T. (2008). Bion's Four Principles of Mental Functioning. *fort da, 14:* 11–35.
Rey, H. (1994). *Universals of Psychoanalysis in the Treatment of Psychotic and Borderline States.* London: Free Association.
Rosenfeld, H. (1964). On the Psychopathology of Narcissism: A Clinical Approach. *International Journal of Psycho-Analysis, 45:* 169–179.
Rosenfeld, H. (1983). Primitive Object Relations and Mechanisms. *International Journal of Psycho-Analysis, 64:* 261–267.
Rosenthal, J. (2009). Perversion as Protection. In C. Clulow (Ed.) *Sex, Attachment, and Couple Psychotherapy* (pp. 199–216). London: Karnac.
Ruszczynski, S. (1993). *Psychotherapy with Couples: Theory and Practice at the Tavistock Institute of Marital Studies.* London: Karnac.
Ruszczynski, S. (1995). Narcissistic Object Relating. In S. Ruszczynski & J. Fisher (Eds.) *Intrusiveness and Intimacy in the Couple* (pp. 33–48). London: Karnac.
Ruszczynski, S. (2005). Reflective Space in the Intimate Couple Relationship: The "Marital Triangle." In F. Grier (Ed.) *Oedipus and the Couple* (pp. 31–48). London: Karnac.
Ruszczynski, S. & Fisher, J. (Eds.) (1995). *Intrusiveness and Intimacy in the Couple.* London: Karnac.
Sander, F. (1993). Foreword to H. Dicks, *Marital Tensions: Clinical Studies Towards a Psychological Theory of Interaction.* London: Karnac.
Sehgal, A. (2012). Viewing the Absence of Sex from Couple Relationships Through the "Core Complex" Lens. *Couple and Family Psychoanalysis, 2(2):* 149–164.
Shmueli, A. (2012). Working Therapeutically with High Conflict Divorce. In A. Balfour, M. Morgan & C. Vincent (Eds.) *How Couple Relationships Shape Our World* (pp. 137–158). London: Karnac.
Siegel, J.P. (1992). *Repairing Intimacy: An Object Relations Approach to Couples Therapy.* Northvale, NJ: Jason Aronson.
Skrine, R. (2001). Emotional Contact and Containment in Psychosexual Medicine. In F. Grier (Ed.) *Brief Encounters with Couples* (pp. 99–112). London: Karnac.
Steiner, J. (1993). *Psychic Retreats.* London: Routledge.
Vincent, C. (2001). Giving Advice During Consultations: Unconscious Enactment or Thoughtful Containment? In F. Grier (Ed.) *Brief Encounters with Couples* (pp. 85–98). London: Karnac.

Wallerstein, R. (1988). One Psychoanalysis or Many? *International Journal of Psychoanalysis, 69:* 16–17. [Reprinted in *The Common Ground of Psychoanalysis*, R. Wallerstein (Ed.). Northvale, NJ: Jason Aronson, 1992, pp. 56–57].

Winnicott, D.W. (1947a). Further Thoughts on Babies as Persons. In *The Child and the Outside World* (pp. 134–140). London: Tavistock Publications, 1957.

Winnicott, D.W. (1947b). Hate in the Counter-Transference. *International Journal of Psychoanalysis, 41:* 585–595.

Winnicott, D.W. (1956). On Transference. *International Journal of Psychoanalysis, 37:* 386–388.

Winnicott, D.W. (1965). *The Maturational Process and the Facilitating Environment.* London: Hogarth Press.

Chapter 2

Couples on the couch
Working psychoanalytically with couple relationships

Stanley Ruszczynski

Is what I do as a psychoanalytic couple psychotherapist "psychoanalysis"?[1] Much literature exists on what defines psychoanalysis. Of course, there is no final conclusion, but I think it is possible to refer to a set of concepts that most psychoanalytic practitioners would hold to – unconscious processes, the conflicts between life forces and anti-life forces or between love and hate, resistances, and the inevitability of transference and countertransference. In my experience, these concepts come very close to what is available for the clinician who has a couple relationship in treatment and who holds the same "neutral role" as any analyst in observing, processing, analysing, and communicating what is experienced in the clinical encounter.

The psychoanalysis of coupling

We are the products of our relationships, and our ways of relating shape our world. Central to the psychoanalytic model of the mind – even though the various schools of psychoanalysis express it differently – is that human nature develops within and is fundamentally based on intrapsychic, interactive, and interpersonal processes – processes necessary to meet the needs and requirements of the developing individual. In fact, I think it is possible to go further and specify the centrality, in both our inner and our external worlds, of couple and family life, whether, as Britton (1995) says, it is "celebrated or uncelebrated, socially contracted or uncontracted, or simply conspicuous by (its) absence …" (p. xi). Britton emphasises that "the idea of a couple coming together to produce a child is central to our psychic life, whether we aspire to it, object to it, realise we are produced by it, deny it, relish it or hate it" (p. xi). The fact of life of the centrality of the couple relationship renders moot the question whether psychoanalytic couple psychotherapy is psychoanalysis. I use psychoanalysis to focus on the couple dynamic as it emerges in its various forms in the consulting room, and I investigate where the experience and nature of coupling fits into the minds of the two individuals and in their shared couple mind.

As suggested by Britton (1995), the normal mind contains a fundamental notion of a couple and of coupling, and this fundamental notion simultaneously has a healthy and creative aspect and a potentially defensive or pathological aspect. The relationship between the two people who make up the couple is the couple therapist's "patient". Contemporary psychoanalysis – especially that influenced by object relations theory – is a way to understand the nature of that relationship and a technique for the couple to gain insight into the nature of their interaction – "for better and for worse".

Conflict and tension are fundamental in human development – occurring and existing between love and hate, between self-interest and concern for the other, between a need for autonomy and a need for attachment, and between a wish for and a fear of emotional knowledge that leads to change. The intimate couple relationship contains significant archaic remnants of many of these aspects of development – sufficiently shared by the couple – providing the source of their love and their conflicts and, therefore, potentially the source for further development and growth.

Projective identification – with its potential for both evacuative defence and for communication and containment – suggests a way of thinking about the nature and unconscious purpose of the intimate couple relationship. Each partner unconsciously uses the other to project into, and both are potentially the object of defensive evacuative projective identification or the object of containment and therefore development.

In addition, the concept of the "total transference situation" (Joseph, 1989) explains that it is not only the person of the partner who is significant, but also the image of the marital relationship as an object itself. Conscious and unconscious images of interaction, relating, intercourse, and sharing are endowed with fears and anxieties as well as hopes and aspirations. In any intimate couple relationship, there are three objects: each of the two partners and their relationship as a psychological entity in its own right, and each are imbued with archaic images. Britton (2003) refers to this phenomenon vividly when he writes that:

> this is something that analysis and marriage have in common: in both, the relationship with the other person is impregnated with transference significance. This means that in marriage, just as in analysis, from the time that the relationship really begins, we lose the ability to treat the partner as rationally, dispassionately or decently as we can other people. It is a relationship we invest with significance transferred on to it – from the past, from an internal world of dream figures, from unrealised ideal aspects of ourselves that we seek in others, or from an aspect of ourselves we repudiate and attribute to others.
>
> (p. 168)

Because of its potential for intensity, commitment, intimacy, and longevity, the couple relationship makes possible an interaction between two people at greater depth than any other, except that of earliest childhood. It offers the possibility of playful infantile needs, for example, in the sexual and physical relationship, but also the possibility of the creation and expression of the more mature aspects of the personality, for example, in the service of parenthood. To what degree these needs and wishes are met depends on the nature of the anxieties and defences of each in the couple and how each interacts with the other.

Choices and behaviour are governed and motivated by unconscious and conscious needs, fears, wishes, and phantasies. People (and situations) are sought out who may meet these unconscious needs – needs which are determined by earliest infantile experiences elaborated in childhood, adolescence, and adulthood. The unconscious choice of partner is, therefore, determined by each partner's receptivity to the split-off, disowned, and projected aspects of the self, creating a shared system with each partner acting to some degree as a container for the other's unconscious hopes of repeating what was good in the past, repairing or discovering what was bad or missing, or carrying that which is felt to be unbearable in the earliest infantile relationships. The mutual acceptance of the other's projections constitutes the unconscious attachment that the couple will make with each other and consists of sufficiently shared phantasies and defences. By making such a choice, and creating what might be described as a marital fit, the couple is embarking on an unconscious contract for the purpose of development and defence. As Bion (1977) wrote, "This could be one of the advantages of marriage; the two partners can, as it were, pool their defects and thereby also pool their wisdom" (p. 52).

Developing the capacity to couple

One of the fundamental issues in couple work, and also in individual work, is the psychoanalytic task of developing the capacity for more mature, depressive functioning and relating, as opposed to more primitive, narcissistic relating. Caper (1999) evocatively describes this capacity as "developing a mind of one's own" (p. 111).

In Freud's "Analysis Terminable and Interminable" (1937), considered by some to be his clinical legacy, he writes about both the potential and the limitations of psychoanalysis as a therapeutic method. This realism extends to his view of human nature. Freud writes:

> A normal ego ... is, like normality in general, an ideal fiction. The abnormal ego ... is unfortunately no fiction. Every normal person, in fact, is only normal on the average. His ego approximates to that of the psychotic in some part or other and to a greater or lesser extent.
> (p. 235)

I want to explore this appraisal of the "normal person" by examining the nature of the intimate couple relationship and how this might be understood as an externalisation of both partners' internal worlds and object relations, inevitably involving, in Freud's words, both the more normal and the more abnormal parts of the ego.

In all intimate couple relationships, inevitably there will be times when one or both partners – consciously and unconsciously – are more preoccupied with themselves than with their partner or their relationship. The capacity to tolerate this inevitable tension between the appropriate and necessary separateness of each of the individuals and the requirements of their mutually aspired-to partnership is a significant sign of the health of any relationship. The tension between narcissism and maturity, or between a more paranoid-schizoid way of functioning and a more depressive way, is played out in all of us throughout our lives.

This dynamic tension among the individual, the partner, and the nature of the relationship invites – or actually is representative of – the unconscious enactment of less mature and more primitively organised ways of functioning and relating, where the differentiation of the self and the separateness of the other is not recognised, respected, or valued. Instead, there is a seeking to control or attack the other whose difference and separateness is felt to be threatening or persecutory. It is also likely that the other will be related to not in the other's fullness but more in relation to particular parts of the other, which come to be experienced as dominant.

An inability to have and manage the capacity to have appropriate concern for the needs of the self, the needs of the partner, and that required of the relationship – not an easy achievement at the best of times – will, of course, be experienced by all couples from time to time. But a reasonably mature relationship will in time re-establish a more benign interaction. Some couples – those who find themselves in treatment – demonstrate this incapacity by a frequent inability to establish or sustain a meaningful intimate relationship by repeatedly creating hostile and violent relationships, either between themselves or in others close to them, or by producing a highly fused undifferentiated relationship. Some couples come together substantially on the basis of this more perverse or violent way of relating. Others become fixed in a sadomasochistic way of relating, sometimes subtle and hidden, other times more overt and dramatic.

Even in the most disturbed and disturbing couples, where the capacity for reflection and thoughtfulness is limited, and the relationship regularly produces emotional or even physical aggression and violence, it is possible to psychoanalytically offer the couple a mutative experience. If the couple therapist can focus on the affective reaction created in him or her by the couple's enactments of aggression, a potential thinking space emerges that such couples normally do not have. With a couple who act out, either the partners cannot share the space between them because rivalry or envy attacks that possibility, or they simply cannot create such a space as a result of having no benign internalities of being contained in that way. With the former, the primary identification might be more with aggression, and with the latter, the primary identification might be more with neglect and deprivation. The internalised couple as an object for identification is either one imbued with this aggression or with depression and emptiness.

The unconscious couple

The strongest bond between a couple – for better and for worse – may be the harmony of their unconscious images and patterns of relating. To some significant degree, each partner will represent or characterise for the other a repressed or split-off part of the self. Often, even quite dissimilar partners may unconsciously find in each other that which they have most sternly repressed or split off in themselves. This is a shared process active in every relationship: by mutually receiving one another's unconscious projections, hopes, and fears, each partner gives the other a feeling of recognition, acceptance, and attachment. The unconscious drive is always both defensive and developmental. Defensively, unwanted parts of the self are disowned and located in the other, who is obliged to carry the projected attributes. Developmentally, the other's capacity to carry, contain, and metabolise the projected attributes may enable the projector to take back the projections in a form more acceptable and manageable.

Freud, while paying no particular attention in his writings to marital and family life, noted that transference – a concept central to psychoanalytic theory and practice – arises spontaneously in all human relationships. Klein, in her writings, agrees, arguing consistently that, in some form or other, transference is universal and operates throughout life influencing all human relationships. In a paper entitled "What Is Transference?", Gosling (1968) writes:

> Falling in love is perhaps one of the most striking examples of transference …
>
> (p. 4)

> [I]n a marriage relationship each partner is constantly, to some extent, relating to the other as if the other were a figure out of his past life, or he is trying to get the other to behave like a figure out of his imagination, be it a consciously known figure or a kind of ghost or shadow-figure who is constantly but unconsciously expected.
>
> (p. 5)

In any relationship, there is always a question as to how much the other is recognised for who and what they are, and how much they are an object of our own hopes and wishes and fears and anxieties – in other words, transference figures. So, when thinking about a couple relationship, are we seeing intimacy, which requires some recognition and valuing of the separate other, or are we seeing something more intrusive, where the other psychically becomes intruded upon and colonised by aspects of our own internal world, split off and projected into the other?

Narcissistic vs. mature object relating

How can the internalised shared image of the nature of the couple develop from a more narcissistic one to one more capable of concern and reparation? But, what do we mean by "narcissism" and by "mature object relating"? In fact, we might be more interested in exploring the relationship between these two states of mind, which Bion (1957), for example, echoing Freud (1937), refers to as the differentiation between the psychotic and non-psychotic parts of the personality. A number of colleagues, including Britton (1998), describe how, in fact, there is always a necessary dynamic oscillation between the more primitive and the more mature ways of functioning and relating.

In 1914, Freud suggested that the study of the erotic life of human beings shows two types of intimate relations: an anaclitic (or attachment) type of love – fundamentally a love of the object which has nourished or protected – and a narcissistic type of love – a love of what he himself is, was, or would like to be, which Freud understood to be an objectless state. However, he did not conclude that human beings are divided into two sharply differentiated groups, according to whether their object-choice conforms to the anaclitic or to the narcissistic type. He writes:

> both kinds of object-choice are open to each individual, though he may show a preference for one or the other. We say that a human being has originally two sexual objects – himself and the woman who nurses him – and in doing so we are postulating a primary narcissism in everyone, which in some cases manifests itself in a dominating fashion in his object-choice.
>
> (1914, p. 88)

As a result of her clinical experience with children, Klein (1952) came to a different view than Freud's concerning an objectless stage of primary narcissism. She postulated a primitive, rudimentary ego in the infant from the very beginning, engaging in primitive object relations. The infant relates powerfully to the mother, or at least those parts or functions of the mother that are needed at any particular time. The impulses felt towards the mother are projected into her and colour the nature of the figure/object subsequently introjected. This normal process of projection and introjection builds up within the infant an inner world made up of a variety of relationships to different objects or, rather more accurately, part objects. As Klein (1952) puts it, "Every external experience is interwoven with ... phantasies and on the other hand every phantasy contains elements of actual experience" (p. 54). It is not, Klein concludes, that there is an initial objectless stage of development. On the contrary, primitive relating is a relating to aspects of the self and to aspects of the other. In fact, this could be put even more firmly. If we acknowledge that through the process of maternal reverie and containment the infant is in part constituted through its interactions with others, then our sense of ourselves is not that we see others as no more than extensions of ourselves but that actually we see the self as originally an extension of our experience of the other (Fonagy, Gergely, Jurist, & Target, 2002).

Klein (1952) went on to describe projective identification as a process, in phantasy, that may be used to dominate and control the object, or as a way of keeping the projection intact in the other, or as a way of avoiding the awareness of separateness and difference and all the anxieties that this awareness might produce. In a couple relationship, this process may operate with particular power.

Klein (1935, 1946) also introduced the concepts of the depressive and paranoid-schizoid positions – fluid constellations of anxieties, defences, and types of object relations. The most important difference between the two positions is the degree of increasing psychological integration as the depressive position is approached, leading to a sense of wholeness in the self and a capacity of concern for the separate other. Though the paranoid-schizoid position predates the depressive position and is more primitive in its form, a continuous dynamic oscillation between the two takes place so that neither position and its anxieties, defences, and types of object relating dominates with any degree of permanence.

The development of this understanding of the schizoid processes of splitting, projection, and introjective and projective identification – operating from the beginning of life – suggests that the paranoid-schizoid position may be synonymous with narcissistic object relations. One of the consequences of projective identification is that the subject relates to the object not as a separate person with his own characteristics but as if relating to himself. Aspects of the object that do not fit the projection may be ignored, or the subject may control or force the object to act the role required of him. This describes the individual who, as Freud (1914) put it, loves, narcissistically, what he himself is, was, or would like to be (p. 90). Such a love of the other is based on the phantasy that parts of the self and internal objects are projected into the other and it is this that makes this other so attractive to the narcissistic individual. The other is, in effect, psychically colonised.

Chronic vs. acute narcissistic relating

In understanding and working psychoanalytically with a couple relationship, even those couples and individuals who do not have a primarily narcissistic psychic structure will, from time to time, find themselves dominated by the anxieties, defences, and types of object relations of the paranoid-schizoid position. Any new life situation or stage of development may arouse fundamental anxieties relating to a sense of insecurity and of lack of control over the internal and external environment. Such disrupting and persecutory anxieties may, therefore, arouse the defences and types of object relations of the paranoid-schizoid position. In a healthy relationship, such ways of relating are usually temporary and worked through towards more mature relating at the depressive position.

A number of writers have stressed the complexity, rigidity, and highly organised nature of the defensive processes employed by those individuals whose internal world is consistently organised by the more primitive and pathological splitting and projective processes. Steiner (1993), for example, coins the evocative term "psychic retreat" to delineate its fixedness. So, in this way, we can differentiate between a temporary, defensive narcissistic withdrawal, which may represent a part of the constant movement between the paranoid-schizoid and the depressive positions, and the more rigidly organised narcissistic psychic organisation, which constructs a more inflexible structure locking the individual and/or the intimate couple into pathological object relations.

There is no doubt that sometimes a couple relationship does atrophy psychically into a rigid pattern of interaction and may on occasion produce something which may be described as a "projective gridlock" (Morgan, 1995) or a claustrum relationship (Fisher, 1995), within which there is really no opportunity for the fluidity of movement between the more primitive towards the more mature ways of relating. If both members of the couple are substantially under the sway of the more narcissistic/paranoid-schizoid type of object relating, a rigidified *folie a deux* may be established that might be extremely resistant or even immune to psychotherapeutic intervention.

Some such relationships might prove to be intractable. Rosenfeld (1971) refined the understanding of narcissistic object relations when he emphasised the notion of "destructive narcissism". He showed how the narcissistic state is not necessarily a withdrawal to, or an identification with, a good internalised object but may be a withdrawal to a more destructive internal object, which, like an internal saboteur, sets out to defeat the efforts of the more benign relating part of the self. Destructive narcissism is produced out of the more envious aspects of the self: the more omnipotent, self-sufficient part of the self is identified with and attacks the more dependent part of the self, which may wish to form attachments and hence arouse the destructive envy of the narcissistic self.

Segal (1983) says that envy, as described by Klein, is "a spoiling hostility at the realisation that the source of life and goodness lies outside" (p. 270). She goes on to say that narcissism defends us against such envy: a narcissistic state of mind is destructive of separateness and is unable to acknowledge the value of the other. It is, therefore, destructive of real object relating. Accordingly, Heimann (1952) writes that:

> The essential difference between infantile and mature object relations is that, whereas the adult conceives of the object as existing independently of himself, for the infant it *always refers in some way to himself*. It exists only by value of its function for the infant.
>
> (p. 142) (italics in the original)

Interestingly, Balint (1968) refers to primitive forms of object relating in which "the object is taken for granted" (p. 70). Balint's description of this primitive type of object relating is very evocative of the pathological and destructive ways in which some more disturbed couples relate to each other:

> [O]nly one partner may have wishes, interests and demands of his own; without any further need for testing, it is taken for granted that the other partner, the object ... will automatically have the same wishes, interests and expectations.... If any hitch or disharmony between subject and object occurs, the reaction to it will consist of loud and vehement symptoms suggesting processes either of a highly aggressive and destructive, or profoundly disintegrative, nature, i.e. either as if the whole world, including the self, would have been smashed up, or as if the subject would have been flooded with pure and unmitigated aggressive-destructive impulses.
>
> (p. 70)

This "hitch or disharmony" between the subject and the object may be the subject's realisation of his dependence on the object and, if narcissistically organised, may arouse destructive envy, splitting to the point of disintegration, and hatred.

However, it may also be possible to consider that the couple relationship – even if this is only in one partner – can be drawn on to contain and process the enactments of the more primitive object relations. In the same way that Freud (1937) refers to the normal and abnormal ego, and Bion (1957) refers to the psychotic and non-psychotic parts of the personality, we may refer to a differentiation between the more defensive and the more developmental aspects of intimate relationships. Even the most perverse or violent marriages might at least be thought about as being a highly organised defensive structure warding off some of the intolerable psychic realities inevitably aroused in any intimate relating, such as dependence and separateness, inclusion and exclusion, and gratitude and envy. Without being seduced by therapeutic enthusiasm, we may be sustained in our clinical work by recalling Betty Joseph's (1984) considered view that, providing we can tune into it, "projective identification is by its very nature a kind of communication, even in cases where this is not its aim or its intention" (p. 170).

Clinical vignette

I have been seeing Mr and Mrs A twice a week for about 18 months. They sought psychotherapy because of the growing tension and distress between them, which, at times, explodes into serious and bitter arguments, occasionally including physical violence. In their late 30s, they have been together for about eight years and have a toddler child. They work in sister institutions in the same profession, actively pursuing their professional ambitions.

Both come from hard-working backgrounds with parents who struggled to better themselves and provide well for their families. Mr A describes a somewhat depressed father who never quite achieved what he might have been capable of. Mr A's mother contributed to the household income, but, in his teenage years, Mr A became aware that she was resentful and angry that she had not been better cared for by her husband. She dealt with her distress by being very involved with Mr A and his younger two sisters, to some degree keeping the father out of the picture. Mr A says that he loves his father but finds it difficult to have the relationship he wants with him because of his father's depression and emotional absence. Mr A does not see his parents as a couple but more as "living in silent antagonism". Mr A did reasonably at school and at his profession, but, before his current job, he tended to move quickly from one concern to another and have periods of independent employment.

Mrs A also has two younger sisters. Her father, reasonably successful, is especially proud that he became a well-known local political figure as a result of activities that gave him status and public admiration but took him away from his family. Her mother never worked. Mrs A experiences her mother as somewhat deflated and often critical of her husband's outside activities. However, Mrs A says her mother devoted herself to her and her sisters. In school, Mrs A did well but felt that this was not recognised by either parent, which made her angry and sad. As a result, she has never quite fulfilled her potential, and, though her professional life is reasonable, she feels that colleagues are better at their work than she is.

So from their histories, we see that this couple shares an image of a depressed, fractured, and unfulfilled couple relationship, with no parent feeling particularly successful much of their lives. Both fathers were absent for different reasons and both mothers harboured resentment.

At the start of the first session of the week, Mr A is very tense and agitated, looking at his wife in an openly aggressive way. Mrs A speaks first, saying that a couple of days earlier Mr A received a very exciting job offer that could substantially enhance his professional ambitions and therefore needs serious consideration. Ever since then, she says, the two of them have been fighting in a state of high tension and mutual antagonism. She adds that she feels attacked by her husband and is very confused, distressed, and angry. Almost immediately, the couple engages in their argument. As Mrs A attempts to offer her thoughts, views, and encouragement about the prospective job – as invited to by her husband – Mr A angrily accuses her of being totally disinterested in his position and of trying to dictate to him how he should proceed in relation to the job offer.

Mr A's violently oscillating perception of his wife is quite extraordinary and almost bizarre. Eventually, repeatedly wrong-footed, Mrs A is left in a state of spluttering confusion, driven to impotent speechlessness by her husband's perverse attacks on her. It is as if Mr A were identified with being the victim of a female figure who is disinterested and antagonistic towards him. The internal couple as a psychic object seems to be a threatened male figure and a threatening critical female figure.

Unsure whether to trust my own observations and experience in relation to the potency of Mr A's misperception of his wife, I, too, am left feeling confused and anxious, and somewhat impotent in that I cannot understand the situation. I feel isolated from my own thinking, and from the couple and their experience, just as they were from each other. I am unable to say much about what is going on. I then notice that Mr A is now looking much less tense and seems calmer. He turns to me and explains, with a barely hidden patronising tone, that he is in the final stages of setting up a number of projects for himself that, taken together, make up a very viable and interesting portfolio of work. He is not sure exactly how this compares to the new job offer, but, he says calmly, he is probably going to pursue his own scheme. He does not need, he says, to discuss it much more either with his wife or here in the session.

I am immediately struck by the dramatic contrast between Mr A's mood and manner now, and how he had been earlier in the session. I also note how his apparently calm and thoughtful state of mind compares with how I observe his wife's to be. I am also aware of my own anxious discomfort in relation to the session so far. It is as if Mrs A and I have been rendered confused, anxious, and speechless while Mr A is now thoughtful and clear. I wonder whether this rather dramatic change in Mr A, and the apparent difference now between his state of mind and that of his wife and mine, suggests that splitting and projective identification are taking place among us. The uncertainty, conflict, and anxiety, which the enticing job offer has created, is completely absent from Mr A. He deals with his anxiety about being in this new job by creating a self-made work project, which means he is less exposed to the other's views. His wife, as I observe her aided by my awareness of my own state, is confused and unsure.

I wonder whether the job offer substantially disturbs Mr A's equilibrium. Rather than being something tempting, for which he could feel ambivalence and uncertainty, or excitement and gratitude, the job offer might be seen as a challenge to Mr A's self-constructed work plans. Mr A could be feeling that the conflict and uncertainty about how he should proceed is an attack on his sense of self by a persecutory bad object. Further, because it is apparently such a tempting offer, it could be provoking his feelings of envy: someone else has something to give that he wants. Finally, if he were to accept the job, he would be working under the authority of his new employer rather than be in charge of his own planned projects, which could raise anxieties about dependence and of not being in control.

Rather than emotionally engage in these various conflicts and anxieties, Mr A splits off his feelings of uncertainty, confusion, and fear of loss of power and control and projects them into his objects that he then identifies as feeling the conflicts and confusion, leaving himself identified with a calm and certain self again. This identification with an internal good object could be a narcissistic withdrawal, created by splitting and projective identification with his wife and me. Mr A is relating to Mrs A as if she were confused about whether he should take up the job or not. In this way he is relating to what he had projected into her rather than to what she herself was trying to say to him. This splitting and projection prevents a more mature object relationship in which the other's individuality and separateness is recognised and related to with interest and concern.

A similar dynamic is experienced in Mr A's transference to me. Can I be allowed to be the employer/psychotherapist who offers potentially interesting psychotherapeutic work or does he turn down my offered interpretations and continue to use his old familiar defences and ways of relating? Does he depend on the psychotherapy and me or does he retain his narcissistic self-reliance, identifying himself with a near-idealised internal object constructed partly by identifying with and introjecting my capacities for thought and reflection, leaving me feeling uncertain and confused?

Mrs A also plays a part in the interaction between them, and in the creation of Mr A's state of mind. It emerges in the session that she herself is disturbed by her husband's job offer because, in fact, it arouses her envy, which she very quickly splits off and denies to herself. But she is left feeling confused and ambivalent about her support for her husband and persecuted by guilt. Unconsciously, she attempts to disown this reaction in herself and project it into her husband. She can then identify herself with a good internal object who wishes to be helpful to her husband. This evacuative projective process, including the split-off projected envy, is unconsciously experienced by Mr A as an attack. He then deals with a Mrs A, who is consciously supporting him but, simultaneously, unconsciously aggressively projecting into him her envy, confusion, and guilt. This latter meshes with Mr A's own envy and confusion and so arouses his paranoid anxieties against which he defends himself by violent splitting and projection.

Mrs A is indeed identified with an envious object who feels threatened by the other's success and achievements. The image of her internal couple is her mother's relatively silent fury at her father's activities, success, and popularity. Whereas Mr A has an internalised image of a couple in conflict because of the father's perceived failure, Mrs A's image is of a couple in conflict because of the father's apparent success. In the case of both sets of parents, and in relation to Mr and Mrs A, the couple relationship is one of conflict, disappointment, and unexpressed antagonism.

It is this complex set of splitting and evacuative projective identification which creates the fights between them, both at home and in the consulting room. Each becomes easily dominated by the more paranoid anxieties, which call up the more primitive or destructive narcissistic defences and types of object relations.

As the treatment develops, I can make better use of my own capacity to relate to my sense of my competence and not become anxious by my uncertainty. It is as if I am able to locate a mature capacity within myself from which I can engage with the couple and especially their shared doubt about being able to manage disappointment and also success. On one occasion, I make an interpretation about Mr A fearing to be seen by his wife as disappointing no matter what he achieves, when actually he is uncertain about his own capacity to demonstrate his competence to others, as with his decision not to take the exciting job offer. He becomes furious with me, saying that I am suggesting that he doubts his own competencies, and that what he is doing is independently creating his own work for himself. How could I undermine him in this way? I respond by saying that if he felt he could be undermined by a comment which he disagrees with, then I thought that perhaps he is indeed less sure of himself than he thinks. Having his own mind means noting differences and being able to live with them.

Mrs A's transference relationship to me was more muted, but I was aware of an underlying tension. On a couple of occasions, she said that I had completely misunderstood her and that she was surprised that I could be so sure of myself in the comments I'd made. In her mind, I'd become the rather powerful but arrogant figure who diminished her through my interpretative activity. I tried to explore with her whether this was indeed what I had done, or, as with her husband and his exciting job offer, she could feel confused and disturbed by the other's apparent success and potency.

For this couple, the object for psychoanalytic investigation is their shared images of a fractured and disappointed couple relationship with both partners feeling threatened by the other and both projecting their own aggression into the other. This is a couple who gets by, but a relatively depressed couple with underlying resentments and an inability to manage at points of stress and tension. Their capacity to offer solace to the other was undermined by each feeling in danger of being found wanting.

The enactment of narcissistic object relations in this couple is an example of an externalised pathological personality organisation. If one partner is less under the influence of the more paranoid-schizoid anxieties and defences, his or her capacity for thought and concern for the other may present the potential for a more containing experience within the couple. At the same time, however, the more destructive aspects of the paranoid-schizoid position will attack this capacity in the partner and so undermine the containing potential in the intimate relationship. This sabotaging led them to seek psychotherapeutic help. And then, of course, the psychotherapy became the target for the attack as it is seen to be in opposition to the existing more primitive ways of relating.

Summary

Tension between the more narcissistic and more mature object relations is present in all individuals as described by Freud's (1937) view of the universal nature of the "normal" and "abnormal" ego within each individual. There is constant movement between the more primitive anxieties and defences of the paranoid-schizoid position and the more mature capacity for ambivalence and concern of the depressive position. Some individuals are more regularly under the influence of primitive anxieties, and the most disturbed can be understood as consistently living in this state of mind and object relating.

Couples in psychoanalytic couple psychotherapy are indeed "on the couch", with the psychoanalytic stance of the clinician offering the opportunity to explore the place of a couple or coupling in the patient's individual and joint minds. Such patients can not only develop more of a mind of their own but also secure a relationship that also offers solace and containment rather than replicating more archaic unresolved experiences with their respective parental couple relationships.

Note

1 Extending the psychoanalytic orientation to other than intensive individual work is sometimes referred to as "applied psychoanalysis". I struggle to understand the distinction between "psychoanalysis" and "applied psychoanalysis". In some quarters, at least in the UK, this differentiation quickly becomes a political question with rivalry and competition between groups who hold differing views about what constitutes psychoanalysis. I am more interested in thinking about what psychoanalysis is, how it is useful as a theory of mind and development, and how it supports certain technical and clinical practice in my relationship with my patients.

References

Balint, M. (1968). *The basic fault*. London: Tavistock Publications.
Bion, W.R. (1957). Differentiation of the psychotic from the non-psychotic personalities. *International Journal of Psycho-Analysis*, 38: 266–275.
Bion, W.R. (1989). Caesura. In *Two papers: The grid and caesura* (pp. 35–36). London: Karnac Books. (Original work published 1977).
Britton, R. (1995). Foreword. In S. Ruszczynski & J. Fisher (Eds.), *Intrusiveness and intimacy in the couple* (pp. xi–xiii). London: Karnac.
Britton, R. (1998). *Belief and imagination*. London: Routledge.
Britton, R. (2003). *Sex, death and the superego*. London: Karnac.

Caper, R. (1999). *A mind of one's own*. London: Routledge.
Fisher, J. (1995). Identity and intimacy in the couple: Three types of identification. In S. Ruszczynski & J. Fisher (Eds.), *Intrusiveness and intimacy in the couple* (pp. 74–104). London: Karnac.
Fonagy, P., Gergely, G., Jurist, E. & Target, M. (2002). *Affect regulation, mentalisation and the development of the self*. New York: Other Press.
Freud, S. (1964). On narcissism. In J. Strachey (Ed. & Trans.), *The complete works of Sigmund Freud* (vol. 14). London: Hogarth Press. (Original work published 1914).
Freud, S. (1964). Analysis terminable and interminable. In J. Strachey (Ed. & Trans.), *The complete works of Sigmund Freud* (vol. 23). London: Hogarth Press. (Original work published 1937).
Gosling, R. (1968). What is transference? In J. Sutherland (Ed.), *The psychoanalytic approach* (pp. 1–10). London: Institute of Psychoanalysis and Bailliere, Tindall and Cassell.
Heimann, P. (1952). Certain functions of introjection and projection in early infancy. In M. Klein, P. Heimann, S. Isaacs & J. Riviere (Eds.), *Developments in psychoanalysis* (pp. 122–168). London: Hogarth Press.
Joseph, B. (1989). Projective identification: Some clinical aspects. In M. Feldman & E.B. Spillius (Eds.), *Psychic equilibrium and psychic change: Selected papers of Betty Joseph* (pp. 168–180). London/New York: Routledge. (Original work published 1984).
Klein, M. (1975). Contributions to the psycho-genesis of manic and depressive states. In *Love, guilt and reparation and other works: The writings of Melanie Klein*, vol. 1. London: Hogarth Press. (Original work published 1935).
Klein, M. (1975). Notes on some schizoid mechanism. In *Envy and gratitude and other works: The writings of Melanie Klein*, vol. 3. London: Hogarth Press. (Original work published 1946).
Klein, M. (1975): The origins of transference. In *Envy and gratitude and other works: The writings of Melanie Klein*, vol. 3. London: Hogarth Press. (Original work published 1952).
Morgan, M. (1995). The projective gridlock: A form of projective identification in couple relationships. In S. Ruszczynski & J. Fisher (Eds.), *Intrusiveness and intimacy in the couple* (pp. 33–48). London: Karnac.
Rosenfeld, H. (1971). A clinical approach to the psycho-analytic theory of the life and death instincts: An investigation into the aggressive aspects of narcissism. *International Journal of Psycho-Analysis*, 52: 169–178.
Segal, H. (1983). Some clinical implications of Melanie Klein's work. *International Journal of Psycho-Analysis*, 64: 269–276.
Steiner, J. (1993). *Psychic retreats*. London: Routledge.

Chapter 3

Discussion of "Couples on the couch: working psychoanalytically with couple relationships"

Rachel Cooke

Stanley Ruszczynski's many papers are a tremendous resource for couple therapists seeking to ground themselves in the application of psychoanalytic theory to clinical practice. His classic paper entitled "Narcissistic Object Relating" (1995) is a staple of my teaching papers, and I couldn't imagine trying to describe the multiple communicative and controlling aspects of projective identification in couples, or how couples fail to see each other as separate beings, without it. "Couples on the Couch" (2013) is another important paper packed with insights into the nuances of narcissistic object relations as these pertain to couple dynamics. He demonstrates throughout how the form of couple therapy that has evolved at the Tavistock Centre for Couple Relationships (TCCR) applies the fundamental tenets of psychoanalysis. In developing his argument, Ruszczynski has given us a very thorough orientation to the psychological functioning of disturbed couples.

In this chapter I will first respond to some ideas Ruszczynski presents and elaborate on them through the lens of other papers he has written, as well as ideas his London-based colleagues have presented over the years, paying special attention to the problem of difference in couples; that is, with how partners deal with the impingement of each other's differences. Ruszczynski states that "the clinical question is whether there is the potential in the couple for a less narcissistic and a more mature or more flexible way of relating." In light of this question, I will next weave in what I believe to be potentially effective, everyday clinical ways of facilitating the movement of couples towards healthier forms of relating.

Theoretical foundations

Ruszczynski's chapter points us towards a recognition of what he calls the "archaic remnants" of mind, including intergenerational transmissions and intrapsychic drama. We are all born into families whose flawed relationships and unresolved traumas mark us from before birth and in perpetuity. We are all – as James Fisher (1999) quips in "Folie a Deux" – the "out-come" of a relationship, and we are all born into relationship, utterly helpless and dependent at first, usually, on a mother, and later on a second parent or other parental figure. Sibling and extended family members complicate and people our worlds, in an assemblage of function and dysfunction, similarity and difference, competitive striving and multiple anxieties, and somehow out of this primordial ooze of dubious inheritance each of us emerge. As Freud (1915) wrote in *The Unconscious*, "It is a very remarkable thing that the unconscious of one human being can react upon that of another without passing through the conscious" (p. 194). We first experience this in our families of origin, and then we take the foundational but unconscious remnants from there into our marriages.

Citing Fonagy's work, Ruszczynski mentions that our sense of ourselves is in part the product of our parents' unconscious projections into us right from the beginning. As Heidegger and the phenomenologists might say, by the time we achieve self-consciousness, we are "always already" formed by intrusive projections as well as (hopefully) by the emotional gifts of real intimacy, which allow for separateness but also proffer a kind of psychic "breaking and entering," in a relentless and incessant relationality that constructs us all.

Ruszczynski explores throughout his chapter how psychoanalytic couple work takes as a given the primacy of unconscious processes. Life forces and anti-life forces, developmental urges and regressive pulls, time past and time present, layers of conflicts that we listen for in order to bring to the surface and determine features of couples' relationship patterns. In contrast to work with individuals, couple work begins with a fully formed set of transferences between the members of the couple, which they offer to the therapist for observation. This already-made-ness of the couple relationship provides the couple therapist with an extraordinary research opportunity into how people choose each other and re-establish patterns from their family of origin. As Ruszczynski describes, in psychoanalytic couple therapy, it is not just the individuals in the couple or the couple who are of interest, but (in his words) "the image of the marital relationship as an object itself."

We must deliberately pursue information early in a couple treatment about each person's experience of their parents' relationship; this will have had such a defining impact on each of their unconscious internal models of relationship. Much of what the couple plays out between them are the patterns and hallmarks of their unconscious beliefs about what it is like to be in a couple. These beliefs influence the kind of couple they become, and making these patterns conscious helps them gain access to previously hidden places and reclaim projected parts of themselves. This assists their movement towards becoming more separate from each other, and also more connected.

Here Ruszczynski's chapter presents a detailed application of psychoanalytic theory to working with couples, with a particular emphasis on some of the more problematic ways of relating. However, Ruszczynski and his colleagues at the TCCR have also used psychoanalytic theory to identify what the qualities and capacities are in healthier couple relating, and technical interventions follow from their theoretical ideas.

If psychoanalytic couple psychotherapy is going to be mutative, there are several key relational dimensions with which it is important to be conversant. These are our stock-in-trade axes of observation, described by Mary Morgan (2001) in her important paper, "The Therapist's Couple State of Mind," and reiterated in the couple psychotherapy literature. One such axis is the capacity to tolerate the other's difference from oneself. Ron Britton's (1989) work on the Oedipal situation and what he calls "triangular space" (p. 83) has been seminal, and Ruszczynski and others have applied his ideas to furthering our understanding of couples. To summarize Britton (p. 85): Adequate emotional containment in infancy and childhood provides the conditions in which a person can begin to be able to think, and moving through the Oedipal situation allows for the capacity to tolerate some degree of separateness as well as exclusion. Britton showed how, if the infant is going to be able to develop the capacity to tolerate his own separateness, the infant–mother dyad has to be intruded on by the father (or another figure). Only by recognizing his exclusion from a relationship that precedes him can the infant-toddler build a foundation on which to experience himself as separate (rather than as adhesively attached or abandoned). This way he can also accept the otherness of his mother and father. From there he can take up a third position in which he is able to observe himself and be aware that there are others who can observe him and who are different from him. Successful completion of this trajectory will result in a much greater ability to create and sustain a healthy couple. These ideas have been translated for use with couples as follows.

> The "creative couple" is one in which there is a capacity for separateness and difference, an awareness of the fact of dependence, and some capacity for self-reflection as well as a capacity to manage inclusion and exclusion. It is ... creative because there is the awareness of the relationship as a third, something that the individuals create between them, nurture, allow to develop and turn to as a resource.
>
> (Morgan, 2001, p. 27)

Ruszczynski quoted Britton on how "the idea of the couple coming together to make a child is central to our psychic life." The couple also come together to make a relationship that, at best, offers a place for nurturance and containment. In another paper, "Reflective Space in the Intimate Couple Relationship," Ruszczynski (2005) developed these ideas even further, introducing a concept he calls the "marital triangle," which builds on Britton's "triangular space" and Morgan's idea of the *relationship* as a third. Discussing how every couple will to some degree inevitably oscillate between narcissistic states and healthier states, he writes that the:

> "marital triangle" [is] where the couple can reflect on their own needs, the needs of the other, and on the needs of the relationship. Often and inevitably, these various needs will be in conflict and require reflection, possible relinquishment, and tolerable, though ambivalent, resolution.
>
> (Ruszczynski, 2005, p. 42)

I think that sentence displays in its form just how hard a project this is! Indeed, couple therapy is frequently a space for negotiation and compromise, for determining whose needs get to come first, and in what circumstances, etc. People in couples have to deal not only with disagreements and differences of opinion but also with real external thirds that threaten to come between them – most obviously, the children they create. Couples sometimes present for treatment because the challenges of parenting have driven a wedge between them and those stresses and strains can be severe. Everyone is faced with negotiating and tolerating exclusion throughout the life span, and how the members of a couple deal with the experience of being excluded displays what level of "creativeness," shall we say, they have achieved.

These capacities (tolerating difference, dependence, exclusion, otherness, and being able to think about all these emotionally demanding experiences) depict the antidote to narcissistic relating as Ruszczynski described it, where separateness is refused, the person's otherness obliterated, and attempts made via projection and evacuation to define and control the other. Both kinds of couple have inside an internal representation of a couple, but their images are altogether different, and they produce very different kinds of coupling.

Ruszczynski's chapter introduced me to Robert Gosling, who he quotes centrally in his chapter. I discovered that Gosling led the Tavistock Clinic in the 1970s, where he was much loved. He also had a long and successful marriage and five children. There is a charming story in his obituary of how the staff at the Tavistock gave him and his wife a goose and a gander when they retired to the country and took up farming. He called them Tavi and Stock, they mated, and gave birth to a whole generation of (lower case g) "goslings!" Ruszczynski quotes Gosling:

> [I]n a marriage each partner is relating to the other as if he were a figure out of his past life, or he is trying to get the other to behave like a figure out of his imagination … a shadow-figure who is constantly but unconsciously expected.
> (Gosling, 1968, as cited in Ruszczynski, 2005)

This evocative statement brings to mind the timelessness of the unconscious, and implicitly references the repetition compulsion, which insists that we have the same experience over and over again. In "Remembering, Repeating and Working Through," Freud (1914) asserts that the compulsion to repeat is the patient's "way of remembering." Freud states, for example, that the patient does not remember being combative towards his parents' authority, but he behaves this way towards the analyst, which signifies it as a transference-repetition (p. 149). This is what draws people towards romantic partners who will unconsciously participate in recreating their disruptive and familiar formative experiences. Assuming the developmental aspect of the unconscious as well as its regressive aspect, there is always at play the hope for a creative or reparative experience as well as the repetition of something damaging.

The last part of the Gosling quote is the description of a state in which what has already happened is "constantly but unconsciously expected." Much as Winnicott (1974) pointed out in "Fear of Breakdown," the disaster most feared has already happened. In couples, that disaster gets encoded unconsciously as a shared belief about the relationship. That shared belief might have its roots in the internal model of parental relationship or in a childhood trauma of some kind. Examples of the belief might be, for instance, that the relationship will inevitably fail (which. of course, will bring about unconscious efforts to sabotage it). It might be that there isn't room for both individuals and therefore it requires a great degree of sacrifice, which then breeds resentment and destructive acting out. It might be that the relationship is not a safe place to be, and therefore requires unconsciously casting the other person as an enemy who has to be warded off. It might be a tendency to idealize or devalue the relationship and to recreate each other as idealized or devalued parental figures.

At the outset of the couple relationship, the disaster has not yet happened, but there is unconscious pressure on the relationship to evolve in the way the couple or patient already know to be the way in which history unfolds. Similarly, when couples fall prey to a more narcissistic form of relating, it is very common for them to go looking to prove unconscious (or even conscious) beliefs they have formed about each other. These beliefs are typically persecutory in nature, such as, "He doesn't really want to be with me" or "Something is wrong with her," and so on. It is incumbent on us as couple therapists to expose and gently confront these beliefs when we hear them, in order to help the couple loosen their attachment to those static and archaic versions of each other.

Projective gridlock in the cocktail party

In his chapter, Ruszczynski very interestingly observes that the "strongest bond between a couple – for better and for worse – may be thought to be the harmony of their unconscious images and patterns of relating" (personal communication, October 5, 2013). Why is this their *strongest* bond? In his exegesis of T.S. Eliot's 1949 play, *The Cocktail Party*, James Fisher (1999) attends to this precise question because it is exactly how the character of Reilly, the couple psychotherapist in the play, describes his patients. Edward and Lavinia, a married couple, are at the brink of the discovery that their relationship has been a pretense in which there is really no loving beginning to recall, the loss of which to grieve, and no real capacity to recognize the other. When they enter the therapist's office, they discover that they do have something very fundamental in common. They have a "shared unconscious phantasy of a 'shared' isolation," which is that, "he is a man incapable of loving, and … she is a woman no man can love" (Fisher, 1999, p. 212). Projective identifications have allowed Lavinia to believe that Edward cannot love any woman, and therefore she is off the hook as the deficit is his. Edward has decided that no man could love Lavinia, and thereby sought to protect himself from the knowledge of his own incapacity. Each comes to the therapy fresh from the failure of an extra-marital affair, which has helped them prepare for psychic reality. Each has hoped for a different experience with a new partner but has been obliged to see it turn into the same exact experience: Edward realizes he doesn't really love his lover, Celia, and Lavinia learns that her lover, Peter, has fallen in love with someone else. The couple begins to despair when each starts to bear their own anxiety in an honest way: he, that he is incapable of loving, and she, that she feels unlovable; that no one can love her. The therapist exhorts them to:

> See it rather as the bond which holds you together.
> While still in a state of unenlightenment,
> You … could accuse each other of your own faults,
> And so could avoid understanding each other.
> Now, you have *only* to reverse the propositions
> And put them together.
> (Eliot, 1949, p. 125; emphasis mine)

Fisher acknowledges the humor Eliot must have intended by having Reilly say "only," as if that project (reclaiming their projections) were easy. He remarks, "Sometimes the intrusive projections are so entrenched in the couple that they, and we as their therapists might wonder ... is that possible?" (Fisher, 1999, p. 212).

The tragedy of this kind of projective defense in couples is that it always occurs at the expense of the possibility of any kind of healthy couple functioning. It represents the individual or individuals in the couple putting their own psychic interests ahead of the couple, and in unilaterally destructive ways! What I mean is that the process of evacuating badness into one's spouse is an entirely pyrrhic victory. Evacuating that bad object into the other might provide a kind of pseudo-relief, but it takes place at the expense of their being on the same team and turns them into each other's dumping ground. One person gets to feel better for a moment but at the expense of the couple.

So the unconscious "fit" *is* the strongest bond, precisely because it allows the couple's narcissistic stasis and pretense about themselves to continue indefinitely, at the same time as it contains within it the clues to helping them relinquish a kind of couple "false self" and thereby enter psychic reality. As Fisher points out, in order for Edward and Lavinia "to be able to face themselves, their illusions and deceptions, it is necessary for each to face the reality of the other" (p. 210). The shared unconscious belief points in both directions: backwards, into a regressive world of narcissistic defenses, and also forwards, into the depressive position, with all its attendant grief and loss.

In all the oscillations between paranoid-schizoid and depressive positions, it is inevitable that couples will experience each other as adversaries at times. Intrusions and environmental failures in early life are more likely to result in narcissistic defenses, which show up in couples in particular ways. In his 2006 paper, entitled "Sado-Masochistic Enactments in a Couple Relationship: The Fear of Intimacy and the Dread of Separateness," Ruszczynski addresses how people from traumatic backgrounds have not received the kind of emotional (or physical) containment which is necessary for healthy development. He references Bion's container-contained relationship, in which parents are the containers and transformers of their children's distress. In a pathological reversal of this relationship, children are expected to be the recipients of their parents' emotional toxic waste or unprocessed anxieties and fears. Worse still: They have often been expected or obliged to provide a containing function of sorts for their disturbed parents. As a result of being colonized and impinged on in this way, people are likely to experience intimate relationships as dangerous. Akin to Henri Rey's claustro-agoraphobic dilemma (Rey, 1994), this situation results in what Mervin Glasser (1986) called the "core complex." Ruszczynski describes it as a "terror of separation, which feels like abandonment, and a horror of closeness, which feels like intrusion" (2006, p. 112).

People with this kind of history are much more likely to create mutually destabilizing relationships where boundaries are violated and abusive paradigms predominate. I have worked with couples where the relationship is parasitic: Their dependent feeding off each other is deadly to both. One person's needs are escalated to such a pitch that the other person is rendered helpless to provide. These are couples whose relationships have broken down – there is no containing structure – yet they are incapable of separating. In these couples the individuals may function better outside their couple, but in the regressive orbit of their relationship, they are prone to cycles of severely disturbed behavior, including suicide threats and domestic violence.

Related to this theme, I see Ruszczynski's comments on the couple relationship as the place where the psychotic parts of the personality get expressed as a fascinating starting point for another paper I hope he will write! It makes sense that the couple relationship, which invites all kinds of primitive states and infantile longings, is also the place in which the psychotic part of the personality gets unleashed. Rosenfeld (1987) believed that the dependent, infantile part of the personality is also the healthy part of the personality because it is the place from which we first experience love for the mother. People whose needs were sufficiently met earlier in life are more likely to be able to bear their own dependent states and longings in couple relationships because these are less anxiety producing than for people whose needs have never been met. A seductive pull towards a state of blissful infantile comfort comes from depending on another whom we want to meet all our needs, but those needs cannot possibly be met. The underbelly of the dependency is a terrifying helplessness. In parasitically dependent couples, people use their romantic partner as compensatory caregivers in the absence of a history of adequate parental care. Most of the time the wish for perfect attunement cannot be met, which sets the scene for further hurt and persecutory experience in the couple. It is then that the cycles of attack and retaliation, or perceived attack and retaliation, get set in motion. These are the cycles we are tasked with observing and describing as closely as possible, and which we attempt to disrupt.

The dependency engendered in romantic couples makes it no coincidence that a frequent term of endearment by partners for each other is "Baby." An individual patient of mine, who suffers from intermittent bulimic episodes, is four months into a relationship she is for once *not* trying to get out of. This is a milestone. She is terrified of becoming emotionally dependent, losing her autonomy, and having her "unloveableness" exposed. She recently described to me that she and her boyfriend have begun calling each other "Baby ... which is like taking little bites of delicious cupcakes." To my mind this sums up her dilemma: Can she bear to keep the sweetness inside, knowing it may leave her wanting more, or will she have to get rid of it so as to ward off an uncomfortably dependent state?

The difficulty of difference

Difference is the real nemesis of narcissism. People in couples have chosen each other for their otherness, and yet, without realizing it or meaning to, they collapse into narcissistic states where the partner's otherness, as Ruszczynski has shown, is, at minimum, protested or denied and, more insidiously, intruded into or controlled. In "Sado-Masochistic Enactments in a Couple Relationship" (2006) Ruszczynski writes:

> In a psychic structure that is more paranoid-schizoid, or where there is a regression to that state, the sense of difference is experienced not as separateness, with the ensuing sense of mourning and loss, but more as an intrusion by a terrifying persecutor.
>
> (p. 114)

This experience of difference as intrusion can happen at varying levels of intensity. At one end of the spectrum, a couple in crisis may well experience each other's conflicting desires as mutually annihilating. At the other end, couples argue about each other's different standards of neatness and messiness, which can be a chronic source of discomforting difference. And in between: One person's benign use of alcohol can be experienced by their spouse as undermining the marriage. One person's desire to move to a new house can provoke a firestorm in the other. One person's relieving expletive is another person's offensive attack.

Ruszczynski and I are both attending to the ways in which narcissistic states refuse difference. There are also states of ordinary or "everyday" narcissism in which people routinely mistake each other for themselves. These are moments when spouses habitually offer each other what they would each want, and in so doing fail to recognize that their partner wants something different. A husband might leave his wife alone in a state of grief or distress, since he would tend to withdraw were he in distress, when what she wants is the comfort of contact but is incapable of asking for it. There are also overlaps between narcissistic states and transference-repetition. People "forget" that their partners are different people and that they do not have the same mind. Spouses commonly assume their partners can read their minds and become enraged to find this is not the case. There are many powerful unconscious pulls towards states of merger and ways in which couple life invites intrusions and boundary crossings. Navigating emotional distance and closeness is a confusing and treacherous terrain: It requires an ongoing attempt to remain separate yet deeply connected; a capacity to cross body and brain barriers yet not stay merged.

Couples, therefore, cannot help but bump into each other, psychically speaking. In paranoid-schizoid states there is often the attribution of intention to harm. Micro-states of perceived and real attack and retaliation occur all the time between couples who come in for treatment. Working to get the couple curious about the gap between perception and reality helps to disentangle the otherwise recalcitrant patterns between them. Insisting on the co-creation of their dynamics also helps shift the weight from blame and accusation to inquiry and investigation. We help couples frame new questions: "What is you and what is me?"; "What do I bring and what do you bring?" Couple therapy offers the possibility of talking through what has been left unspoken, and making explicit partners' different wishes and needs, alongside a discussion of how to decide whose needs to accommodate. The hope is that their dialogue becomes fuller and more continuous outside of the therapy as a result.

The countertransference impact of two people's primitive emotional states puts great pressure on the therapist, who may retain his or her reflective capacity by virtue of being outside the couple and remaining to some degree an observer. I particularly admire Ruszczynski's use of his countertransference with his case, observing as he does his shifts in consciousness and how these link with the affects the couple are trying to get rid of. He is tremendously skilled at retaining his reflective function in the face of extreme pressure to become controlling, dominant, or enraged in response to the husband's attempts to control him. More generally, the couple therapist's visceral barometric sense of hopefulness or hopelessness about a couple is often an invaluable guide. The feelings patients elicit in us of love and care towards them can be transformative. Loving moments of maternal provision offset the anxieties and unpleasant affects that the couple therapy requires them to feel. These moments also help install more resilient good internal objects, and a sense of goodness about what their couple can create. I'm sure there are many couple therapists who have had couples use therapy to get ready psychically to make a baby and then do it!

Conclusion

Psychotherapists are rightly concerned with what is mutative in therapy, and I think there are specific ways in which couple therapists may help a couple to change and grow. Ruszczynski mentions empathy in some of his work, which, to my mind, is a cardinal quality that needs to be developed – not just in therapists, whose capacity for connection with their patients depends upon it, but in the individuals who come to us in couples and, crucially, between each other. Couples come in because of failures in empathy: They have lost or have not developed sufficient separateness to access the other person's experience. In a paranoid-schizoid state, empathy is not a viable proposition because it amounts to feeling taken over or annihilated by the other. Spouses fall into habits of projecting unwanted parts of themselves into each other and then hate what they see, becoming less kind or less "decent" (Britton, 2003, p. 168) than they would be towards a stranger. It is not uncommon for one member of a couple to complain that their spouse speaks in an uninhibitedly hostile or insulting tone, without provocation or in the context of a fight. Of course, John Gottman (1995) has made a career of demonstrating how nothing kills a marriage faster than contempt (p. 79). What if there was a culture-wide attempt to bring about the capacity for empathy? The Canadian educator Mary Gordon's (2009) program, "Roots of Empathy," has demonstrably shown how children's capacity for empathy can be greatly increased. The program, now widely used in schools across Canada, consists of weekly, yearlong access to a mother and baby in a classroom setting, where first-graders gather with that mother–baby dyad in a kind of "infant observation for children" (p. 11). They speculate and discuss how the baby is experiencing her world and through observation they come to a much fuller awareness of the baby's emotional states, including how and what the baby and mother communicate to each other.

As Ruszczynski has said, we are tasked with retaining our thinking minds and not retaliating impulsively. We privilege thought over action and attempt to galvanize our patients' reflective capacity. The therapist's curiosity also models for the couple the possibility of retaining a state of not knowing, instead of jumping to paranoid conclusions. We help patients become curious about each other to find out what they do not already know. We make joint interpretations to the couple to signify the co-creation of their difficulties, and resist their pulls to blame one of them or the other. We provide as safe a space as we are able, by recognizing the dangers of mutual exposure and by not pathologizing what they bring but, where possible, acknowledging its ordinariness. We do not shy away from what is destructive in the couple, nor from acknowledging their strengths. We do attempt an unyielding pursuit of psychic reality, listening to as many layers as possible and bringing them to light. All this is done in the service of assisting the development of more mature and flexible states.

References

Britton, R. (1989). The missing link: Parental sexuality in the Oedipus complex. In *The Oedipus complex today: Clinical implications* (pp. 83–101). London: Karnac.

Britton, R. (2003). *Sex, death and the superego*. London: Karnac.

Eliot, T.S. (1949). *The cocktail party*. London: Faber.

Fisher, J. (1999). *The uninvited guest*. London: Karnac.

Freud, S. (1914). Remembering, repeating and working through. In J. Strachey (Ed. & Trans.), *The standard edition of the complete psychological works of Sigmund Freud* (vol. 12, pp. 145–156). London: Hogarth Press.

Freud, S. (1915). The unconscious. In J. Strachey (Ed. & Trans.), *The standard edition of the complete psychological works of Sigmund Freud* (vol. 14, pp. 159–215). London: Hogarth Press.

Glasser, M. (1986). Identification and its vicissitudes as observed in the perversions. *International Journal of Psychoanalysis*, 67: 9–16.

Gordon, M. (2009). *The roots of empathy*. New York: Experiment/Workman Publishing.

Gottman, J. (1995). *Why marriages succeed or fail.* New York: Simon & Schuster.

Morgan, M. (2001). First contacts: The therapist's couple state of mind. In F. Grier (Ed.) *Brief encounters with couples* (pp. 17–32). London: Karnac.

Rey, H. (1994). *Universals of psychoanalysis.* London: Free Association Books.

Rosenfeld, H. (1987). *Impasse and interpretation.* London: Karnac.

Ruszczynski, S. (1995). Narcissistic object relating. In S. Ruszczynski & J. Fisher (Eds.), *Intrusiveness and intimacy in the couple* (pp. 13–32). London: Karnac.

Ruszczynski, S. (2005). Reflective space in the intimate couple relationship: The "marital triangle." In F. Grier (Ed.), *Oedipus and the couple* (pp. 31–48). London: Karnac.

Ruszczynski, S. (2006). Sado-masochistic enactments in a couple relationship. *Psychoanalytic Perspectives on Couple Work*, 2: 107–116.

Winnicott, D.W. (1974). Fear of breakdown. *International Review of Psychoanalysis*, 1: 103–107.

Chapter 4

Unconscious beliefs about being a couple

Mary Morgan

Introduction

When a couple comes into the consulting room we are presented with a relationship in some kind of difficulty that gradually unfolds before our eyes and within the emotional experience we find ourselves having with them. If one listens closely to the material, the emotional tone of the session, and the countertransference, then I think it is possible to pick up and open up what might be described as the couple's unconscious beliefs about a couple – or perhaps, more specifically, unconscious beliefs about what a couple relationship is. Unconscious phantasies about the nature of relating will be active as couples bring their relationship to therapy for treatment. Some unconscious phantasies become beliefs and strongly influence the kinds of the relationships we make and how we are in those relationships – our expectations, desires – and our beliefs about the other.

In this chapter I want to explore the usefulness of the concept of unconscious beliefs in working with couples. It is not the only thing of significance happening in the unconscious of the couple, but I think it is central to what is going on unconsciously all the time in the relationship that, made conscious, can be shared and thought about with the couple. Once a couple is able to see that their beliefs about a couple are beliefs and not facts or truths, then it opens up the possibility of looking anew at their perception of the relationship and of the other.

Unconscious beliefs

In discussing unconscious beliefs about a couple, I am following closely the way unconscious belief has been conceptualised by Ron Britton (Britton, 1998). Unconscious beliefs have a particular feeling about them

– although they are "beliefs", they reside in the unconscious like facts until we become aware that they are in reality only beliefs. Britton gives a lovely personal example of this.

Following on from Descartes who in his "First Meditations" describes being "struck by the large number of falsehoods that I had accepted as true in my childhood, and by the doubtful nature of the whole edifice that I have subsequently based on them", Britton (1998) describes his own "doubtful edifice" accepted without question as a young child, which included the existence of God:

> As a child I did not realise until I first encountered the word "atheist" that I believed in God; until that moment I thought God was a fact. There was an unnerving precedent for this discovery, which was that at a much earlier age I met a child sceptic, and it was only then I realised that Father Christmas was not a fact but a belief of mine. This transmission from assumed knowledge to belief was to be followed eventually by disbelief. I can remember thinking when my friend shocked me by telling me what an atheist was, "I hope this doesn't turn out to be like Father Christmas". *I needed the discovery that it was possible not to believe to discover that I had a belief and did not know a fact. It is the shift from thinking one knows a fact to realising one has a belief which is linked to self-awareness.*
>
> (p. 14; my italics)

It is this capacity that can be so crucial for a couple developing insight into their relationship – the shift from thinking one knows a fact to realising one has a belief. It helps make sense of the emotional intensity accompanying some of the things couples say, argue about, and feel distressed about.

For example, a husband started a session by complaining that he had hit a very low spot during the week and his wife did not give him the comfort and reassurance he needed. He felt extremely angry and upset about this. It was absolutely clear to me that I was to join in with his sense of outrage and explore with his wife her difficulty in supporting him. It felt that not to do so would be experienced as me holding some appalling alternative view that couples don't have to give each other emotional support. One could sympathise with his disappointment and wonder why she was unable or unwilling to provide this. However, if one has the concept of unconscious beliefs, then what also becomes very interesting is the particular emotional quality in the room – the fact that he felt so certain about this and there was no room to think about it, along with the pressure I felt under in my countertransference to accept this belief. In fact, as I did try and look at this with them, rather than confirm his view it made him more furious and he appealed to me incredulously – "Look, isn't this what is supposed to happen in relationships?" Certainly he seemed to think so. This is what an unconscious belief feels like – in his mind, at that moment it was simply a fact that a couple relationship should be like this.

Unconscious beliefs, shared phantasy, proleptic imagination, and the internal couple

Before continuing I would like to touch on some other concepts that relate or overlap with the concept of unconscious beliefs. The concept of shared phantasy and shared defence has some overlap, perhaps even a lot with the idea of unconscious beliefs. However, Britton does make an important distinction between phantasies and beliefs. He points out that while "phantasies are generated and persist unconsciously from infancy onwards … the status of a belief is conferred on some pre existing phantasies, which then have emotional and behavioural consequences which otherwise they do not" (Britton, 1998).

Simply put, unconscious phantasies are the stories we create to explain our experiences of relating externally and internally. The explanation provides the best way of managing the event and feeling that you are taking some control. As Susan Isaacs (1948) put it, "Phantasy is (in the first instance) the mental corollary, the psychic representative, of instinct. There is no impulse, no instinctual urge or response which is not experienced as unconscious phantasy." These phantasies accumulate in our unconscious and affect how we experience reality. Many unconscious phantasies are initiated in infancy but are modified as they get reworked through the processes of development. For example, the young infant may experience the mother's sudden absence as being "dropped". However, with development and an increased capacity to take in and tolerate external reality, which would include awareness of the mother as a separate person with a life outside the baby, this phantasy may become, with Oedipal development, less about being dropped and more about being shut out. Later if development goes well, this phantasy too becomes modified, so that the adult no longer has the same original phantasy when its primary object leaves the room. As Melanie Klein (1958) saw it, some unreconstructed infantile phantasies remain in the deep layers of the unconscious in their unchanged original form. A defence system builds up around the phantasy and the phantasy becomes a belief and part of the personality. A challenge to the belief is felt as threatening as this feels like a challenge to the self.

Shared unconscious phantasy usually refers to something significant in the psyches of the two individuals that is shared or that dovetails in some way with the other's unconscious phantasy. In the literature it tends to be used either explicitly (Bannister & Pincus, 1965) or implicitly to refer to a shared anxiety the couple have that they then set up a shared defence to deal with. Thus, if a couple's shared anxiety is fear of intimacy, their shared phantasy may be that intimacy leads to being taken over by the other (perhaps having roots in an intrusive early relationship to the primary object), then the shared defence may be that the couple always manage to find a third (children, work, parents, interests) to be a barrier between them. These shared unconscious phantasies can be seen as what unconsciously draws a couple together, as part of the unconscious phantasy is projected into the other. As Stan Ruszczynski (1993) describes, "The exploration of shared phantasies in couple psychotherapy may allow the projected attributes to be found less terrifying and eventually felt to be capable of being taken back." In the idea of a defensive or developmental marriage, unconscious phantasies can be something the couple defend against or are able to work through together. They are not necessarily unconscious beliefs (though some may be), and the fact that the unconscious phantasies are shared or something that dovetails together perhaps places them closer to an unconscious belief. The couple, rather than finding in the other someone who doesn't fit their unconscious phantasy, finds that the other does. The couple may then form a system, like a joint personality, around the phantasies that then becomes a belief. This way of thinking about shared phantasy has been put forward by Helen Tarsh and Elaine Bollinghaus (1999), who suggest that phantasy "is more in the nature of an absolute conviction or belief system than the rather ephemeral-sounding word 'phantasy' would suggest. At bottom it is a belief about what being in a relationship with another means".

James Fisher has used the notion of proleptic imagination to capture a state of mind in which something imagined, wished for, or believed feels to that individual like reality. He says, "whatever is pictured – at the moment as well as in the future, something feared as well as something wished for – is taken concretely as a reality" (Fisher, 2009). Drawing on his clinical work and Shakespeare's *Macbeth* he shows clearly the disturbing impact of this on a couple's interaction. Shelley Nathans (2009 and this volume), in a commentary in *fort da* on James Fisher's chapter, eloquently describes how this is experienced in the consulting room with couples.

> Thinking of the proleptic imagination state of mind in this way we can think of it as a form of relating which propels certain types of action between the partners, driving it forward in time. It is the mental leap into future time – the certain assumption that we know what will be – that escalates the interaction. This is also what gives many couple interactions a scripted quality. They know where this story is heading and where it will end. And as we, as therapists watch the couple over time, we too can know exactly where the disinterested look on someone's face, the interruption, the late arrival, the rolling of the eyes, will lead. We can predict each partner's response and the subsequent back and forth, because we have witnessed it many, many times over. Once a couple is caught up in such a dynamic, it can feel like there is no getting out of it; they are trapped and we are trapped in the consulting room with them.
>
> (p. 59)

Not all proleptic imagination is based upon a belief; it could simply be an unconscious phantasy or even a conscious fantasy and the necessary abdication of the capacity for curious questioning. To take an example in which one partner feels rejected by the other – in that partner's mind this equates with being rejected. I feel it, therefore it is. This is the same kind of emotional experience that occurs with unconscious beliefs: the belief feels like a fact. The idea of the proleptic imagination helps us see how unconscious beliefs get lived out in the mind and in the interaction between two people. If one has an unconscious belief that being in a relationship leaves you vulnerable to being abandoned, then there will be a tendency to filter what the other does or says through the lens of this unconscious belief. For example, a wife is waiting to meet her husband at the theatre; he doesn't turn up on time, she feels anxious. Soon she feels perhaps a bit paranoid – *Can everyone see that she is on her own, exposed, and abandoned*? Her fantasies about her husband begin to flourish, some conscious, some unconscious: he has left her, he is with his female colleague, he is abandoning her in a cruel and humiliating way. They meet three quarters of an hour later, he having been stuck on the tube without mobile phone contact. What happens next is crucial for the couple. Can she recognise that her distress is about the impact of her unconscious beliefs and that they are beliefs but not facts? Or does her emotional experience so colour her experience of reality that, although he did not abandon her, it felt as if he did, and therefore, her emotional reality is that he did. Emotionally there is a sense of conviction and certainty from which she cannot escape. Even though she might have some awareness that she is being driven by an unconscious belief, this awareness is not strong enough to counter the emotional impact of that unconscious belief. The couple then has a terrible evening in which she relates to him as if he has abandoned her.

Finally, when talking about an unconscious belief about a couple, is this another way of describing the internal couple? We often talk about the internal couples of our couple patients in treatment. We sometimes wonder if there is an internal couple at all as we come across couples that do not seem to have inside them any idea of what a couple relationship is. The internal world is made up of objects, some of which we identify with, others we relate to. For example, we can turn to a good internal object when we need to, we identify with various internal objects when we empathise, or we can get overtaken by objects when provoked. Where unconscious beliefs are present this interplay between the ego and one's internal objects, or identifying and dis-identifying with internal objects, doesn't exist. The internal world is static – this is the way things are; a couple relationship is like this. It is as if there is no third position in the unconscious from which one can imagine being like the internal couple – perhaps some version of the parental relationship, but also not being like them. It is like the difference between a couple who question what a couple relationship is and what kind of relationship they would like or are capable of, and those for whom the question never arises as it is already a given.

What kinds of unconscious beliefs exist about a couple?

The kinds of unconscious beliefs we encounter in those couples that come for help will be many and varied. Sometimes the unconscious beliefs are shared by the couple; sometimes they are different but dovetail with the other partner's in some way. I will describe just one broad area of unconscious beliefs couples have about being a couple, which is that an adult couple relationship is a version of a mother–baby relationship. This should come as no surprise since the intimate adult relationship, although much later developmentally, is the first intimate relationship of such intensity since the mother–baby relationship. For some couples their early experiences of relating are not modified by development but become fixed in the unconscious as a belief about all subsequent relationships.

This mother–baby idea about a relationship has many versions from more or less primitive, symbiotic, and psychotic. There is a primitive version in which there is a belief that the other should meet all one's needs, as if one was a tiny baby. If I, the baby, have a tummy pain, this is something bad out there (the tummy pain projected) and I need Mummy to take it away. If all is going well Mummy does want to take it away and provides the breast or comfort. The unconscious adult equivalent of this is "I feel bad and it's your (the partner's) responsibility to make it better", rather like the example I described earlier. In an adult couple this can either operate symbiotically or one partner is set up as mother and the other as baby. For many couples this can feel good, at least for a while, and it is extraordinary the length that some couples will go to in order to maintain this illusion. If one has this kind of belief about a couple then there is no need to be interested in or curious about the other. You are so inside the other or the other is so inside you that you are one. The relationships that are built around this kind of belief can feel very idealised but gradually move towards a gridlock in which neither partner feels sufficiently separate (Morgan, 1995).

There are other versions of this mother–baby couple that never feel good. Where there has been a very disturbed early relationship, the couple may feel the reverse of containment is happening. Instead of their projections received and contained, they feel the other is constantly projecting into them. Here we get an unconscious belief that being a couple is dangerous and one has to protect oneself from intrusion. If there is this kind of belief then intimacy will be felt to be very dangerous, as there is the danger that something toxic will get inside you from the other. There are also mother–baby couples in which the other is experienced as impenetrable and unable to take in any of the other's communications (Fisher, 1993). There is the desperate need and expectation that the other will contain anxieties, but the object merely deflects them.

How do we become aware of a couple's unconscious beliefs?

Things happen in a therapy session with a couple that I believe alert one to the presence of unconscious beliefs. There is often a particular kind of emotional atmosphere in the room, certain kinds of experiences in one's countertransference and sometimes enactments.

The emotional tone of a session is often one of certainty. There may be a sense of outrage, taking the moral high ground, or the individual or couple relating to the therapist as if "isn't it obvious that this is how it is". This sense of certainty nearly always accompanies unconscious beliefs. There is a noticeable lack of curiosity; the partners in one couple would often become slightly agitated when I made an interpretation that tried to open things up, and I noticed them often glancing at the clock when I spoke, which I thought was a kind of panic reaction to me speaking, almost as if simply my otherness felt like a challenge to their beliefs. Beliefs occur in a paranoid schizoid state, not in a depressive one, which allows for doubt, uncertainty, ambiguity, and ambivalence.

With some couples there is a feeling of "here we go again". The couple or one of them gets going in a familiar way, maybe using a particular kind of voice, complaining whiny or verbose, and the therapist starts feeling that from that point on in the session there is nothing she is going to be able to do. The couple stops listening and the therapist feels deadened. Here the unconscious belief is in full swing. The therapist feels she is being subtly or not so subtly pressurised to give up on having a separate view or any helpful thoughts. She might also start to feel uncomfortable as the couple relate to her as if she shares the belief, as after all, it is felt emotionally to be a fact, or if the therapist is felt to hold a separate view, she is experienced as a threat and possible threatening, as a different view is felt as an opposing belief. There is the feeling that you cannot make the interpretation you want to make, and if you could think of it, you would be afraid to make it. Therefore, the therapist's interpretation, which offers another view, will feel like an attack on a truth. Think of the reaction initially to Darwin's scientific finding about the Ascent of Man. For some people at the time – and for some people today – these findings were and are experienced as an attack on a truth or fact. They are not experienced as scientific facts that might reveal what was felt to be a fact, to be a belief, but instead as an alternative belief challenging a known truth. This exemplifies the power of unconscious beliefs – here we have an actual belief given the status of a fact and an actual fact dismissed as a heretical belief.

As one can imagine in this kind of situation, it becomes very difficult to think. There can be an alarming experience of becoming very repetitive with interpretations and not getting anywhere. One might be overtaken by the couple's unconscious beliefs or experience an inability to take a third position not only in relation to the couple's beliefs but to one's own thoughts. One might notice a lecturing quality to interpretations or a feeling that you have the moral high ground. Even worse, the therapist can feel in the grip of her own unconscious beliefs about a couple. Here the therapist's unconscious phantasies about a couple are temporarily "promoted" to beliefs in the face of what feels like an attack by the unconscious beliefs of the couple.

In this situation enactments can easily occur. The therapist may completely lose a third position and find herself caught up in the couple's unconscious belief and acting it out with them. But sometimes one has to allow oneself to be caught up – hopefully not in a gross way, but as has been demonstrated time and time again in analytic work, it is these very difficult moments in which the therapist cannot think or manage an emotional experience that lead to a deeper insight.

So far I have only identified and tried to describe the emotional experience of unconscious beliefs, but I have not discussed how we might address them with a couple. I will describe some aspects of the work with two couples who came for psychotherapy; their different presentations have helped me bring together some of the ideas in this chapter. I hope to illustrate some of the phenomena I have been describing so far, the emotional tone, the countertransference, and tendency towards enactment.

Stephanie and Richard

Stephanie and Richard were a couple in their thirties with three young children. Their unconscious beliefs about a couple relationship had a serious effect on their development individually, as a couple, and on the therapy. The early sessions with this couple often followed a particular format in which one of them would start and the other would be required to listen. Who would start might be agreed between them before a session with one of them bringing written notes to read out, having reached agreement with the other to listen without interruption for a full five minutes. Whoever was speaking was at the same time trying to ensure that the other did not interrupt and would frequently state, "I'm not finished yet, please don't interrupt, please let me speak", while the silent or silenced one would be sitting there holding their breath. Occasional attempts at trying to interact with the one who was speaking was experienced as intrusion or disorientating interruption – so that the speaker could quite literally lose the thread of what they were trying to articulate. When the other's turn came to speak, it was striking that very little of what the other had said was responded to. It was then a different story about how that one was feeling without always being able to connect to what the other had just conveyed. This left them both feeling unheard, except gradually by me. For much of this early part of the therapy, during these exchanges between them I also felt I could not interrupt. This paralysed feeling is one indication of an unconscious belief operating. When this feeling lessened in me and I was more able to interrupt and make links between them, I could see this was an indication of the unconscious belief lessening its grip.

Both Stephanie and Richard said that what they needed was for the other to "hear them". He felt that she did not hear him accurately and made false assumptions about him, and she felt that he was not really available to her, too preoccupied with himself or his work. They could not risk taking in what the other said. When one of them expressed a feeling, it was responded to as if a "statement of fact" were being delivered, and this felt like an assault obliterating the other's feeling, an example of the proleptic imagination in action. Curiosity about the other was replaced by a certainty each had about what was going on between them.

As I understood it, at this early stage of the therapy this couple were completely in the grip of an unconscious belief about what it meant to be a couple. They held the belief that being in a couple relationship was dangerous; if you opened yourself up to the other, something toxic would get inside you. This unconscious belief was entirely at odds with what could be described as their conscious belief, that they should be sharing all their feelings with each other. For this couple there was a painful struggle between their conscious attempts to create a relationship in which they could feel heard and understood, and a much more powerful unconscious belief that to do so was extremely dangerous.

Richard described his mother as remote and self-absorbed and having glazed eyes that he couldn't penetrate, nor could he work out what was going on behind them. He couldn't get his mother to hear him, or if she did, he felt she misheard or she would make statements with the expectation that he agreed; it made him feel mad. He was acutely sensitive to feeling misheard or misunderstood by me and could experience this as me pushing something sharp into him like being "stabbed". Stephanie's mother had debilitating illnesses throughout her childhood and she struggled to separate from her without abandoning her. Both their fathers were in different ways a mixture of uninterested and intrusive. Richard's parents divorced when he was five; Stephanie's mother had been a single parent, and her father came and went in and out of her life.

In one session Richard started by saying he wanted to say something about "eyes". He was aware that when he didn't look at Stephanie he felt more separate from her and avoided eye contact with her for much of the time. When Stephanie spoke, she said she felt Richard could "drill into her with his eyes" – when he was angry she felt she had to avert her eyes from him in order to stop him. Sometimes she felt she would actually like more eye contact from him and had said to him, "Look at me", but when he did, it could feel too much. She was aware of how they positioned themselves around the house; for example, eating side by side at the breakfast bar, so that they could avoid eye contact. Stephanie said she was always scanning Richard to try and establish his mood before sharing anything. I was very interested in this because I'd noticed it in the first consultation I had with them and then in the sessions, and I had wondered what it was about. I was aware, for example, of how Richard gazed past me – looking in my direction but not at me – and how Stephanie often darted anxious looks at me.

I saw this material as a description of a fundamental disturbance in the relationship to the primary object. They were describing a wish to look and be looked at, but this was fraught with anxiety. I think they experienced their mothers as using eyes as a vehicle for projection and had to protect themselves by avoiding contact, closing their eyes, or turning away. It was like a short circuit taking place – in the moment of turning to the primary object for containment, something instead was projected into them. Of course, I don't know this for a fact, but I felt they were showing me and involving me in a here-and-now version of their primary relationship. A picture of "glazed maternal eyes", an impenetrable mother, and worse, the eye contact leaving you vulnerable to being intruded on by a misunderstanding object, experienced perhaps, as Bion (1962b) suggests, as "wilfully misunderstanding". This illustrates what can then be such a complex problem in couple relationships. Both were trying to get heard while at the same time trying to keep the other out. It becomes too threatening to take in what the other was feeling, as instead of this being a loving thing it felt like an attack. So this couple's cry of "I just want you to hear me" could be experienced as a threatening request, as to open up communication channels made them each feel very vulnerable to unwanted projections from the other. One can see how this early experience led to a belief that relating to another was dangerous.

With this kind of unconscious belief there can be a problem in the therapy as the therapist, too, is experienced as dangerous and therefore interpretations cannot be taken in; what they wanted was validation of experience, rather than an enquiry into experience. As the therapeutic relationship developed sufficient safety, they did begin to feel understood by the therapist, but their understanding of themselves, the other, and the relationship was more difficult to achieve. To enable this, the interpretation of what happens with the therapist – in other words, transference interpretations – becomes essential. The therapist needs to track carefully the impact of what the couple says or does with her interpretations. Without this kind of attention and interpretation, the sessions feel mad or chaotic or repetitive because things that were being said – either between the couple or interpretations from the therapist – were being subtly ignored or impacting and deflected or taken in momentarily before becoming lost. When the therapeutic situation itself gets gripped by unconscious beliefs, then the therapist can only function by taking a third position in relation to what is going on between all those in the room (Joseph, 1989). The concept of unconscious belief can also inform these transference interpretations that engage with the emotional experience of unconscious beliefs, which for this couple was often in the area of their conviction that relationships were dangerous. Safety in the therapeutic relationship was extremely important for this couple, which over time enabled them to risk allowing, though not without some apprehension, the other in.

Grant and Elizabeth

This couple came for help because they felt the very special relationship they first had together and enjoyed for a few years had given way to a deep unhappiness between them. They were in their late forties, both very involved in their careers, and without children. Perhaps one of the most important descriptions of them is the feeling state in the room: Grant's sense of deep disappointment, verging at times on despair, and Elizabeth's tangible distress – many sessions were dominated by her continuous crying and sense of helplessness. After some exploration it became clearer that the problem was that Grant wanted a closer emotional and sexual relationship with Elizabeth, which she could not provide without feeling she lost her sense of self. If she moved too far towards meeting Grant's needs, she felt too far from meeting her own. She had this kind of relationship with her mother growing up, in which she needed to be perfectly attuned to her mother's needs, and she had been very good at it. Grant was an only child sent away to boarding school at a young age. When he was reunited with his parents and younger sisters who were at home, he felt he had had to be a good grown-up boy in his family, which meant making little demands on his troubled parents, but he never felt attended to or acknowledged or even loved properly. He longed for attentiveness and reassurance, which he felt he never had sufficiently but did get in this relationship when Elizabeth was physically and sexually close.

As the therapy progressed we talked about how things were when the couple first got together. They were then in their early forties, both established in successful careers and at that time living a long distance from each other, but when they were together they got along extremely well and felt quite perfectly attuned. They had decided when they met that they would not try and have children, feeling it was a bit too late, and they were enjoying the "twosomeness" of their relationship. As time went on Elizabeth felt that maybe they should think again about the question of children, though she was unsure. They managed to talk about it on occasions, but it seemed that their deep ambivalence never brought their discussions to a conclusion. Then it started to dawn on Elizabeth that as they had not become pregnant and were quite lax with contraception, they might not get pregnant anyway without help. There was a moment in which she wanted to find out if there was an infertility problem; they talked about it but didn't resolve it. It got left, though there remained some part of her – maybe the main part of her – that did want to try for a baby. She felt Grant should have known this and if he could have supported her with this, their lives might have been very different, with children in it. For whatever reasons, he hadn't been aware of how much of an issue this was for her (and perhaps for him).

For Elizabeth this took on the quality of a betrayal. I don't know how conscious she was of all of this until it came to light in the therapy. But I started to realise that what I was seeing in the room was a couple in mourning – not just for a non-conceived baby, but for the lost relationship of being perfectly attuned. In their case, as must happen to many people, like Ron Britton and the child sceptic, reality intervened and shifted their unconscious belief – or at least the benign version of it. They still believed unconsciously that couples should be perfectly attuned, but at the point of entering the therapy with me this was a serious problem between them, no longer an idyll. Their unconscious belief about what a couple relationship is or should be then came out in the open between us. The therapy had to deal with a pull towards a way of being that interfered with something more reality-based and creative, which they were trying to establish.

How did we get to this place? Interestingly one of the turning points was a session in which Grant suddenly became so furious with me that he shouted very loudly for what seemed like several minutes, culminating in throwing a tissue he had been holding in my direction landing at my feet. It affected me sufficiently that I reflected during the week before the next session that I may not be able to continue with them. I didn't know why he was so angry or what it was I had done or he thought I had done to cause such anger, but it was quite disturbing to me. In the following week's session it was clear that Grant felt very ashamed, though it seemed this had come after Elizabeth had told him how he'd behaved; he hadn't been aware of how angry and threatening he'd been. It was only then that we could begin to look at what had happened in the previous session. It seemed that Grant felt I had not picked up how he had been feeling and perhaps even made an incorrect joint interpretation when I had suggested that he and Elizabeth shared a feeling. I have no reason to doubt that this was the case, but at this stage what I was interested in was his sense of outrage that I had got something so wrong. I'm sure I had got things wrong before, but it seemed at that moment it really hit him that I could get things wrong, and the emotional atmosphere in the room was like a catastrophe.

This was a useful though difficult experience because I felt through my own emotional experience that I understood his sense of outrage (after all, I felt outraged to the point of considering ending their therapy) but also when we could look at what had triggered this, it was a belief that I should not get things wrong and that his needs should be met. This was very close to Elizabeth's view; they both felt the other should meet their needs perfectly.

This case is an example of a couple acting something out and the therapist also considering taking action as feelings in us all were very heightened. As Britton (1998) points out, the individual is unconscious of his or her beliefs, but the effects of the belief will be evident in action. The acting out, once it could be processed, enabled me to see something that I hadn't seen clearly before. I now knew what a catastrophe it felt when the other was not attuned. It was following my interpretation about this that they told me more about how they used to be perfectly attuned. They felt that something rather incredible had happened between them – they had each felt the other was able to meet more of their needs than they had to meet of the other's. At some point this phantasy was challenged. Although they didn't know why at the time, in the therapy we came to understand that a crucial point of disillusionment had been Elizabeth's sense of betrayal when Grant could not detect her tentative feelings about having children.

Even though they had experience that challenged this belief, the fact that they had not been in tune about having children and had now left it too late, the belief still gripped them – although one might say it mutated into a different form. He demanded attunement from her and she felt she should provide it (as she had for her mother), but this now conflicted with her taking care of herself and her sense of self. When I became properly aware of the belief, things fell into place. It was possible with this couple to address the belief as a belief, and the work was then about mourning the belief and trying to move towards a position in which the couple could be more separate and therefore more creative.

The awareness of the belief, and all the various ways it manifested in their relationship, became a helpful concept to the couple. We could notice when they were slipping back into the belief and address it. Although one might say there was a "eureka" moment when this couple discovered this unconscious belief and realised it was not a fact, it still took a lot of working through. In particular, this involved helping them bear the disappointment when the other did not know what they needed or knew what they needed but was unable to provide it.

Technique: listening, the countertransference, and interpretation

Although I have been referring to technique throughout this chapter I will summarise my thoughts about this here.

Listening

First of all, there is a way of listening to the couple. I think this is similar to that which John Zinner (1988) described as listening "with the third ear" – for the latent communication as well as the manifest. We try and do this but couples put enormous pressure on us to work with the manifest content. I am suggesting a kind of listening that asks the question, "What story is going on unconsciously in each partner as they speak?" While we might often think the way the couple are talking to each other is slightly "mad", perhaps with the concept of unconscious belief, we can think, "It is mad because they are relating to each other as if relationships are like this" – my two examples: "There should be perfect attunement" or "Relationships are fundamentally dangerous."

Countertransference

Second, we have to monitor our countertransference and I think there are particular kinds of countertransference experiences that may indicate the presence of unconscious beliefs:

- repetitiveness in the couple or in the therapist;

- a feeling of losing control of the session, when the couple "goes off" and you feel from that point on in the session "you've lost it", meaning, you have lost emotional contact and any kind of thinking space;
- feeling afraid to make the interpretation you want to make because you are in touch with the likelihood that your interpretation will be experienced as an attack on a belief;
- you notice a lecturing quality in your interpretations – the couple's unconscious belief has triggered an unconscious belief response in you;
- enactment – when we become aware that we too are caught up in the couple's unconscious belief.

Interpretation

Third, we need to think about when we interpret and how we interpret. When we interpret follows when we become aware of an unconscious belief in the ways I have described. We might wish to time our interpretation of unconscious beliefs when we feel a couple will not feel too threatened, but interpretation of unconscious beliefs always feels threatening. The points I want to make about how we interpret are, first, we will often need to interpret what is happening in the therapy as a whole, not only what is happening in the couple; and second, it is important to interpret in the language of the emotional experience of unconscious beliefs – the certainty and the lack of doubt and curiosity. For example, following the incident in which Grant threw the tissue, I needed to find a way of formulating an interpretation that communicated my understanding that from his point of view his fury with me was justified; in his mind my attunement to him was an expectation based on a "fact" about our relationship.

Conclusion: curiosity – the discovery of the other

The problem about unconscious beliefs is that they stop the relationship developing. The relationship is required to fit into the unconscious belief about what a couple is. Therefore, instead of curiosity about the other and discovery of the other leading to something potentially creative, the feelings or behaviour of the other that oppose the belief are experienced as problems. As well as this, they do not feel like problems that can be engaged with or thought about. Unconscious beliefs are like a fundamentalist state of mind – you don't have to find out about the other because you already know what is true. It is through a genuine wish to know the other that one learns from experience and what was once believed may no longer be appropriate. When my partner goes away, I am not, as I believed as a young infant, being "dropped".

Listening carefully to any session with a couple we can detect that each partner has their own story going on unconsciously that affects the way they perceive and react to the other. To take the example of Grant and Elizabeth, before they were aware of their belief about attunement, they felt the other not being in tune was a fault in the other, as in their minds this was what a couple relationship was all about. Later in the therapy, following the awareness that this was not a fact, they felt a range of feelings when the other was not attuned – disappointment, anger, frustration and so on – but the feelings were now available to be thought about.

In some previous papers (Morgan, 2001, 2005) I have written about how important it is for a couple to be able to get into a third position from which they can see themselves and their relationship. At the beginning this capacity rests with the therapist, but over time (if things go well) it becomes installed in the couple. One of the reasons I like the concept of unconscious belief is that it feels useful not only as an essential dimension for the therapist to grasp but as something that can stimulate the development of a third position in the couple.

In a sense, curiosity is the cure for an unconscious belief and equally the dissolution of an unconscious belief brings about curiosity. We need to maintain our own curiosity not only about the couple but about ourselves, our countertransference, and the way in which we can get caught up in enactments with the couple. The couple needs us to be curious about them but also to be seen as curious about what is happening between the three of us (see Fisher, 2006), such as in the example of Elizabeth and Grant.

Once curiosity is alive the couple can start to think about their relationship, what it is and could be and who the other is. If you have a belief that you are perfectly attuned to the other, then you really don't have to find out about them because you believe that you already know. If you have a belief that relationships are dangerous because you fear something toxic will get into you, then you are so busy trying to defend yourself that there is little space to be curious. Stephanie and Richard each wanted the other to be curious about them, but opening receptive organs to the other – eyes and ears – made them feel too vulnerable, so they could not easily be curious about the other.

When unconscious beliefs about relationships are revealed as phantasies, desires, or fears but not as facts, the couple has the opportunity to look anew at their relationship. This creates a different kind of space in the therapy, and it is not easy, as the belief has to be mourned. Even though the belief is no longer felt to be a fact, there may still be enormous resistance to relinquishing it, and this may take some time. But the difference between, for example, knowing that you long for attunement and believing attunement is a fact is enormous.

Curiosity is the essential quality that differentiates us from the other higher mammals; it is described by Freud and Klein as the epistemophilic instinct, and by Bion as K, the urge to know. The activity of this drive, which requires us constantly to explain to ourselves what is happening to us, is what creates the inner world and, as a consequence, consciousness. We can only use what we already know as models to explain our experience. If we are open to taking in information, our original "explanations" about what is happening can be modified by that experience, as Bion (1962a) described, learning from experience. However, as this chapter has attempted to point out, we sometimes do not modify our internal explanations; they become fixed and take the form of unconscious beliefs. Essential to this development is the requirement of disabling curiosity – otherwise it will lead to an experience that might challenge the belief and, thereby, reveal that it is only a belief and not a fact.

References

Bannister, K. & Pincus, L. (1965). *Shared phantasy in marital problems*. London: Institute of Marital Studies.
Bion, W.R. (1962a). *Learning from experience*. London: Karnac Books.
Bion, W.R. (1962b). A theory of thinking. In *Second thoughts*. London: Karnac Books.
Britton, R. (1998). *Belief and imagination: Explorations in psychoanalysis*. London and New York: Routledge.

Fisher, J. (1993). The impenetrable other: Ambivalence and the Oedipal conflict in work with couples. In *Psychotherapy with couples: Theory and practice at the Tavistock Institute of Marital Studies*. London: Karnac Books.

Fisher, J. (2006). The emotional experience of K. *International Journal of Psycho-Analysis*, 87: 1221–1237.

Fisher, J. (2009). Macbeth in the consulting room: Proleptic imagination and the couple. *fort da*, 15(2): 33–55.

Isaacs, S. (1970). The nature and function of phantasy. In M. Klein, P. Heimann, S. Isaacs & J. Riviere (Eds.) *Developments in psycho-analysis*. London: Hogarth Press. (Original published in 1948).

Joseph, B. (1989). Transference: The total situation. In M. Feldman and E.B. Spillius (Eds.) *Psychic equilibrium and psychic change*. London: Routledge.

Klein, M. (1975). On the development of mental functioning. In R. Money-Kyrle, B. Joseph, E. O'Shaughnessy & H. Segal (Eds.) *The writings of Melanie Klein, vol. 3*. London: Hogarth Press. (Original work published in 1958).

Morgan, M. (1995). The projective gridlock: A form of projective identification in couple relationships. In S. Ruszczynski & J. Fisher (Eds.), *Intrusiveness and intimacy in the couple*. London: Karnac Books.

Morgan, M. (2001). First contacts: The therapist's "couple state of mind" as a factor in the containment of couples seen for consultations. In F. Grier (Ed.), *Brief encounters with couples: Some analytical perspectives*. London: Karnac Books.

Morgan, M. (2005). On being able to be couple: The importance of a "creative couple" in psychic life. In F. Grier (Ed.) *Oedipus and the couple*. London: Karnac Books.

Nathans, S. (2009). Discussion of: "The Macbeths in the Consulting Room," by James V. Fisher. *fort da*, 15: 56–65.

Ruszczynski, R. (1993). The theory and practice of the Tavistock Institute of Marital Studies. In *Psychotherapy with couples: Theory and practice at the Tavistock Institute of Marital Studies*. London: Karnac Books.

Tarsh, H. & Bollinghaus, E. (1999). Shared unconscious phantasy: Reality or illusion? *Sexual and Marital Therapy*, 14(2): 123–136.

Zinner, J. (1988). Listening with the third ear in couple therapy. Unpublished paper.

Chapter 5

Discussion of "Unconscious beliefs about being a couple"
Beliefs about a couple and beliefs about the other

Milton Schaefer

One can discern from the seriousness and complexity of her chapter Mary Morgan's unique ability to simultaneously hold in mind the emotional tone and interactional dynamics of the couple; the conscious and unconscious ways this gets played out in the transference and countertransference with the therapist, and to track how that is informed, moment to moment, by the haunting trajectories of both the inevitable everyday and more traumatic failures and disappointments of the individual's early object relations. Morgan's writing is suffused not just with intellectual rigor and an abiding curiosity but also with a deep sense of compassion for the ways that these couples are imprisoned and unaware in their unconscious phantasies, projections, and as she shows in this chapter, their unconscious beliefs about what it means to be a couple.

Over the past decade Morgan has generated many of the most central concepts in psychoanalytic couple therapy, especially within a neo-Kleinian and Bionian framework. I will touch on her concepts of "projective gridlock" and the "creative couple" as they provide a backdrop to her chapter on unconscious beliefs. In all of her writings Morgan is concerned about the essential tension in the individual between having an intimate relationship with another while at the same time maintaining a sense of autonomy and separation. Central to the work of theorists at the Tavistock Centre for Couples Relations was the role of projective identification as both a means of communication and a way of ridding one of unwanted parts of the self. Their notion of the "unconscious choice of a partner" entailed choosing someone who could serve the function of reclaiming those disowned aspects of the personality. Her concept of "projective gridlock" was an extension of this idea to more pathological processes where:

> Projective identification is used less as a way of projecting aspects of the self into the other and more as a way of *maintaining* a particular state of mind dominated by the phantasy of being one with, or residing inside, the object.
>
> (Morgan, 1995, p. 38)

Morgan has poignantly described how in the countertransference with these patients one can feel pulled into a state of nirvana-like oneness or a feeling of being controlled by an intruding object, but that what is central is the denial of separateness between the members of the couple and between the couple and the therapist.

In a later paper, titled "On Being Able to Be a Couple: The Importance of the 'Creative Couple' in Psychic Life," Morgan (2005) extends psychoanalytic notions of envy and exclusion that are central to Oedipus to show how the resolution of these conflicts does not solely involve renunciation and identification of respective parents. She adds – and it is central to our work with couples – that the parental couple is also internalized and serves as a model for intercourse with another. I take this to mean that one has in mind an idea of how two separate subjects can come together and that this internalization can serve as a container for the anxieties and regressions involved in the inevitable assaults to one's narcissism that are the unavoidable consequence of being with another. As Morgan (2005) states:

> The aim of couple psychoanalytic psychotherapy ... could be conceptualized as helping the couple towards more creative couple relating.... The "creative couple" is primarily a psychic development, one in which it is possible to allow different thoughts and feelings to come together in one's mind, and for something to develop out of them.... In this way the relationship is subjectively experienced as a resource, something the individuals in the relationship can turn to in their minds, with the whole being greater than the sum of the parts. This is tremendously helpful to a couple that is having a difficult time together because somewhere there is a belief that the relationship can withstand it.
>
> (p. 22)

Thus, this third is also related to a movement into a depressive position and so feelings of mourning and loss are always implicated in our efforts to help the couples we see.

In the present chapter Morgan is extending her views about the difficulties couples have in tolerating difference into the ways that they hold knowledge of themselves and the world. Thus, her focus on beliefs is both a clinical and an epistemological perspective. In this regard, the chapter's aim shares much in common with Fisher's recent work on the proleptic imagination where internal events unfold in preformed, predictable, though perhaps psychotic ways (Fisher, 2009). What seems important in both phenomena is this sense of certainty about not only one's experience of self and other but that this is the only way it could possibly be. The central difference, as I see it, between a phantasy, which is always unconscious, and an unconscious belief is that a belief is held to be true in relation to the external world. Britton has stated that, "Beliefs require sensory confirmation to become knowledge, conversely, what is perceived requires belief to become knowledge" (1995, p. 20). Thus, beliefs are central to our making sense of our experience and the way we put together both the beta-elements of our internal experience and the confusion of the world outside us. In this way I think of a belief as akin to what Thomas Kuhn (1970) talks about as a paradigm, which serves to structure and understand our experience of self and other.

While there is no disagreement with Mary on this point, I want to emphasize that these beliefs are how we live and only sometimes are pathognomonic in the vivid ways that Morgan has described. There also may exist the belief that one will be cared for, that one will be loved, that one's neediness is not too much for the other to bear, and these a priori beliefs are what allow us to pursue, with more or less conflict, our innate wish to be with another. In fact, it is in the awareness of just this tension, between the individual and couple as object, seeking and yet also needing to protect themselves, that Morgan provides a model of attunement and compassion, which has implications for both technique and what is mutative in our work.

Describing the "dance of eyes" between Richard and Stephanie, the children of psychotic mothers, Morgan says, "Both were trying to get heard while at the same time trying to keep the other out ..." So this couple's cry of "I just want you to hear me" was actually quite a threatening request, as to open up communication channels made them feel vulnerable to the unwanted projections from the other. Increasingly, I have also found it most useful with couples when I can track how they react to each other's and my own comments. However, I am also aware of how pointing this out to the couple can be seen as a hounding pursuit, and I think Mary is alerting us to the difficulties of working with these couples who have the belief that it is terribly dangerous and threatening for something new to be taken in.

Following on Britton and Morgan's religious examples of belief, there is, of course, nothing wrong with believing in God, or even believing in Creationism. However, when the result of the belief is a shutting out of the new so that increasingly one must limit internal and external experience, then instead of beliefs being a way to make the world a dependable and predictable place they become an increasingly self-fulfilling fundamentalism where the other must be denied and controlled, perhaps like the difference between a religion and a cult. Morgan states that:

> One of the most common kinds of unconscious beliefs that couples have about a couple is that it is a version of the mother–baby relationship. This should come as no surprise since the intimate adult relationship, although much later developmentally, is the first intimate relationship of such intensity since the mother–baby relationship.

Examples she describes include the parent who takes away all pain and provides endless support, or the parent who is dangerously intrusive and controlling, or the parent who is impenetrable. It seems that the importance between these being beliefs and not just phantasies is that they extend to how one sees the world and one's being in the world. In this way Morgan is also talking about the way the parent helps the infant make sense out of experience, and the ways in which learning, including the possibility of new learning, does and does not take place.

Going back to Richard and Stephanie, Morgan notes the problems inherent in the couple taking in anything from the therapist, as she, too, is experienced as dangerous. In fact, she alerts us that the therapist's countertransference caution of saying what she thinks because of a fear of it being dangerous may evidence an unconscious belief in the couple. Unfortunately, the result can be that nothing new happens and one often feels caught in the same unproductive struggle as the couple. Morgan advises that:

> In this situation the interpretation of what happens with the therapist – in other words, transference interpretations – becomes essential.

> The therapist needs to track carefully the impact of what the couple does and says with her interpretations.... When the therapeutic situation itself gets gripped by unconscious beliefs, then the therapist can only function by taking a third position in relation to what is going on between all those in the room. In this case I think it would need to be an interpretation that addresses their deep conviction that relationships are dangerous and the way they feel extremely threatened when they are required by each other or the therapist to listen and take something in.

I think Morgan is telling us what she believes is mutative in therapy and that it is the awareness, the making conscious, that one has an unconscious belief that leads to the possibility of change. However, I wonder why the interpretation, regardless of how accurate, is not just felt as more of the same; a drilling in with a more precise instrument. I think Morgan is also describing the ways in which the interpretive function of the therapist serves both as a third to allow thinking between the couple *and* as a way of showing the couple what a curious mind looks like. But I also wonder the extent to which her compassion – perhaps another word for her ability to metabolize the anxieties of the couple slowly, over time – allows her interpretations to make a dent. Perhaps in this way I am closer to Winnicott than to Klein. I also would wonder the extent to which a curious mind is, almost by necessity, a confused mind and thus the extent to which the therapist's letting herself be part of these unconscious, perhaps destructive moments and then surviving and being curious – confused – provides a model for the couple; that these things can be thought about with others.

The case of Elizabeth and Grant also brings up for me the question of what is mutative in our work. Morgan instructs us that mutative interpretations need to address not just the manifest emotional content of what is occurring in the room but more importantly the underlying unconscious belief and the lack of curiosity and doubt. So it was important to talk about Grant's belief in "perfect attunement." I again wondered what enabled this couple to take in that interpretation at that point in the treatment and the extent to which it was related to the enactment. From an American Relational standpoint, his throwing the tissue would not be considered by itself an enactment but more an acting out. However, Morgan's intense response where she considered ending the therapy in reaction to his intense anger does make this a shared, intersubjective experience, co-created by the participants, which would be understood as an enactment of an unconscious aspect of the relationship. Morgan states:

> I'm sure I had got things wrong before, but it seemed at that moment that it really hit him that I could get things wrong, and the emotional atmosphere in the room was like a catastrophe.

I have had many similar experiences where I felt that something I did, I said, or I didn't say led to intense eruptions with the feeling that one or the other or all of us in the room had been hurt; that the treatment has been ruined, that I am no longer of help to the couple, and that they or I will/should stop meeting. The feeling is that it is all just too damaging. There have been times when this experience does lead to a termination. Sometimes enactments are damaging. But more often the treatment survives and the eruption/enactment leads to both greater insight and a feeling of tremendous relief and gratitude in both therapist and couple. I wonder if there was some way that for Grant and Elizabeth the work with Morgan had progressed to a place where this enactment was possible and in this way the event represents a forward-moving articulation in action of an unconscious belief, not dissimilar to how control-mastery theory posits progress in analysis where testing out of pathognomonic beliefs is central.

Over the past few years John Steiner has entered into a series of discussions/arguments with analysts aligned to more relational approaches, such as Edgar Levinson and Henry Smith, over how enactments should be viewed and used by the analyst. I want to extend this discussion to couples therapy and its relation to unconscious beliefs. Briefly, Steiner (2006a, 2006b) sees enactments as unavoidable and mostly a regrettable form of acting out on the part of the analyst and that they represent the analyst's failure at self-control. Enactments for him are, in essence, anti-analytic in that they are action instead of talking. In this way he feels they represent some form of boundary violation, and "the most worrying enactments take place when the analyst sanctions or even idealizes enactments without becoming nervous" (2006b, p. 327). Relational analysts, on the other hand, have a focus on the interpersonal or intersubjective as well as the intrapsychic and believe that the enactment becomes a tool to understand how the couple's interpersonal life is played out. I think this also relates to how insight and curiosity are seen in regard to therapeutic change. The question that I would pose is whether it is insight – that is, knowledge of an unconscious belief – that promotes change or is it the willingness of the couple's therapist to take on a different position, to employ a new relational belief that promotes change? Curiosity, then, is a type of relational flexibility in dealing with the world and thus opens up possibility for the couple, as much as interpretation and insight, into enactments of unconscious pathognomonic beliefs.

The enactment between the couple and Mary Morgan was the result of both an inevitable misattunement on the therapist's part and a way that Grant felt ready to test the sturdiness of his therapist. While this drama unfolds between Grant and Morgan I also wonder how this enactment affected Elizabeth. There is often a way that each of the three parties in the room can become a third for the other two if the therapist allows this to happen. In some ways, it is not just that the therapist is interpreting a shared unconscious belief or a shared defense, but also I wonder the extent that he or she gives the couple a new experience. Winnicott's ideas regarding the use of an object are useful in understanding the mutative aspects of this type of enactment. He theorized that the infant has to see that the object who is mainly need-gratifying and under his omnipotent control can withstand his attack and that it is this process that leads to being able to see the other as a separate subject. In this case, and in this chapter, Morgan shows us the ways that giving up a belief entails a type of mourning process and is a movement to a more depressive position where uncertainty, doubt, and hopefully curiosity predominate. I also want to reiterate that it is not just the interpretation of unconscious beliefs or just the ability of the therapist to survive that is mutative, but it is also the relationship that develops over time that has the quality of attunement and compassion, and so shows the couple a different way of being with another.

Morgan states at the end of her chapter that:

> One of the reasons I like the concept of unconscious belief is that it feels useful not only as an essential dimension for the therapist to grasp but as something that can stimulate the development of the third position in the couple.

Having access to this third position facilitates thinking as well as being able to have a holding function for both therapist and analyst. Certainly theory can serve that function and, in fact, I wonder if it can take on the quality of a belief at times. For example, as I have immersed myself in Morgan's work in preparation for this discussion, I have had a palpable sense of her calming presence in my couples' sessions that has been helpful. Most of the Tavistock theorists talk about the internalization of the parent–child relationship as providing an internal couple, but there is little mention to my knowledge of the actual parental couple and the ways that this affects the couple's beliefs about what constitutes a couple.

I also think our current relationships with our significant others provide a backdrop and perhaps a "thirdness" in our work with couples. I know that in my work with couples my associations, my reveries, often go to my own relationship. In fact, it is in these internal musings in the session that I often become aware of my own beliefs about what it means to be a couple, which cannot help but to significantly impact my work, probably in both positive and negative ways. It has been striking, the absence of any mention in the literature of this factor in the work, and to me it often feels like an inhibition, like not wanting to talk about sex. While a topic for another time, it nonetheless points to the intensely private nature of couples' lives, the intensity of desperation that drives couples to seek treatment, and the courage that enables them and their therapist to endure.

References

Britton, R. (1995). Psychic reality and unconscious belief. *International Journal of Psychoanalysis*, 76, 19–23.

Fisher, J. (2009). Macbeth in the consulting room: Proleptic imagination. *fort da*, 15(2), 33–55.

Kuhn, Thomas S. (1970). *The structure of scientific revolutions*. Chicago: University of Chicago Press.

Morgan, M. (1995). The projective gridlock: A form of projective identification in couple relationships. In S. Ruszczynski & J. Fisher (Eds.), *Intrusiveness and intimacy in the couple* (pp. 33–48). London: Karnac Books.

Morgan, M. (2005). On being able to be a couple: The importance of a "creative couple" in psychic life. In F. Grier (Ed.), *Oedipus and the couple* (pp. 9–30). London: Karnac Books.

Steiner, J. (2006a). Interpretive enactments and the analytic setting. *International Journal of Psychoanalysis*, 87, 315–320.

Steiner, J. (2006b). Reply to Dr. Levenson. *International Journal of Psychoanalysis*, 87, 325–328.

Chapter 6

The Macbeths in the consulting room

James V. Fisher

Introduction

I want to explore some ideas about couple relationships and therapy with couples. Although I will be describing dynamics that are largely familiar, I have found them difficult to work with effectively without a clear conceptual framework. In order to help clarify the nature and structure of these dynamics, I want to introduce new terms into our psychoanalytic vocabulary. These ideas derive from three sources. One source is Wilfred Bion's (1967a, 1967b) early clinical thinking that draws on his analysis of psychotic patients in the 1950s. These ideas constitute an important extension and development of Freud's discussion of the reality principle. The second source, perhaps surprisingly, is Shakespeare's tragedy *Macbeth*, a play in which we are presented with a remarkably astute picture of a psychotic state of mind, which I am describing as the "proleptic imagination". The third source is my experience working with couples, which is an important source for exploring psychoanalytic theory, especially, perhaps not surprisingly, Bion's (1967a, 1967b) theory about the origin and nature of psychotic states of mind.

Consider the following scene from a session last week. I heard the outside door exactly at 7:10, the time the session was due to begin. However, when I went to the waiting room, only Mrs A was there. She had talked with Mr A half an hour ago and he said he might be late, she thought perhaps 10–15 minutes late. I said we would wait for him and went back to my room, leaving her in the waiting room. After half an hour I heard her on her mobile phone and went to check, finding her very distressed and saying he would be another eight minutes. He finally arrived 40 minutes late. I told them we could carry on for an additional 10 minutes, giving us half an hour.

Just to give you a flavour of what happened next, she launched into an explosive account of how she felt betrayed and abandoned. He got lost coming from a different direction, although she had a map and when he phoned she figured out exactly where he was. She could have directed him since she is an excellent map-reader, but he refused to be helped by her. Becoming increasingly distraught, she pictured him as deliberately sabotaging the session and trying to torment her. Though she said she was angry and sad, it was her anguish that was palpable. It was as if she were being physically tortured.

Mr A was silent through this. Finally he said he was sorry he was late and sorry she felt so strongly about it. This triggered off more from her until he said, in a very cool and detached way, that it's always like this. He is some sort of monster and always to blame. They had to decide how they were going to use the little time left, and turned to me to thank me for giving them the extra 10 minutes. At that point I felt Mrs A was about to get up and walk out – again.

How do we understand what is going on here? And, perhaps more to the point, how do we work with a dynamic like this? I'll come back to Mr and Mrs A at the end of the chapter, but first let's get some conceptual tools for thinking about what is happening here.

Macbeth and the proleptic imagination

Now, let's turn first to Shakespeare to help us clarify our thinking, although he is not unfailingly insightful about human experience, especially when it comes to the exploration of marriage. This lack may have something to do with Shakespeare's own experience of marriage, or at least that is the thesis Greenblatt (2004) puts forward in his recent biographical study, *Will in the World*. Taking all of Shakespeare's plays together, Greenblatt concludes that, with two exceptions, Shakespeare found it "difficult to portray or even imagine fully achieved marital intimacy" (p. 128). In one marital relationship he did explore, that of the Macbeths, Greenblatt describes "the extent to which they inhabit each other's minds" as startling. Freud (1916b) goes further in his reflections on the Macbeths, speculating that husband and wife represent two complementary aspects of the same person (pp. 318–324).

From a contemporary psychoanalytic perspective, we would doubtless be thinking in terms of projective identification as the mechanism for "inhabiting each other's minds" and thus the "two becoming one". However, I want to introduce a concept drawn from my work on Bion and from Shakespeare's *Macbeth*: the dynamic of proleptic imagination. It is a dynamic that can include experiences of projective identification, though that will not be my focus here.

The term "proleptic" has not found its way into our psychoanalytic vocabulary, although in 1963 Spitz did describe the anticipation of gratification as the *proleptic function* of emotions.[1] It is defined as "the representation or taking of something future as already done or existing". In introducing the notion of a *proleptic state of mind*, I want to extend that definition to include situations where whatever is pictured – at the moment as well as in the future, something feared as well as something wished for – is taken concretely as a reality. When we encounter it in therapy with couples, it can be the picturing of something distressing or even something disturbing, intimidating, horrible. Obviously, when what is pictured in the proleptic imagination is desirable, even wonderful – as we see initially with the Macbeths – it leads to couples getting together, not coming to us in desperation. It is related to what has been referred to as "concrete thinking" or "symbolic equation" (Segal, 1957).

In the proleptic imagination, whatever it is that is pictured, there is no space between the image or the idea and the fact or the reality. The critical question, not just in understanding this state of mind but in working with it, is: *why is there no space*? Or better, what is it that makes for the space between the picture and the reality? I don't mean what differentiates what is in my mind from what is in the world. That should be clear. We are talking about states of mind here. That is one of Bion's great clarifications in developing Freud's account of the reality principle. We're talking about a reality-oriented state of mind in which it is possible to differentiate between talking about what is in my mind and talking about what is in the world.

Before we try to answer the question of what makes for a reality-oriented state of mind, let's get a better picture of the proleptic state of mind. I doubt there is a better picture of the proleptic imagination in action than in Shakespeare's story of the Macbeths. In his version, Shakespeare pivots the drama on the moment when, returning from having led the army of the Scottish King Duncan to a bloody victory over Norway, Macbeth and Banquo are met on the heath by apparitions that are identified as the three witches or the Weird Sisters:

MACBETH: Speak, if you can: – what are you?
WITCH 1: *All hail, Macbeth! hail to thee, Thane of Glamis!*
WITCH 2: *All hail, Macbeth! hail to thee, Thane of Cawdor!*
WITCH 3: *All hail, Macbeth! that shalt be King hereafter.*
(*Macbeth*: Act 1, Scene 3, Lines 47–50)

Now the audience knows that, because of his military victories and the treason of the current Thane of Cawdor, Macbeth has been given this additional fiefdom – but Macbeth doesn't know that. He's shocked:

Stay, you imperfect speakers, tell me more.
By Sinel's death I know I am Thane of Glamis;
But how of Cawdor? the Thane of Cawdor lives,
A prosperous gentleman; and to be King
Stands not within the prospect of belief,
No more than to be Cawdor.
(*Macbeth*: Act 1, Scene 3, Lines 70–78)

When Macbeth discovers a few moments later that he has, in fact, been made Thane of Cawdor, he seems to react as if the thought, the wish, had become a reality just by being thought – the thought only had to be put into his head for it to be a reality. Harold Bloom (1999), from whom I borrowed the term, describes this as Macbeth's "proleptic state of mind": "He scarcely is conscious of an ambition, desire, or wish before he sees himself on the other side or shore, already having performed the crime that equivocally fulfils ambition" (p. 517). It is known to us in different terms in our psychoanalytic vocabulary, as C.L. Barber has observed: "The witches in Macbeth lure the hero on through the expectation of a magical omnipotence of mind by which what is envisaged must come true, a child's assumption" (Barber & Wheeler, 1986, p. 33). This "magical omnipotence of mind" is familiar to us. We will find, however, that it is more than a child's assumption as we look more closely at the drama of the Macbeths. I want to focus on the effect of Macbeth's proleptic imagination on his wife as it generates what can be described as a *shared* proleptic state of mind.

Lady Macbeth's proleptic imagination

In *Macbeth*: Act 1, Scene 5, Lines 1–73, we observe the emotional impact on Lady Macbeth of her husband's letter from the front. In her actions we almost literally see the crown with which, in her proleptic imagination, Macbeth has already been crowned by "fate and metaphysical aid". As she takes out his dress uniform, she suddenly worries that this bloody warrior will be unable to do what is necessary to make real what already feels real, the murder of the current King Duncan. As she prepares for Macbeth's return, she is told Duncan and his entourage are coming as well. One of the most chilling speeches in all of Shakespeare is spoken in this production by Lady Macbeth in her bath: "Unsex me here." And then as she welcomes her battle weary husband, she tells him that his letters have "transported her beyond the ignorant present" and she "feels now the future in the instant". However, Macbeth at this point is less sure and says only that they will speak further about it.

Shakespeare opens this scene showing Lady Macbeth reading her husband's letter from the battlefront telling her of his uncanny experience. An interesting dramatic device – a communication from his mind to hers. What is the effect of her husband's news on Lady Macbeth and on her state of mind? We certainly hear it unmistakably in her greeting to her returning warrior husband:

> Great Glamis! Worthy Cawdor!
> Greater than both, by the all-hail hereafter!
> Thy letters have transported me beyond
> This ignorant present, and I feel now
> The future in the instant.
>   (*Macbeth*: Act 1, Scene 5, Lines 54–58)

"This ignorant present" – look around … none of them know … you are King and I your Queen … "I feel now the future in the instant". "Glamis, Cawdor" … you are "greater than both by the all-hail hereafter"! The picture evoked in her husband's letter has sparked her own proleptic imagination, just as the "All Hail" of the witches seemed to have sparked Macbeth's.

In this scene, I'd like to call attention in particular to a critical couple dynamic. Note Lady Macbeth's first thoughts after reading the letter as she pictures her husband crowned with that golden round. How do we reconcile her thoughts with the portrayal of him in previous scenes? For example, in this report from the battlefront:

> For brave Macbeth (well he deserves that name),
> Disdaining Fortune, with his brandish'd steel,
> Which smok'd with bloody execution,
> Like Valour's minion, carv'd out his passage,
> Till he fac'd the slave
> Which ne'er shook hands, nor bade farewell to him,
> Till he unseam'd him from the nave to th'chops,
> And fix'd his head upon our battlements.
> ...
> ...so they
> Doubly redoubled strokes upon the foe:
> Except they meant to bathe in reeking wounds,
> Or memorize another Golgotha,
> I cannot tell –
>
> (*Macbeth*: Act 1, Scene 2, Lines 16–23, Lines 38–42)

Shakespeare goes to great pains to picture Macbeth as a fearless warrior, one who "unseam'd" his opponent "from the nave to th'chops,/And fix'd his head upon our battlements" – one who seemed to intend "to bathe in reeking wounds,/Or to [create a memorial to] another Golgotha". We hear Lady Macbeth fearing for what she perceives as her husband's nature – "too full of the milk of human kindness". Is she talking about the same Macbeth we've just been hearing about?

I want to focus on the couple dynamics in two respects. First: why is Lady Macbeth herself so ready to act, almost as if his becoming king is her responsibility? Second: why is she becoming so impatient and angry with him – what is it that so unnerves her? We might take Shakespeare in this play to be describing a kind of excited impatience, a kind intolerance for waiting that we are all familiar with. It is true that an inability to tolerate frustration is a factor in the state of mind I am trying to describe – here the frustration of the Macbeths perhaps having to wait for their "moment of greatness". And Bion (1967a, 1967b) points to the capacity to tolerate frustration as a key element in the differentiation between psychotic and non-psychotic states of mind.

Consider a patient I saw a number of years ago. He regularly reported experiences in which, for example, he would be walking along the street and would suddenly picture the person opposite as having a terrible accident, perhaps falling over and breaking an arm. For a long while I found it difficult not to feel simply amused by these accounts. They seemed so naïve, a childish malevolent wishful thinking. Finally, however, his intense agony made it impossible to ignore the hallucinatory quality of these experiences. It was the agony, not just of witnessing a calamity, but having caused it, and having caused it simply by his picturing it. It was like Midas and the nightmare of his touch that turned everything to gold.

The Macbeths, as Shakespeare pictures them in this tragedy, are on the cusp of this kind of experience, at this point somewhere between an excited impatience and the certainty characteristic of a hallucination. We will subsequently see both Macbeth and his wife plagued by nightmare hallucinations. And in the couple dynamics I am trying to describe, it is a hallucinatory sense of certainty that marks the experience of the proleptic imagination.

That still doesn't answer why, if she "feels the future in the instant", she feels responsible for making it happen. If what is imagined, what is pictured, is felt as a present reality, why this dramatic speech we have just heard in which she is picturing *her* "keen knife and the wound it makes"?

> Come you Spirits
> That tend on mortal thoughts, unsex me here,
> And fill me, from the crown to the toe, top full
> Of direst cruelty! make thick my blood,
> Stop up th'access and passage to remorse;
> …
> Come to my woman's breasts,
> And take my milk for gall, you murth'ring ministers,
> …
> Come, thick Night,
> And pall thee in the dunnest smoke of Hell,
> That my keen knife see not the wound it makes,
> Nor Heaven peep through the blanket of the dark,
> To cry, "Hold, hold!"
> (*Macbeth*: Act 1, Scene 5, Lines 38–54)

It is a chilling speech – "fill me, from the crown to the toe, top full of direst cruelty" – "make thick my blood" – "stop up th'access and passage to remorse" – "come to my woman's breasts, and take my milk for gall" – "unsex me here". It is as if she is the one who knows what is required. Her husband is too full of the milk of human kindness. She is the one who must make it happen. It is almost as if she must be unsexed and become the Macbeth who proved himself in bloody battle. In a sense she does seem to inhabit his mind.

But there is something more here than a process of identification, or projective identification. It is a dynamic in the adult couple relationship that mirrors that earlier, more primitive couple relationship of mother and baby. It reveals a complementary dynamic often seen in the shared proleptic imagination. We see and feel the almost irresistible power of it in the sense of responsibility the mother feels for her baby. She experiences her baby's wishes and needs as demands that must be fulfilled. It is an almost instinctive feeling based on the reality that the baby is essentially helpless. If there were no one to make the baby's wishes into reality, especially insofar as the wishes are actually needs, the baby would not survive.

I suggest something like that is happening here. Lady Macbeth does not experience her husband as communicating in this letter a picture of his emotional experience – she feels the future in the instant. His picture of himself as king is experienced by her as compelling, literally demanding that she act. Since Macbeth *is* king, Duncan must be dead:

> Duncan comes here to-night.
> And when goes hence?
> To-morrow, as he purposes.
> O! never
> Shall sun that morrow see!
>   (*Macbeth*: Act 1, Scene 5,
>   Lines 59–61)

Kings must do terrible things – not in order to become kings, but because they *are* kings.

You've seen it over and over in couple dynamics. She cannot express her *wishes* as he always experiences them as *demands* – and then attacks her for being so demanding. Gender is irrelevant in this. In a proleptic state of mind no distinction can be made between a wish and a demand. And either, or both, can be oppressed and controlled by what is experienced as the other continually being so demanding.

Furthermore, having been drawn into this proleptic state of mind by the partner, any ambivalence on the part of that partner is experienced as a betrayal. What we are beginning to see here is one of the dynamics in what I am calling the *shared proleptic imagination*, as the proleptic state of mind is passed back and forth. And in this dialectic of certainty and doubt, there is panic and distress as emotional reality in the form of doubt sabotages any shared sense of certainty.

The shared proleptic imagination

In Act 1, Scene 7, lines 1–83, we see that Lady Macbeth has correctly anticipated her husband's complex, conflicting emotions. And she experiences them as evidence of his betraying both himself and her. Whatever state of mind Macbeth was in when he wrote that letter, we see him now shocked at how adamant his wife is in contrast with his doubts. In this remarkable scene, we feel with Macbeth as he explores the range of his emotions. That is, he explores not just his ambition and the feeling that the crown is already his, but also his respect, even admiration for Duncan and the guilt he imagines he will feel after the assassination. It is a dramatic illustration of what I am calling the reality-testing of the full range of one's emotional experience. This reflective state of mind is opposed to the proleptic imagination which seeks to "jump the life to come," as if one emotion – in this case vaulting ambition – would become the only emotional reality, to the exclusion of those other emotions Macbeth, at least in this state of mind, knows he will feel. Lady Macbeth faces the dilemma of how to pull her husband back into a state of mind in which there is one single emotional reality. She does in an intensely erotic exchange between these childless lovers about what it is to be a man, evoking in Macbeth the longing that she should "bring forth men-children only".

How do we understand what is happening here? Consider what function his doubts play. I propose we think about the dynamics at work here in terms of the reality principle. Bion's (1962b) key contribution is his expansion and development of Freud's account of the institution of the reality principle. The first is his proposal that the reality principle be viewed, not subsequent as to the pleasure principle, nor as subordinate to it. In Bion's view the two principles of mental functioning are dynamically co-existent. This view emphasizes the fact, true for Freud as for Bion, that the establishing and sustaining of a reality-oriented state of mind is the central task of the developmental process and the central arena of the psychoanalytic process. The second is his proposal to apply the reality principle to internal reality as well as to external reality as Freud originally had in mind. If emotion is the "heart of the matter", the establishing and sustaining of a reality-oriented state of mind vis-à-vis our emotions is at the heart of both the developmental process and the analytic process.

This reality-testing of the internal world – and the curiosity, the capacity for doubting, the wanting to know that drives it – is the process that provides the space between the image (the picture of the wished for or the feared) and reality. And this, I suggest, is what Macbeth is doing. His reflections, cast in some of Shakespeare's most elegant poetic language, show him in the process we can call reality-testing.

In Scene 7, Macbeth's reflections begin with a practical consideration: if the assassination were the be-all and the end-all. But would it be? Here Macbeth articulates what is critical to thinking his emotions:

> – But in these cases
> We still have judgment here.
> (*Macbeth*: Act 1, Scene 7,
> Lines 7–8)

And what does his judgment look like? He reviews the whole range of his feelings and not just his "vaulting ambition". If the emotion of "vaulting ambition" is all he knows, it will indeed "overleap" all and land him on the other side of complex emotions. But the reality-testing of emotional experience involves an imaginative awareness of more than the immediate emotion; an awareness of one's feelings "in the round", so to speak.

Meanwhile, Lady Macbeth is desperate to stop this thinking feelingly. She faces the dilemma of how to pull her husband back into a state of mind in which there is one single emotional reality, the picture of the two of them on the throne. She does it in an intensely erotic exchange between these childless lovers about what it is to be a man, evoking in Macbeth the longing that she should "bring forth men-children only".

It is important to recall that at the beginning of the play Banquo is told that he will be the father of kings, though never king himself (*Macbeth*: Act 1, Scene 3, Lines 65–68). Macbeth, however, is only told he will be king. Whatever our view on that old debate about whether Lady Macbeth herself actually had ever given birth, there is no doubt that the Macbeths were childless. Shakespeare makes clear that Macbeth was increasingly preoccupied with the idea that he would never be the father of kings. It is Macbeth's anxiety about having no heirs that allows Lady Macbeth, in her desperation in the face of her husband's profound ambivalence, to pull him back into a shared proleptic state of mind.

The shock of her words is like the shock I have sometimes felt at moments of similar intensity with couples in my consulting room:

> I have given suck, and know
> How tender 'tis to love the babe that milks me:
> I would, while it was smiling in my face,
> Have pluck'd my nipple from his boneless gums,
> And dash'd the brains out, had I so sworn
> As you have done to this.
> (*Macbeth*: Act 1, Scene 7, Lines 54–59)

It seems to be a disturbing image of a woman's attack on her own maternal feelings. However, Macbeth hears it not as a rejection of herself as mother, but to the contrary as the possibility of the conception of the children, the *male* children, the heirs this couple do not have.

> Bring forth men-children only!
> For thy undaunted mettle should compose
> Nothing but males.
> (*Macbeth*: Act 1, Scene 7, Lines 73–75)

Greenblatt (2004) describes Macbeth as "weirdly aroused by this fantasy" (p. 139). Is it weird or is this the form their shared proleptic imagination takes? With this speech Lady Macbeth draws her husband back into a proleptic state of mind in which he sees not only himself as king, but as the father of kings.

In this state of mind Macbeth appears now to see the murder of Duncan as somehow equivalent to the procreation of male children, securing his crown in an unbroken line into the future – an image those of you who know the play will recognize as a nightmare Macbeth later experiences. His wife has become in his mind the mother of soldiers who, like their mother, would show no hesitation, no weakness, no ambivalence. Her words now take on a new meaning: "What cannot you and I perform."

From this point on the drama revolves around the struggle over fathers and sons as it becomes clear that the image of murder as a kind of procreation was in reality a cruel delusion enacted over and over by Macbeth. And as this becomes increasingly clear, both Macbeth and his wife slip irretrievably towards the madness of the negative proleptic imagination – first a hysterical desperation leading to suicide and then a schizoid nightmare of meaninglessness.

Before we see where the negative proleptic imagination can lead, let's return to our attempt to understand this dynamic psychoanalytically.

The reality principle and thinking feelingly

It is important to note that the germ of the idea of a proleptic state of mind is at the heart of psychoanalytic theory as part of the differentiation between what is variously termed primary vs. secondary processes or the pleasure principle vs. the reality principle. Freud first discussed these fundamental distinctions in his unpublished 1895 paper "Project for a Scientific Psychology"[2] and then in 1900 in Chapter VII of *The Interpretation of Dreams*. About a decade later in 1911, he formulated a somewhat more systematic account in his "Two Principles of Mental Functioning", a paper that shaped Bion's thinking during that creative decade leading up to his 1962 *Learning from Experience*.

We see the *proleptic imagination* in Freud's assumption that the "primary psychical processes" do not by themselves make any distinction between an idea and a perception, that is, its reality. A few years later in his paper on a *Metapsychological Supplement to the Theory of Dreams*, Freud (1916a) developed this point using the idea of hallucination. His concern was to determine how in normal life one is able to distinguish between phantasy and reality. Listen to how he formulates the process related to the differentiation between phantasy and reality in his "Two Principles" paper:

I shall be returning to lines of thought which I have developed elsewhere when I suggest that the state of psychical rest was originally disturbed by the peremptory demands of internal needs. *When this happened, whatever was thought of (wished for) was simply presented in a hallucinatory manner*, just as still happens today with our dream-thoughts every night. It was only the non-occurrence of the expected satisfaction, the disappointment experienced, that led to the abandonment of this attempt at satisfaction by means of hallucination. Instead of it, the psychical apparatus had to decide to form a conception of the real circumstances in the external world and to endeavour to make a real alteration in them. A new principle of mental functioning was thus introduced; what was presented in the mind was no longer what was agreeable but what was real, even if it happened to be disagreeable. This setting-up of the reality principle proved to be a momentous step.

(Freud, 1911, p. 219, my italics)

The problem here is that in the formulation of wishes (and whatever was thought) there is a tendency for it to be experienced as a reality. That's what Freud means by "presented in a hallucinatory manner". And it is the experience of frustration, the lack of satisfaction, that leads to another process he calls the "setting up of the reality principle".

In this paper Freud begins to work out the details of this reality-orienting process by proposing five adaptations in the "mental apparatus" that the process requires. As a shorthand I'll call these the five reality-testing ego functions: (i) attention; (ii) notation/memory; (iii) judgment; (iv) thought; (v) action. Bion (1962a) goes on to develop this schema, calling attention to another function one could say was implicit in Freud's account, linking. The result is that the schema of reality-testing ego functions now looks like this:

(i) attention (to current perceptions, the internal as well as external sense impressions out of which our knowledge of reality is constructed);
(ii) memory (of what has been attended to);
(iii) the capacity to join, articulate and link (perceptions and memories);
(iv) judgment (assessing the relative validity of current perceptions and memories linked together);

(v) thought (in the sense of imagined action contemplated on the basis of the judgments, i.e. thought experiments);
(vi) action (in the external world aimed at either adapting reality in a chosen direction or facilitating the acceptance of reality).

As Bion reflected on this schema he defined as the components of the process of thinking, he began to build on the dichotomy of phantasy and reality that he saw underlying it. He came to recognize that the ego functions of attention[3] and notation/memory required something that organizes the disparate elements (the sense impressions) before they could be properly attended to and remembered. He considered various terms for this hypothesized underlying ego function – "α", "dream-work", "dream-work-α", "reverie", and at one point settling on the term "attention" itself (Bion, 1992, p. 73). In the end he decided to call it "alpha-function".

1 *Imaging-state-of-mind.* One pole of the process that establishes and maintains a reality-oriented state of mind, therefore, is this organizing function. I am proposing that we call this dimension of the reality-orienting process the *imaging-state-of-mind*. Insofar as it has to do with external reality it refers to a complex mental process that makes it possible to focus on some sense impressions and to ignore all the others in order not to be overwhelmed. While it would be interesting to explore this further from the perspective of the psychology and neuro-physiology of perception, it's not really a problem for the couples we see in therapy.

   The confusions and tensions arise in the imaging of emotional experience. It is important that both Freud and Bion came to their central ideas in reflecting on the process of dreaming. Bion (1962b) proposed that in dreaming, whether in night dreams or in the process he called "waking-dreaming", we see this alpha-function, this organizing or imaging function, at work. In this Bion was essentially giving prominence to the aspect of dream formation Freud called "conditions of representability". If we had time it would be helpful to discuss the few psychoanalytic groups currently making significant contributions, primarily in France, such as the work of the Botellas (Botella & Botella, 2005). They describe it as the "work of psychic figurability", after a French neologism *figurabilité*. Although dreams are a prime example of the imaging-state-of-mind, it also takes place in the analytic process (as the Botellas so dramatically demonstrate) in Bion's sense of the session as dreaming. And in ordinary life, drama on the stage, poetry, music, the arts in general are all means of giving shape and form to emotional experience.

Confusions arise in relation to this imaging-state-of-mind largely because of two related features concerning the sense of reality. One is what Freud discussed in reference to dreams, where there is an inevitable sense or feeling of reality. Inside the dream what happens is simply taken as real. Nightmares wouldn't be nightmarish if that weren't so. The natural inclination is to take the organization, the imaging, of sense impressions – and here we mean the internal sense impressions that are the raw material of emotions – as real. In the arts we can usually distinguish between the realism of the presentation and the reality of everyday life; we don't rush on to the stage to rescue Desdemona from Othello.

But that leads to the second feature of the process of imaging emotional experience. While the images that organize the physical sense impressions of the external have their own language, so to speak, the imaging of emotional experience for the most part has to borrow the language of the external world. There are some words that more or less convey emotional experiences, but mainly we use narratives from life in the external to picture our internal emotional experience. Macbeth might have been communicating his emotional experience of the "All Hail" to his wife. The problem, if it were a communication of emotional experience and not a proleptic state of mind, is that he told the story in such a way that involved his "partner of greatness". Therefore, she takes him as talking about an external reality and simply as picturing for her his emotional experience. To be clear, he could have said, it feels as if I am already king and you my queen, though I know it might not happen – still it feels so real! Or something like that.

2 *Reality-testing-state-of-mind.* That, however, would have involved a state of mind appropriate to the second pole of the process, which establishes and maintains a reality-oriented state of mind. Bion never explicitly formulated this dimension. What he did, however, was to emphasize both the functions of linking and judgment, which are critical to what I propose to call the *reality-testing-state-of-mind*. Motivated by the impulse to be curious, the desire to know, it is essential for our awareness of internal as well as external reality.

In external reality-testing we link, compare and make judgments regarding the information from the sense impressions. With internal reality-testing it is similar, though it may not seem so at first. And yet that is precisely what Macbeth was doing when he was reflecting on his feelings "in the round". The sense of certainty that accompanies strong emotions can make it difficult to think feelingly, that is, think about one's feelings in the round – attending to them, remembering, linking, imaginatively exploring them, and finally acting in the sense deciding the emotional priorities.

In the proleptic state of mind there is a reluctance, a refusal to entertain the doubt and curiosity required to think-feelingly. The sense of certainty precludes any questioning and, as we have seen, experiences doubt as a betrayal.

This sense of certainty that marks the proleptic imagination, while comforting when what is imagined is positive, becomes a nightmare when what is imagined is negative.

Hallucinations and the negative proleptic imagination

By the expression "negative proleptic imagination" I simply mean the state of mind where what is imagined is feared or hated. Shakespeare uses the experience of hallucinations to portray this negative proleptic imagination. For example, Macbeth seems to picture his wife's influence leading him to murder Duncan as a hallucinated dagger "marshalling him in the way he should go" (*Macbeth*: Act 2, Scene 1, Lines 33–49). After the bloody murder, his doubts still torment him as he slips out of the certainty of his proleptic state of mind. Again this disturbs his wife and she warns:

> These deeds must not be thought
> After these ways: so, it will make us mad.
>   (*Macbeth*: Act 2, Scene 2, Lines 32–33)

Macbeth's response, some lines later, marks the turning point for him and a turning point in the play.

> To know my deed, 'twere best not know myself.
>   (*Macbeth*: Act 2, Scene 2, Line 72)

From here on Macbeth moves irretrievably into a schizoid form of madness, preceded for a time by intense hysterical hallucinations. The story now fast-forwards, so to speak, and we find Macbeth increasingly aware that the image of Duncan's murder as the procreation of male children was a delusion:

> Upon my head they plac'd a fruitless crown,
> And put a barren sceptre in my gripe,
> ...
> No son of mine succeeding.
> (*Macbeth*, Act 3, Scene 2, Lines 4–7)

Not only has he no son to succeed him, Banquo, the one who was told he was to be the progenitor of kings, *does* have a son:

> O! full of scorpions is my mind, dear wife!
> Thou know'st that Banquo, and his Fleance, lives.
> (*Macbeth*: Act 3, Scene 2, Lines 36–37)

But the pain of thinking feelingly is becoming unbearable. It is indeed best, he concludes, not to know himself. So he acts, not as the consequence of thinking feelingly, but in order to destroy the reality of what he feels – that is, he feels "a barren sceptre in his hand", childless. No, he seems to protest – it is other fathers who will be childless! The rest of the play turns on a series of murders. Having ordered the death of Banquo and his son, he finds, though the father is killed, the son escapes. When McDuff escapes, Macbeth has his family killed, including especially, of course, his son. But murder is not procreation.

What is critical here is that the proleptic state of mind is a hallucinatory state, and hallucinations do not satisfy, as Freud pointed out. They are the appearance of reality, the feeling of reality, but they are not reality. Notice, however, that, while hallucinations are not realities in the external world, they are nevertheless related to reality – to the reality of the internal world.

In *Macbeth*, Act 3, Scene 4, Lines 31–143, we are presented with a scene of what we could call a "nightmare dinner party", another very disturbing form of the proleptic imagination. Macbeth has just been informed that the murderers he has hired to kill Banquo and his son were successful with the father but had allowed the son to escape. Invited by his guests to sit at the royal table, he now experiences Banquo sitting in the empty chair he is offered. Lady Macbeth tries to pull him out of this hallucination by telling him it is a "painting of your fear". It is true that it is a painting of his emotional experience, as she says, like "the air-drawn dagger". However, given that Macbeth's first words to the image of the murdered Banquo are "thou canst not say, I did it", they are more probably a painting of his guilt. In this terrible scene of her husband's hallucinatory madness, Lady Macbeth repeatedly tries to interrupt his proleptic imagination. But in the end she has to face that, if what is wished for can be felt as real just by wishing, so what is feared can be experienced as real just by fearing. In this production she leaves the empty dining table carrying a candle, just as we will see her in her own hallucinatory nightmare of the next scene.

The primary difference between this disturbing scene and structurally similar scenes in our consulting rooms lies in the nature of the hallucination. Think now, what is it that Macbeth sees that no one else sees? What is the content of his hallucination? Isn't it simply that he sees Banquo sitting in his chair? No one else sees that Banquo is displacing him. In fact, no one else, Lady Macbeth included, knows that Banquo is dead.

What is a hallucination? I suggest that it is a picture, an image of an emotional state – but a picture, an image, invested with an intense sense of reality. That sense of reality is an expression of the reality of the emotional experience, not the reality of the external world with which it is confused. Hallucinations are a significant problem in disturbed couples and in their therapy. The problem is precisely this same confusion. The certainty accompanying the hallucination derives from the reality of the emotional experience confused with the reality of the external world.

In my consulting room working with a couple a few weeks ago, he is telling me about taking his son to buy a pair of shoes and the row that ensued. Though familiar, it now threatens to blow away the fragile ability to think together that we have desperately, slowly created in the previous sessions. She asks, several times, did the son try on both shoes, following this with an incredibly detailed account of how the right shoe was laced up, obviously indicating that the clerk had switched the right shoe and given him an identical one from another pair. It is so convoluted and he is feeling so attacked that he smiles – involuntarily or not, I cannot tell. She explodes, crying and shouting at the same time: *now you see, he is a vile, horrible man trying to poison me with his vicious hatefulness*! She is able to return after storming out only with the greatest effort since we have worked hard to understand these hallucinatory explosions.

A hallucination? What that means here is that he, as he is in the real world, is simply equated with what he is in the picture in her mind. I'm not going to tell you the rest of that story, except to say that, after much tedious, delicate work, it became possible, just, for both of them to see her "hallucinatory" picture of a vile man as a genuine picture of her emotional experience. And, critically, both can enter sufficiently into a *reality-testing-state-of-mind* in order to explore the relationship between the image and the reality. Once we can get to that point, and he doesn't then walk out, we can begin to tackle the dynamics of the relationship that lead to these explosions.

But we cannot do that work until we get past the proleptic confusion of her hallucinatory state in which both participate – or until both partners can begin to see the images, the stories, even the accusations, as "a communication of emotional experience".

The same is true for Macbeth's hallucination. It is his emotional experience that Banquo is displacing him, taking his place as the father of a line of kings. It is not wishes alone that motivate the dreams that picture our emotional experiences. Fears are another of the myriad of emotional experiences pictured in dreams – and, of course, hallucinations. Proleptic fears are those that, as soon as they are imaged, are experienced as real actual events. Macbeth is not merely afraid that Banquo will displace him – that would be the interpretation we would make to him. No, his proleptic nightmare reality is that Banquo has already taken his place.

As Shakespeare pictures the shared proleptic imagination in the relationship of these two desperate people, we now see Lady Macbeth drawn into her own hallucinatory nightmare by that of her husband. And it is a negative proleptic state of mind from which she will not escape. In *Macbeth*, Act 5, Scene 1, Lines 1–76, the court physician and the nurse attending her observe her carrying a candle as she sleepwalks. Having tried to tell her husband that his hallucination was but a painting of his fear, there is no one who dares to tell her the same thing. Rubbing her hands, trying to get the blood off them, it is clear the picture of the emotional experience has become the reality. It is as if the only way she can face the reality of her emotional experience of having murdered Duncan is to experience it as the physical reality of actual blood on her hands.

But it is not the hallucination that makes this scene so difficult to watch. It is the emotional reality portrayed by that hallucination.

After the murder it had been Macbeth who had cried:

> Will all Neptune's ocean wash this blood
> Clean from my hand?
> (*Macbeth*: Act 2, Scene 2, Lines 59–60)

Now it is his wife who, sleepwalking in the night, cries,

> Out, damned spot! out, I say!...
> What, will these hands ne'er be clean?
> (*Macbeth*: Act 5, Scene 1,
> Lines 33, 41)

It's true, as she says:

> What's done cannot be undone.
> (*Macbeth*: Act 5, Scene 1,
> Line 65)

But why is she unable to shake herself free from this picture, this hallucination of blood on her hands? Why cannot Lady Macbeth simply picture that is a wish, her hands clean? After all, it was she who told her husband in his panic after the murder that:

> ...a little water clears us of this deed.
> (*Macbeth*: Act 2, Scene 2, Line 64)

The answer to that question is clear if we keep in mind that hallucinations, like dreams, are true – true insofar as they picture an emotional experience. In that sense they are true to that emotional experience. It is only when we forget that and become confused, confusing a picture of the internal world with a picture of the external world. The confusion is tempting because dreams – and hallucinations – use images from our experience of the external world to picture our emotional experience. But it is a disaster in life, in relationships and in our consulting rooms when we succumb to that confusion.

That Lady Macbeth has blood on her hands is a true picture of her emotional state. And the intense feeling of reality, which she experiences as part of that picture, simply articulates the reality of her emotional experience of having blood on her hands. Can these hands ever be clean again? Perhaps. But only by a real process, not by a proleptic imagination – a real process that would begin with her remorse, had she not stopped up "the access and passage to remorse". In the absence of that process, all that is left for her is suicide.

And what of her husband who knows of her desperate state of mind? He demands the physician to do something for her:

> Cure her of that:
> Canst thou not minister to a mind diseas'd,
> Pluck from the memory a rooted sorrow,
> Raze out the written troubles of the brain,
> And with some sweet oblivious antidote
> Cleanse the stuff'd bosom of that perilous stuff
> Which weighs upon the heart.
> (*Macbeth*: Act 5, Scene 3, Lines 39–45)

Not "give sorrow words" but attack the memory, which is critical for thinking feelingly. In its place some longed-for, sweet, oblivion-making medicine.

Lady Macbeth finds her oblivion in suicide. Her husband finds his own "sweet oblivious antidote" in a cynical, schizoid state of mind that is, in the end, but another form of suicide.

Before we conclude with Shakespeare's unforgettable picture of this schizoid state of mind, sadly so familiar to us in our consulting rooms, let me bring you briefly back to that couple at the beginning. He: very late, having gotten lost, in a state of emotional detachment that was driving her mad. She: already nearly mad by his deliberate, malicious betrayal and abandonment. Ironically, although in the six weeks prior to this session we had several walkouts, with the therapy always on the edge of disintegration, this time there was no explosion. There was just – just barely – enough curiosity in the room for him to be able to think she might be describing her emotional experience, the attack having little to do with him in reality. And for her to be able to listen to and think about his experience, as if he might not be the monster who over and over betrays and abandons her.

However, with all such couples one is always on the edge of suicidal hallucinatory moments mirrored by suicidal schizoid ones. Shakespeare portrays it so elegantly, it is almost possible to forget how terrifying it can feel.

In this scene in Act 5, we see Macbeth under siege, accompanied by the court physician who could do so little for his wife despite her husband's pleas that there must be "some sweet oblivious antidote" that would be able to "pluck from the memory a rooted sorrow", which "weighs upon the heart". Instead the cry of women marks the news that the queen, Lady Macbeth, is dead. We now hear Macbeth's own "sweet oblivious antidote" in the form of one of Shakespeare's most eloquent speeches put in the mouth of a Macbeth trying to find oblivion in cynicism:

> Out, out, brief candle!
> Life's but a walking shadow; a poor player,
> That struts and frets his hour upon the stage,
> And is heard no more: it is a tale
> Told by an idiot, full of sound and fury,
> Signifying nothing.
> (*Macbeth*: Act 5, Scene 5, Lines 23–28)

Notes

1 The only previous use of the term in the psychoanalytic literature I have found is in Ernest Jones's review of Stanley Hall's study of fear during WWI (Jones, E. [1922]. Stanley Hall: A synthetic genetic study of fear. *American Journal of Psychology*, Vol. XXV, April and July 1914, pp. 149, 321; *International Journal of Psychoanalysis*, 3: 335–341). Jones quotes Hall:

> In fear the future dominates the present and gives it a new significance in addition to its own, and but for fear pain could do little of its prodigious educative work in the animal world. Fear is thus the chief paradigm of psychic prolepsis as well as the chief spur of psychic evolution.

2 The thesis was stated in Section 1 of Part I of the "Project" and elaborated in Sections 15 and 16 of Part I and in the later portions of Section 1 of Part III.
3 There is a close link in Freud's thinking between attention and besitzung, unfortunately translated as cathexis. Although Bion does not mention this connection (and perhaps was not aware of it), I suggest it is important in taking Bion's thinking forward.

References

Barber, C.L. & Wheeler, R.P. (1986). *The whole journey: Shakespeare's power of development*, Berkeley: University of California Press.

Bion, W.R. (1962a). The psycho-analytic study of thinking. *International Journal of Psycho-Analysis*, 43: 306–310.

Bion, W. (1962b). *Learning from experience*. London: Karnac. (Reprinted 1984).

Bion, W.R. (1967a). Differentiation of the psychotic from the non-psychotic personalities. In *Second thoughts* (pp. 43–64). London: Karnac Books. (Original published in 1957).

Bion, W.R. (1967b). On arrogance. In *Second thoughts* (pp. 86–92). London: Karnac Books. (Original published in 1958).

Bion, W.R. (1992). *Cogitations*. Bion, F., editor. London: Karnac.

Bloom, H. (1999). *Shakespeare: The invention of the human*, London: Fourth Estate Ltd.

Botella, C. & Botella, S. (2005). *The work of psychic figurability: Mental states without representation* (A. Weller, Trans.). (The New Library of Psychoanalysis), Hove & New York: Brunner-Routledge.

Freud, S. (1895). Project for a scientific psychology. In J. Strachey (Ed. & Trans.), *The standard edition of the complete psychological works of Sigmund Freud* (Vol. 1, pp. 281–387), London: Hogarth Press.

Freud, S. (1900). The interpretation of dreams. In J. Strachey (Ed. & Trans.), *The standard edition of the complete psychological works of Sigmund Freud* (Vols. 4 & 5, pp. 1–82), London: Hogarth Press.

Freud, S. (1911). Formulations on the two principles of mental functioning. In J. Strachey (Ed. & Trans.), *The standard edition of the complete psychological works of Sigmund Freud* (Vol. 12, pp. 213–226), London: Hogarth Press.

Freud, S. (1916a). Metapsychological supplement to the theory of dreams. In J. Strachey (Ed. & Trans.), *The standard edition of the complete psychological works of Sigmund Freud* (Vol. 14, pp. 217–235), London: Hogarth Press.

Freud, S. (1916b). Some character-types met with in psycho-analytic work. In J. Strachey (Ed. & Trans.), *The standard edition of the complete psychological works of Sigmund Freud* (Vol. 14, pp. 311–333), London: Hogarth Press.

Greenblatt, S. (2004). *Will in the world*, Jonathan Cape: London.

Segal, H. (1957). Notes on symbol formation. *International Journal of Psychoanalysis*, 38, 391–397.

Spitz, R.A. (1963). Ontogenesis: The proleptic function of emotion. In P.H. Knapp (Ed.), *Expression of emotions in man* (pp. 36–64), New York: International Universities Press.

Chapter 7

Discussion of "The Macbeths in the consulting room"

Shelley Nathans

Until the past decade, there has been a dearth of literature in the psychoanalytic canon devoted to couples, and I am deeply grateful to Dr. Fisher for his continued dedication over many years to writing on this topic. His many publications have enriched our theoretical understanding of both couple relationships as well as psychoanalytic couple psychotherapy. It is a particular honor for me to discuss his rich and thought-provoking chapter "The Macbeths in the Consulting Room" (Fisher, 2009), a chapter that offers us the opportunity to grapple with complex theoretical ideas about the nature of couple relating and deepens our understanding of one of Shakespeare's most famous tragedies.

Dr. Fisher's influence on the theoretical development of the contemporary Tavistock model for psychoanalytic couple psychotherapy is undeniable. I want to begin my discussion by attempting to briefly locate his important theoretical contributions in an historical context. The Tavistock model, begun in the late 1940s, constituted the first attempt to apply psychoanalytic concepts to the understanding and treatment of marital difficulties. Born out of a desire to address the needs of couples and families in distress, the founders of what would become the Tavistock Institute for Marital Studies turned to psychoanalysis for assistance in deepening their understanding of the emotional pressures inherent in relationships. It is significant that some very well-known psychoanalysts were involved as consultants and/or organizers in the early stages of this model, including Enid Balint, Michael Balint, and Elizabeth Bott Spillius.

The early Tavistock model relied on the familiar Freudian ideas of transference, countertransference, and the repetition compulsion and worked within the presumption that early experiences with significant others are internalized and structured into unconscious mental life.

Moreover, these ideas were brought to bear directly on the understanding of the couple, specifically in terms of how partners choose one another through unconscious partner choice, how individual unconscious fantasies and defenses become projected between partners, how these projections become structured and patterned into couple dynamics, and how these processes develop into what they termed the couple's "shared unconscious" (an idea ahead of its time, I might add, and one that seems to have prefigured contemporary intersubjective and relational theory).

Ruszczynski (1993), in a paper detailing the history of the Tavistock Institute for Marital Studies, describes the therapeutic aim in treating couples:

> The dynamic nature of the interaction is, as it were, between the two partners' split off and projected parts of themselves, as located in the other, the force with which these are projected, and how they are recovered and dealt with by the other.... The exploration of shared phantasies in couple psychotherapy may allow the projected attributes to be found less terrifying and eventually felt to be capable of being taken back. The psychological boundaries between the two partners become more clearly established, and so internal and external object relationships are subsequently modified.
>
> (p. 8)

Over time, the Tavistock model has drawn deeply from the work of Klein and Bion, to some extent from Winnicott and Meltzer, and especially from the contemporary British Object Relations theorists such as Britton, Steiner, Feldman, and Joseph. As a result, the model has broadened and evolved under these influences, moving from a focus on shared unconscious fantasy and defense to a greater emphasis on the forms of relating per se.

As Morgan (2001) writes, in the Tavistock model the couple psychotherapist positions him or herself as someone who strives to understand and hold each of the partner's separate experiences in mind while at the same time, holding in mind the couple relationship itself. In theory, this capacity for triadic relating gets internalized by the couple over time, along with the development of the therapist and the therapeutic setting as internal objects upon which the couple can rely. This promotes the possibility that the couple relationship itself can represent something created between the couple, something that is more than each of the separate individuals. The relationship itself then becomes a resource for the couple, something that enables understanding of the self, the other, and the dynamics between the partners of the couple (Morgan, 2005).

But what do we do when these processes go awry, as with couples like the Macbeths? How can we begin to organize and apprehend the extreme affects, the primitive imagery, the violent acts, and the fusion that characterizes such relationships? In Dr. Fisher's chapter, as well as in his many other publications, we can see how closely he mines both Freud's and Bion's ideas, linking them up for the purpose of understanding this couple, and offering us a way to think about issues that are central to the difficulties we all face in relating to one another.

Psychoanalysis has relied on the idea of transference and concepts like projection and projective identification as the mechanisms by which history gets thrust upon the current interpersonal stage. In this chapter, Dr. Fisher is orienting us to the future, rather than the past, or rather the way in which a fantasy of the future substitutes for the present. The repetition compulsion might have its origins in past unresolved conflicts, but the engine that drives the repetition of the pathological dynamics is fueled by certainty about the future. The proleptic imagination is then a state of mind in which a representation of something in the future is related to as if it has already occurred or currently exists.

The first time I read this description of the proleptic state of mind and its omnipotent quality, I was reminded of a former patient of mine. For years, each time I would inform him of an upcoming break in our work, he would respond by saying, "I knew before I arrived at your office today that you were going to tell me that." This patient's omnipotent fantasy of believing he knew the contents of my mind before I spoke to him illustrates the concept of the proleptic imagination and its defensive function.

However, Dr. Fisher extends the notion of the proleptic imagination beyond this future orientation. He also wants us to think of this concept in a very broad way, as when anything that is imagined, thought of, believed, pictured, feared, or wished for is taken as a concrete reality (Fisher, 2007). He equates this with a hallucinatory state, where the appearance of reality, or the feeling of reality, substitutes for reality. In these states of mind, there is a marked absence of curiosity and an inability to entertain doubt. Instead there is absolute conviction and certainty – qualities that in couple relationships can produce battles for the rights to the truth. In such scenarios, the mental functions of attention, memory, linking, judgment, exploration, and informed action that would be employed to modify the proleptic imagination are not available or are not at play.

While it is clear that individuals or couples when functioning in this manner are, in a very real sense, stuck in the realm of the concrete, the concept of the shared proleptic imagination is, in my view, a dynamic, non-static concept. I think one of the most appealing aspects of this idea is the way in which it might be used to understand the movement of a couple's interactions: the pace, the flow, the rapid shifts and oscillations in the exchange. We don't have a very good lexicon for this in psychoanalysis; one needs to search elsewhere, perhaps to music, for the right descriptors.

Thinking of the proleptic imagination state of mind in this way, we can think of it as a form of relating that propels certain types of action between the partners, driving it forward in time. It is the mental leap into future time – the certain assumption that we know what will be – that escalates the interaction. This is also what gives many couple interactions a scripted quality. They know where this story is heading and where it will end. And as we, as therapists, watch the couple over time, we too can know exactly where the disinterested look on someone's face, the interruption, the late arrival, the rolling of the eyes will lead. We can predict each partner's response and the subsequent back and forth because we have witnessed it many, many times over. Once a couple is caught up in such a dynamic, it can feel like there is no getting out of it; they are trapped and we are trapped in the consulting room with them. These are the difficulties for which couples seek our help. They are repetitive and they feel irresolvable. We often hear them say, "We keep getting into the same fight over and over again." I think that it is in part this repetition that breeds the feeling of familiarity and the sense of inevitability about the outcome of such interactions. What is also crucial in these dynamics is the irony that, while the experience is so very familiar, the participants actually know or understand very little about it. There is the sense of being swept up in something that has its own momentum and cannot be understood because they have been thrust into an experience suffused with some mysterious mélange of shared unconscious contents.

For Dr. Fisher, these stuck moments arise out of the difficulty with managing difference. What enables the individual or the couple to extricate themselves from this cycle? It is reality testing, being able to think about emotional experience and to bear the ambivalence felt in the face of reality. Dr. Fisher, following Bion and his idea that the mind contains both thoughts and an apparatus for thinking about those thoughts, finds hope for the couple in the possibility of a schema that enables thinking about feelings, including the near Herculean task of thinking simultaneously about the very different and usually contradictory feelings between oneself and one's partner.

Dr. Fisher has so beautifully described how Macbeth and Lady Macbeth seem to function as if they are of one mind; they act as if they are two sides of the same person, not separate individuals. He tells us that if Macbeth had been able to think about his emotional experience in the round it would have pulled him out of a proleptic state of mind. But of course, he can't do this because he is in relation to Lady Macbeth, whose own desires and fears commingle and conspire with Macbeth's to fuel the shared proleptic imagination state of mind from which neither can fully escape. If thinking together – communicating, not evacuating, or *thinking feelingly* together – provides the vehicle for reality testing in the couple, the absence of thinking in couple dynamics can create a state of shared proleptic imagination and interfere with one or both partners' capacity to reality test. In contrast, a couple relating from a reality testing state of mind might be able to listen to highly charged emotional statements as communications. Or perhaps later they would be able to sit together after the heat of the conflict is over, listen to one another, explain and discuss their separate experiences, and live with awareness of their differences. For Dr. Fisher, this constitutes the "fulcrum of the dynamic of intimacy" (Fisher, 2007, p. 34).

It is important to understand that he is challenging the idea that the major goal of psychoanalytic couple therapy is to get each of the partners to reclaim their projections. Rather, he encourages a different kind of activity. He says we cannot tackle the dynamics of the relationship that lead to explosions until we get past the proleptic confusion – as he put it, not "until both partners can begin to see the images, the stories, even the accusations as 'a communication of emotional experience.'" But what would this mean and how would we think about a couple listening to one another in this way?

In an earlier paper, called "The Role of Imagination in the Apprehension of Difference" (2008), Fisher offers us some ideas about what this might look like. He discusses what he termed "the apprehension of difference" and reminded us that understanding is not a way of overcoming difference.

> I propose a view of understanding in which it is essential to sustain difference.... The dilemma of how to apprehend difference without annihilating it is not only at the heart of the therapeutic enterprise with couples, it constitutes a fundamental developmental process.
>
> (p. 18)

Fisher believes that insights into the unconscious motivations are not in themselves therapeutic:

> What is therapeutic, because it is the fundamental dynamic by which the mind develops and matures, is the capacity emotionally to sustain within the mind conflicting feelings, thoughts, beliefs.... What makes for development and maturity in a relationship is the mutual capacity to imaginatively enter into emotional experiences that feel not just different but mutually contradictory. In therapy with couples, the therapist's imaginative involvement in mutually contradictory emotional experiences can be the focal point for this process.
>
> (2008, p. 34)

While "The Macbeths in the Consulting Room" is not a technique chapter, I think there are a number of intriguing issues about couple psychotherapy technique that are implied by it.

First, Dr. Fisher is explicitly advocating a shift away from the use of interpretations directed toward each of the individual partners in attempts to get them to reclaim their split-off projections. He stresses the importance of the therapist's capacity to listen to these projections as communications and notes that insistence on their withdrawal would be to reject them as communication. Although he doesn't directly say so, I assume that couple interpretations to the shared unconscious anxieties and defenses would also be considered to be secondary to the focus on the proleptic processes Dr. Fisher is describing.

Second, he tells us that the dynamics of proleptic imagination can include experiences of projective identifications, but he doesn't clarify this idea. Because his model relies less on the concept of projective identification as defensive (as in Klein's use of the term) and instead orients us to a more Bionian interpretation of projective identification as communicative of emotional experience, this has some technical implications that I will discuss a bit later.

Third, he is recommending an active involvement by the therapist in the mutually contradictory emotional experiences of the partners. What this would specifically entail he does not say, but we can glean some hints of his methods from some of his other published work. For example, in the "The Role of Imagination in the Apprehension of Difference," Dr. Fisher states that most of his clinical work with couples consists of "detailed, intense, and usually fraught explorations of … differences and the consequent *mis*understandings" (Fisher, 2008, p. 18). It seems an integral part of this exploration involves helping the couple listen to what the other is saying, "as if it were a picture of emotional experience" (p. 21).

A clear example of this technique can be found in his 2007 paper, "The Marriage of the Macbeths," where he describes a couple interaction in which the wife announced that she no longer wanted to be with her husband and that she wanted to end the therapy. Dr. Fisher writes:

> I have learned the hard way with this and other couples how difficult it is not to respond to such comments that are couched as decisions as if they were, in fact, decisions. Communication of emotional experience does not always come with the preface, for example, "I feel as if I never want to see you again." In fact, it seldom does, especially when strong feelings have been suppressed, but it is extraordinarily challenging to remain in a state of mind to hear them as communication of emotional experience … [And later on he says] I try to talk with them about what she has said as an emotional communication of how she feels at this point about the therapy and the marriage.
>
> (p. 33)

I think there is enormous utility in pursuing the direction to which Dr. Fisher is orienting us, and I have been trying to incorporate these ideas into my own clinical practice. But I confess that I am not yet ready to give up my own attachments to the idea of interpreting projections. I think my reluctance may have several sources.

First, it seems to me that people, particularly when they are relating to one another in narcissistic ways, are actually doing things to one another all of the time via unconscious activity. Each of the partners is being subjected to the onslaught of projective processes and they often desperately need our explicit recognition of this precisely because their partner is unable to provide it, typically because the partner is unaware of the intent and impact of their unconscious modes of relating. Usually the therapist's recognition and naming of this is the first step in promoting sufficient containment so that any type of listening might begin. I do not imagine that Dr. Fisher would disagree with me about this point; perhaps it is only a difference in technique, perhaps a difference in style. I tend to think it is a difference in emphasis.

A second reason for my ambivalence about abandoning interpretation of projection has to do with my increasing awareness over the years of working with couples where so much of what is said or done in the name of communication between the partners serves an evacuative function, what Bion conceptualized as a primitive form of communication (Fisher, 2007). In the earlier paper I quoted, Dr. Fisher (2007) distinguishes between a projective identification that aims at an evacuation of something into the other as opposed to the process of the shared proleptic imagination, which he says does not involve evacuation, but relies on the unconscious certainty that both individuals share exactly the same emotional state of mind. I think this is a very useful idea from which we can gather a lot of clinical mileage. I believe that this evacuative functioning exists within us all and consequently is a feature, to a greater or lesser degree, in all couples. In my experience, many couples benefit enormously from help sorting out this distinction between evacuation and communication. Thus, if one side of the technical coin focuses on helping people listen to their partner's rants as communications of emotional experience, the other side of the coin might be to help the ranting partner contain some of their evacuations.

Another reason for my hesitation about giving up the attempt to get people to reclaim some of their projections rests with my interest in the specific contents of the couple's narrative. Again, I suspect that the difference between Dr. Fisher and me is one of emphasis only, but I find it useful to keep the option open of working with a large set of interventions. I think that there are always numerous themes and modes of intervention that warrant our attention. For example, in addition to thinking about the Macbeths' shared proleptic imagination, we would do well to consider other issues. My purpose here is to highlight some of what is relegated to the background when we focus on only one dimension of the relationship between Macbeth and Lady Macbeth. Here are but a few of the many possibilities that might be explored.

First, there is the complex way in which Macbeth can be seen as having unconsciously used Lady Macbeth as the repository for his own unacknowledged murderous impulses. Correspondingly, Lady Macbeth projects her own impotency and weakness into Macbeth and this allows her a safe distance from which she can disdainfully attack him for these qualities. There is a powerful mother/son dynamic between Lady Macbeth and her husband. The play is replete with themes of sexuality, phallic castration, denigration of the maternal, and gender identities and confusions. There is strong symbolic imagery of both the good and bad breast. There is a prominent Oedipal story about the violent overthrow of a father portrayed in the murder of the king. Envy and greed abound, and in place of the recognition and mourning for their childlessness, the Macbeths create a manic plan that contains their own self-destruction because of the denial of reality upon which it is built.

In the earlier paper, "The Marriage of the Macbeths," Dr. Fisher writes, "the disturbing reality is that, no matter how painful to watch, for the Macbeths there is nothing we can say or do that will illumine their way back from these destructive couple dynamics ..." (Fisher, 2007, p. 40). I think this describes very well the desperation and hopelessness of the countertransference experience in working in the psychic terrain I have been discussing here.

In Shakespeare's *Macbeth*, the character of the physician expresses the feelings of futility and impotence with which we as therapists can identify. The physician, called in to help with Lady Macbeth's hallucinatory descent into madness, proclaims:

> Foul whisp'rings are abroad; unnatural deeds
> Do breed unnatural troubles: infected minds
> To their deaf pillows will discharge their secrets;
> More needs she the divine than the physician.
>   (*Macbeth*: Act 5, Scene 1, Lines 79–82)

Unlike the physician in the play, Dr. Fisher does not advise us to turn to the divine as the only source of help for the Macbeths. Perhaps more than any other writer, he has consistently attempted to root the psychoanalytic model of the couple in solid theory, and moreover, he has used his clinical observations of couples to develop theory that extends beyond the domain of couple treatment. "The Macbeths in the Consulting Room" is a very rich paper, in which he offers us an entry, as well as a theoretical model, for beginning to address these incredibly difficult phenomena so frequently encountered in our work with couples.

References

Fisher, J. (2007). The marriage of the Macbeths. In M. Ludlam and V. Nyberg (Eds.), *Couple attachments: Theoretical and clinical studies* (pp. 23–41). London: Karnac.

Fisher, J. (2008). The role of imagination in the apprehension of difference. *fort da*, 14(1), 17–35.

Fisher, J. (2009). Macbeth in the consulting room: Proleptic imagination and the couple. *fort da*, 15(2), 33–55.

Morgan, M. (2001). First contacts: The therapist's "couple state of mind" as a factor in the containment of couples seen for consultations. In F. Grier (Ed.), *Brief encounters with couples: Some analytic perspectives* (pp. 17–32). London: Karnac.

Morgan, M. (2005). On being able to be a couple: The importance of a "creative couple" in psychic life. In F. Grier (Ed.), *Oedipus and the couple* (pp. 9–30). London: Karnac.

Ruszczynski, S. (1993). The theory and practice of the Tavistock Institute of Marital Studies. In S. Ruszczynski (Ed.), *Psychotherapy with couples: Theory and practice at the Tavistock Institute of Marital Studies* (pp. 3–23). London: Karnac.

Shakespeare, W. (1973). Macbeth. In H. Craig and D. Bevington (Eds.), *The complete works of Shakespeare, revised* (pp. 1043–1070). Glenview, Ill: Scott, Foresman & Company. (Original play written in 1623).

Chapter 8

Psychotic and depressive processes in couple functioning

Francis Grier

Much has been written regarding the differences between the psychological universes of the paranoid-schizoid and depressive positions for the individual. In this chapter, I wish to explore how these differences affect couple relationships, especially when their shared paranoid-schizoid frame of mind is extreme, bordering on psychotic functioning. I wish to give especial attention to how these differences express themselves in the regions of couples' *ideals*, and the results of the betrayal of those ideals; also, I wish to emphasise how couples' different experiences of *the passage of time* fundamentally affect their psychological functioning.

Ideals

Couples in trouble often bring up, in the initial consultation, the centrality of ideals in their view of what should constitute the core of a relationship. They will often say how sad or angry they are that the hopes and ideals they used to cherish at the start of their relationship have by now become so dim, or spoiled, or lacking. Although it may not be conscious, each partner at the start of a relationship tends to hold an ideal, often absolute, of a specifically desired relationship to which he or she feels entitled. When a relationship with a real partner does not meet the requirements of the ideal, typically the partner is blamed for betraying the ideal relationship (an identical version of which he or she is expected automatically to share).

An essential development in couple relationships entails the psychological separation and movement of the partners from a more or less fused conglomerate unit toward a more flexible couple structure, consisting of two separate partners who can move in and out of combined and individual psychological functioning. The less this development can occur, the more the couple will remain in the orbit of narcissistic, paranoid-schizoid functioning, in which the reality and the consequences of the difference and separateness of the partners will not be tolerated. A defensive clinging to the ideal that the couple should function as a single, almost undifferentiated, unit can push the couple towards psychotic functioning.

Many couples also cling to an ideal of perfect and perpetual harmony, unable to perceive that they are thereby insisting on forcing each other (and often their children and other close relatives, and, if they are in treatment, their therapist) to try to realise an ideal, which, however superficially attractive, is actually tyrannical and destructive. This is ironic, given that the principal motive driving this ideal is usually the desire, often manic, to institute a vigorous defence against facing and owning destructive impulses within the couple. This can also be seen as a couple variant on Melanie Klein's (1952) description of the infant's relationship to the "good breast," which it

> tends to turn into the "ideal" breast which should fulfil the greedy desire for unlimited, immediate and everlasting gratification. Thus feelings arise about a perfect and inexhaustible breast, always available, always gratifying.
>
> (p. 64)

One "solution" for a couple facing the dilemma of how to remain "ideal" is to draw even closer together into a kind of fusion, denying and ejecting differentiating and problematic aspects of their own relationship into others, e.g. children, relatives, therapist. The very notion of being less than perfect can evoke catastrophic anxiety and hatred, and correspondingly extreme defences. As Klein (1952) writes,

> another factor which makes for idealisation of the good breast is the strength of the infant's persecutory fear, which creates the need to be protected from persecutors and therefore goes to increase the power of an all-gratifying object. The idealised breast forms the corollary of the persecuting breast; and in so far as idealisation is derived from the need to be protected from persecuting objects, it is a method of defence against anxiety.
>
> (p. 64)

It is this conflictual relationship between fear of persecution and consequent defensive idealisation that marks out the psychological territory of many an immature couple. The idealisation also derives from a jointly conceived primitive and ferocious superego, which threatens terrible persecution unless the partners are able to maintain ideals, which, being impossible in their objectives (e.g. that the couple and their family should be able to maintain perfect harmony at all times), are utterly bound sooner or later to plunge the couple into crisis. They may feel that they can only protect themselves via renewed manic denial that their combined psychologies contain anything negative, such as jealousy, envy, aggression, hostility or covetousness, which qualities they are then forced to disown and project into others. This is the couple version of the terrible infantile dilemma set out by Klein (1952):

> ... the infant's feeling that both an ideal breast and a dangerous devouring breast exist, which are largely kept apart from each other in the infant's mind. These two aspects of the mother's breast are introjected and form the core of the superego. Splitting, omnipotence, idealisation, denial and control of internal and external objects are dominant at that stage.
>
> (p. 70)

In this situation, it is hardly possible for the couple to have genuinely loving relations with each other, since their relationship is permeated by suspicion and fear, even if this situation is highly camouflaged by their defensive attempt to adhere to ideals of perfect harmony. They are effectively in the territory marked out by Rosenfeld (1987) where he describes his own work on destructive narcissism:

> ... destructive aspects of the self are idealised and submitted to; they capture and trap the positive dependent aspects of the self ... they oppose any libidinal relations between the patient and the analyst.
>
> (p. 109)

On the level of the couple relationship, adherence to an idealised relationship is destructive to more libidinal, loving, couple relations. The ideals the couple shares are often defensive against experiences of vulnerability and dependence on the partner, which have to be denied or at least highly controlled.

It is the mark of a developmental moment when a couple can start to bring their ideals to consciousness and subject them to critical scrutiny. If a process of thoughtful examination can take place in a relatively benign emotional atmosphere, the couple may begin to move towards the kind of "third position" reflectiveness described in current psychoanalytic theory, for example, in the field of individual analysis by Britton (1989), and in the context of couple work by Ruszczynski (2005) and Morgan (2005), who writes:

> As well as being an observer of a couple from which he is excluded, the child can start to develop an idea of himself in a relationship excluding a third, and being observed by a third. Eventually this third becomes internalised as an aspect of himself, the capacity to observe himself in his own relationship. This development, what linguistics calls the "meta" position, is crucial for the individual in an adult, couple relationship.
>
> (p. 22)

But this is easier said than done. The whole area is overlaid with such intense emotion that, in the attempt, couples regularly find themselves in serious conflict. The very act of falling in love has often been seen to have a kind of madness about it. According to Freud,

> The popular mind has from time immemorial … [spoken] of love as an "intoxication" … believing that falling in love is brought about by love-philtres.
>
> (1917, p. 388)

And

> At the height of being in love the boundary between ego and object threatens to melt away. Against all the evidence of his senses, a man who is in love declares that "I" and "you" are one, and is prepared to behave as if it were a fact.
>
> (1930, p. 66)

Although most adults may try to relate to others in more or less mature forms in most non-domestic areas of their lives, when it comes to their partner or spouse, things are often very different. Many couples unconsciously keep their relationship as a sort of reservation in which overt paranoid-schizoid relating is implicitly deemed permissible. Sexual intercourse involves the loosening, if not abandonment, of normal physical and psychological boundaries and inhibitions, and many couples share some version of an ideal that they ought to be allowed to go in and out of each other's minds, sharing their most intimate thoughts, feelings, and impulses, in much the same way that, on a physical level, their relationship entitles them to go in and out of each other's bodies. The journey to the depressive position is especially difficult for those couples who just cannot tolerate depressive pain and guilt, particularly if they have made huge investments in defences against just such pain – coupled with addictions to excited states of mind in maintaining paranoid-schizoid "highs," which they are very invested in "enjoying" to the full – hostile to any threat of their being spoiled, undermined, or contaminated by depressive position doubts.

Arguments and conflicts as such are inevitable in a close relationship, and couples need to be able to accept that as a fact of life. The emotional quality of their arguments is also important. For example, does respect for the partner vanish, and, similarly, do memories of their loving relating effectively disappear, which is frequently the case in paranoid-schizoid couple conflict; or can these other, more loving and constructive dimensions be held in mind? If so, even serious and hurtful differences may be marked by a much more depressive quality, such as concern. The irony is that it is usually those partners with the apparently highest ideals of harmony who are most likely to drive each other toward a destructive, at times psychotic relationship through their non-comprehension and intolerance of disharmony.

The experience of time

In all of this, the dimension of *time* is crucial. The journey from predominantly narcissistic, paranoid-schizoid to predominantly depressive couple relating cannot but take place over a period of time, usually of many years' duration, involving and fundamentally affecting the couple's basic unconscious attitude towards time itself. A specific feature of the depressive position is that the partners become conscious of the passage of time in various ways. The ideal of perfect harmony goes hand in hand with attempting to live in a kind of timeless zone, where nothing changes because nothing ought to need changing, since all should be perfect. When this totalitarian ideal is inevitably experienced, sooner or later, not as liberation but as denial and suffocation of individuality, the partners will usually feel confused, resentful, accusing and guilty.

When they begin seriously to face the fact that something fundamental in their relationship is wrong (perhaps expressed by a symptom arising from a feeling of sexual dissatisfaction, such as a partner having an affair or feeling drawn to do so), if all goes well, a shift begins to occur from a predominance of blame, which inevitably splits the couple, to the insight that the partners are jointly responsible, expressing or triggering a movement towards integration. This entails trying to investigate the nature of the problem, moving toward a deeper and fuller account of what has really happened, and probing the underlying reasons. The partners can only genuinely begin to try to repair their relationship if and when they can begin to face their depression and guilt, moving on to an awareness that the relationship cannot right itself magically and instantly, but that repair will require them to take real and particular steps – which takes time – to help the relationship move out of its malfunctioning and depressed state. This involves becoming thoughtful about the past and concerned and realistically anxious for the future.

The awareness of the passage of time and the importance of using it to make developmental changes to the relationship is therefore a crucial psychological dimension a couple has to mature into appreciating. This is the couple perspective of one of the basic facts Money-Kyrle (1971) selects as central to the successful completion of an individual's analysis:

> the recognition of the inevitability of time and ultimately death. ... to fear death is not the same as to recognize its inevitability, which is a fact forced on us much against our will by the repeated experience that no good (or bad) experience can ever last for ever – a fact perhaps never fully accepted.
>
> (pp. 443–444)

It is also the same territory explored by Jaques (1965) in his famous paper, "Death and the Mid-life Crisis," in which he writes:

> late adolescent and early adult idealism and optimism accompanied by split-off and projected hate, are given up and supplanted by a more

contemplative pessimism. There is a shift from radical desire and impatience to a more reflective and tolerant pessimism. Beliefs in the inherent goodness of man are replaced by a recognition and acceptance of the fact that inherent goodness is accompanied by hate and destructive forces within, which contribute to man's own misery and tragedy.

(p. 504)

More recently, David Bell (2006) has commented with regard to his own paper, which deals with very much the same themes as I am exploring in this chapter,

The title ..., "Existence in Time: Development or Catastrophe," serves to express the idea that feeling oneself as existing in time is an important developmental achievement. For some, however, it is felt as a fixed, imminent catastrophe to be evaded by the creation of a timeless world in which, apparently, nothing ever changes, where there is an illusion of time standing still. However, the attraction of the illusion is undermined by the ever-present terror of expulsion from this world, this Garden of Eden, precipitating a situation that brings the possibility not of development, but instead of a sense of sudden deterioration and death. It as if all the accumulated time that they have managed to ignore suddenly catches up with them. They feel they will suddenly grow old without ever having grown up.

(p. 784)

Clinical examples

I will explore through two clinical examples how easy it is for a couple to get stuck in the paranoid-schizoid position. I will attempt to highlight the deadly and destructive transferences partners get caught up in when they get fixated in and cling to unrealistic and highly persecutory ideals and to a psychotically eternal present, resistant to developmental, chronometric time. In one case, the inability to give up and move on from the psychotic narcissism inherent in the couple relationship resulted in its destruction, though one partner regarded the result as a liberation; in the other, the couple was narrowly able to avoid disaster and to change tack, as it were, to a developmental journey into a more depressive mode of joint functioning.

Mr. and Mrs. X

In the case of Mr. and Mrs. X, the wife had had an affair, and so, understandably, the husband appeared aggrieved. She had ended her affair, racked with guilt. The husband was voluble about his sense of betrayal but said he now forgave his wife. The couple had got back together again, but they explained that the problem was that they could not just forgive and forget and settle down. The harmony, peace, and happiness that they felt had been the hallmark of their previous "ideal relationship" – their phrase – had deserted them. The hopes and aims of the early stages of their relationship, which they felt they had to a large extent achieved, were now proving horribly elusive. Each felt constantly irritated with the other. Eventually they sought therapy.

They had been married for many years, and, for a considerable period, each had been happy enough with their choice of spouse. But Mrs. X had begun to chafe at the bit, experiencing her marital relationship as claustrophobic and infantilising. This remained the case after the couple's formal reconciliation. Mr. X angrily experienced his wife's feeling this way as a breach of contract.

The couple gave the impression of being very enmeshed, as if they were living inside each other's pockets. I soon felt quite anxious and claustrophobic myself when meeting with them, and found it difficult to think my own separate, different thoughts in their presence. The atmosphere between them was constantly tense. Mr. X needed to know and control as much as he could about his wife as much of the time as possible – her dealings with her professional colleagues, with any social engagements, with relatives, and with her thoughts and feelings. He would taunt her for having many times, in the years before her actual affair, flirted provocatively with various men. She would exasperatedly respond that it was he who had often set these meetings up – all she had done was to flirt. But, in the face of his dogged insistence on his hurt and anger, she would eventually backtrack and apologise. The couple seemed, therefore, to operate in such a way that the husband could constantly be reassured that he could control when his wife was attracted by a rival, threatening him with rejection, and could also control her subsequent rejection of the rival and her turning back repentantly and obediently to him. He could not allow her to have her own separate existence. For her part, Mrs. X, in other aspects of her personality a confident woman, seemed to have been willing to be inordinately manipulated by her husband. They operated as a single unit, in which he dominated and she colluded.

Salient features of their history were that Mrs. X, an only child, felt that her father had consistently sought her out to form an intimate couple with her (though nothing overtly sexual had occurred), relegating her mother to a denigrated background position. Mr. X, also an only child, had slept in his parents' bed until he was about nine, when, on his father complaining, it was father who left the room.

Although Mrs. X gave a superficial impression of receiving a measure of excitement and satisfaction from tantalising her husband sexually with her flirtatious advances towards other men – myself included, in the transference – the bigger picture was that she would always reassure him (and herself) by compliantly moving back under his control. She seemed as invested as her husband (= symbolic father) in keeping her primary identification as daughter rather than woman. This seemed to serve the purpose of defending herself (and him) from their joint anxieties about developing psychologically and sexually, particularly from her alarming unconscious phantasy that, if she became a sexual woman, like her mother she might well lose her husband's interest. Mrs. X's personality and relationship to her husband seemed to be powerfully stuck in an eternally present tense, clearly deriving from her past, hostile to development. This hatred of development in almost any dimension, whether to do with time, aging or sexual development, had a psychotic quality in its utter refusal to recognise and make realistic accommodation to "the facts of life."

Both Mr. and Mrs. X had been very caught up in nearly actualised oedipal relationships with their parent of the opposite sex. For Mr. and Mrs. X, then, their unconscious ideal appeared to have been to continue to enact these archaic, enmeshed relationships, in which each spouse almost perfectly fitted the projective identifications of the other, which each was therefore quite happy unconsciously to introject. Mrs. X was to be dominated and never quite to be respected as an autonomous, adult woman. Mr. X, too, would never grow psychologically into an adult male, but would retain the gratification of remaining always a boy, controlling his wife's (= mother's) sexuality, keeping her for himself away from other men, who were feared and/or mocked as representing father or the real husband. The couple's avoidance of having children was perhaps in part the outcome of these amazingly strong, joint phantasies.

Eventually, Mrs. X began to tire of this arrangement. The balance of conflicting drives and desires within her unconscious appeared to alter, so that her frustration and anxiety over her psychological stuckness began to affect her more strongly than the gratification she experienced through her masochistic submission and triumph over her and her husband's development. Real, chronometric time began to impinge on her, through her incipient awareness that, although time was passing, she was not developing. The almost servile quality of Mrs. X's attachment to her husband she had soon repeated toward me in the transference. However, when I had interpreted how I was apparently meant to find this flattering and seductive, she started to wake up to what she was doing, and then began to find a freer, more autonomous relationship to me. Mr. X resented and resisted this development. When his wife had been servile to me, I think he felt not only that she but also I was under his control. From his point of view, an unnervingly chaotic situation was now threatening to unfold, in which his control was waning.

Mrs. X now began to turn away from Mr. X in earnest. Her flirting began to change its character, both toward me and also, as I heard, toward other men, growing into more genuine – if initially desperate – attempts to seek out a more adult, autonomous relationship. This entailed opening her eyes to what she had been immersed in enacting. This she found very painful. It was also very distressing for her to gain new insights regarding the historical antecedents of her present predicament in her childhood relationship with her parents, particularly to begin for the first time to grasp her own part in perpetuating it. She began to experience herself as a person with a past, a present, and a future, whereas, by contrast, for Mr. X these dimensions of time seemed only to meet a superficial comprehension. She began, in other words, to withdraw her projections from her husband, to see him more as he really was, in all his omnipotent, virtually psychotic triumphant immaturity. This enabled her to look at herself more dispassionately and to begin to see and experience the couple much less as an agglomeration and more as a relationship between two different people.

Mrs. X's developmental drive was not able to trigger a corresponding effect in her husband. Had that been possible, their shared, marital ideal might have changed. Mrs. X might have discovered her "real" husband, i.e. a separate, adult man, ironically enough within her actual husband. Mr. X, too, might have moved towards exchanging someone who symbolised for him primarily a mother for a real, separate adult woman, a wife. But he was quite fixated in his position of clinging on forever to the old ideal, the old arrangement.

As Mrs. X began to move towards more depressive functioning and became more autonomous, Mr. X begun to realise that "the party was over" (his words), at least with regard to *this* wife. From this time on, he quite consciously began to plan to remarry when – not if – he could find someone else to restore his former happiness to him. He thus began to let Mrs. X go, although, as might be expected, this more reality-oriented attitude oscillated with thinly veiled emotional blackmail, whether along the lines of anticipating his own overwhelming grief, which seemed intended to stimulate maximum anxiety and guilt in Mrs. X (and me), or to threaten her by placing before her an imagined scenario of his future happiness with another wife whilst she was pictured as forever pining for him.

Mrs. X then began to mourn not having had children. Until then the prospect of children had only signified to them the mad idea that they would voluntarily create siblings as rivals for their exclusive relationship of child–parent with each other. Having never experienced ordinary oedipal defeat in his childhood, in his adulthood Mr. X could only conceive of it as catastrophic, not survivable, and thus to be avoided at all costs. Now that Mrs. X's ideal of a marital relationship was changing toward an adult woman to adult man relationship, if possible with Mr. X himself, the irony was that it was precisely this which Mr. X experienced as such a betrayal.

Mr. X had remained consistent with his sense of the couple's original contract and its underlying psychotic, anti-reality, anti-developmental ideal, and, therefore, could be quite clear about what constituted betrayal. For Mrs. X, things were becoming different. When she began to respond to her own non-psychotic, developmental drive, she then reconsidered her history with her parents, and now came to feel that her father had betrayed her, no longer excitingly but on a much more serious level. She began to speak more sadly about how she wished that her parents had been happier with each other, and that her father had been less caught up with her and less dismissive of his wife. In other words, she began to have intimations of what she had lost through not suffering ordinary oedipal defeat as a child.

Maintaining my analytic stance became increasingly difficult in this therapy. It could so easily seem as if I were siding with Mrs. X and against Mr. X. I interpreted exactly this, and also made certain that I balanced any interpretations of Mrs. X's difficulties and hopes with empathic interpretations of Mr. X's situation. However, the fact that this did not lead to a change of heart in Mrs. X, coupled with my not attempting to force Mrs. X to re-submit to her husband, led Mr. X to feel let down. I had to bear the anxiety that, far from containing this couple, I might have exacerbated the split between them. And yet it is a maxim of couple psychotherapy that equating a good couple outcome only with a couple resolving their differences and remaining united is mistaken: sometimes a "good" outcome consists precisely in a couple coming to recognise their differences as insurmountable and making the choice to separate, from a more informed position, rather than remaining locked in a mutually destructive and hateful relationship.

This therapy ended with the couple separating. Although both spouses found this traumatic, Mrs. X experienced relief from breaking away from her husband's control and from their joint, psychotically collusive system. Mr. X also felt relief. If his partner could not repent and submissively rejoin him in the "ideal," archaic relationship, he felt it was better for her to go. He was confident that he would find someone else to replace her, which was his defence against his anxiety of being abandoned. But he clearly felt betrayed by me and the therapy, as well as by his wife.

The ending seemed to me to express the elemental difficulty, sometimes insurmountable, of achieving a "healthy" oscillation between paranoid-schizoid and depressive components of couple relating. In this couple the paranoid-schizoid current had intensified to a psychotic level, which lived in unremitting enmity with the depressive position and psychological reality. When the couple's commitment to enacting their jointly structured archaic phantasy broke down, through one of the partners reneging on the original unconscious contract, an un-healable split developed between the spouses, so that one spouse represented the belated acceptance of developmental reality whilst the other remained implacably hostile to it.

Mr. and Mrs. Y

In some fundamental ways, Mr. and Mrs. Y presented similarly to Mr. and Mrs. X. But the dynamic differences were strong enough to enable this couple to move toward a different outcome. Mr. Y's fecklessness and unreliability were immediately presented as the main problem. In this marriage, it was the wife who came across as very controlling, constantly nagging her husband, whilst the husband was presented not only by his wife but also by himself as little more than an irresponsible boy. Whilst he had not actually had an affair, nonetheless emanating from him was an unmistakable aura of potential infidelity. His wife felt keenly undermined by this, in addition to her sense of having been drastically betrayed by his inability to support her psychologically when she had become a mother to twins a few years earlier.

It came as no surprise to learn from Mr. Y's history of a very troubled childhood relationship with his mother, of whom he had been very critical for not being able "to get her life together." His father, whom he professed consciously to admire greatly, had left the family home when Mr. Y was a young boy. Following analysis of the way his idealisation of me in the transference masked a much more critical, private attitude – particularly after my cancellation of a session at short notice – it soon surfaced that for a long time, Mr. Y had been attempting to suppress and deny bitter, internal criticisms of his father, whom he felt had betrayed him by not staying at home. He resented his father for not helping him, neither to cope with his mother nor with his growing up, except at a safe distance. His memory of a strong father defended and camouflaged an internal image of a weak father and husband, hiding behind a veneer of charm, designed to deny his pattern of fleeing from psychological difficulties. Mr. Y seemed to be identifying strongly both with this internal paternal object, as well as with his maternal object, becoming a person who could not "get his life together."

Nevertheless, underlying and disguised by these feelings, there lay another scenario of oedipal triumph over his rivalrous father, who had left, defeated, leaving Mr. Y in sole "possession" of his mother. This emerged very clearly in the transference when I had cancelled the session: Mrs. Y had felt extremely unsupported and upset by my sudden absence; by contrast, Mr. Y's concern for his wife barely concealed his greater pleasure in grasping the opportunity for showing up my failings and successfully taking over my role.

Mrs. Y had been adopted when she was ten weeks old. She felt she had been looked after very lovingly by the couple she had thought of as her parents. However, when she was 12 they eventually informed her of her adoption. She felt furiously betrayed about "having been lied to" about her parentage until that moment, whereas, in marked contrast, she was inclined to be forgiving regarding the original adoption in itself, claiming that no child could have felt very much at such an early age – this despite her often acute observations of her own young children's emotional development.

She came across as very forthright and excessively sure of herself, restrained by no inhibitions in aggressively criticising her husband or, from time to time, her therapist. But fairly soon she revealed that this over-assertive self-presentation masked extreme uncertainty and anxiety. A possible understanding emerged that her experience of the handover of herself as a ten-week-old baby might have led to deep repercussions in her unconscious, pushing her to reorder and create a defensive internal world in which any apparently "good" objects were absolutely *not* to be relied on; instead she had to exert the tightest control over them. Betrayal was always to be expected. The intensity of her feelings about the so-called betrayal when she was 12 appeared to be over-determined, unconsciously invested with the terrible significance of the earlier betrayal. When I had cancelled the session at short notice, Mrs. Y had experienced a panic attack and had nearly broken down. When we met again, she was depressed and very hostile. It took some weeks before she felt she could trust me again. What had helped in the meantime was my solidly interpreting the negative transference rather than attempting to reassure her of my "goodness," which was what she had expected, or, rather, dreaded. She appeared to have been, for a time, quite in the grip of an inner world scenario of catastrophic betrayal, and could hardly envisage any alternative explanation for my cancellation.

Mrs. Y lived in constant anxiety that, in her current life, her husband would let her down and betray her, particularly if she allowed herself to be persuaded into the "weak" position of depending on him. She had managed in the main to stave this danger off until her pregnancy and delivery, when, as if on cue, Mr. Y had apparently found the whole situation of the arrival of the twins emotionally overwhelming, aided and abetted not only by his wife's projections but also by the dynamics of his own inner world. Like his father, he fled, if not literally, nevertheless psychologically. The couple, then, found themselves in a jointly created impasse: they seemed timelessly fixed in the roles either of nagging mother and guilty, resentful boy, or betraying father and abandoned wife/daughter.

Like Mr. and Mrs. X, it could be understood that the Ys had created and were now living in a closed, mutually projective system that external reality seemed only to confirm, rather than providing the oxygen of difference. Mrs. Y was, for Mr. Y, a carbon copy of his internal mother. Mr. Y created himself in an almost exact identification with his internal father, in his fecklessness, his dislike of his wife, and his defensive but shallow jovial image. For Mrs. Y, therefore, her husband was too perfect a fit for her projection of an unreliable object, one who promised well but delivered badly, finally committing the ultimate act of betrayal and rejection. For each of them their spouse represented too closely their opposite sex parent, and, in addition, they unconsciously viewed and structured their marriage as an almost literal repetition and representation of their unconscious, internal version of their parents' marriages. Mr. Y had not experienced ordinary oedipal defeat in his childhood, whereas Mrs. Y had experienced the news of her adoption as tantamount to annihilatory oedipal defeat. The result was, as with the Xs, that Mr. and Mrs. Y were living in a virtually psychotic domestic universe, their relationship structured more like an agglomeration than being able to provide freedom of psychological movement between two separate persons.

Mr. and Mrs. Y had each been whipped relentlessly by their superegos for not managing to create an ideal, happy family; and each was unconsciously expecting their therapist to become the embodiment of these intensely critical figures, much as each of them did for their partner. They were surprised and, on the whole, responsive to a different, non-judgemental approach, to which they initially responded by taking risks in moving out of these fixed positions. Both in his professional situation and at home, Mr. Y appeared to grow in stature. Mrs. Y relaxed her moralising ascendancy, risking trying once more to trust and regard her husband afresh, noticing his finer points. They began to find a more satisfactory sexual life, in which Mr. Y's tendency to impotence righted itself, and his wife could begin for the first time to enjoy being penetrated.

But maintaining these achievements proved difficult: they were regularly hauled back by their previous, powerful identifications and styles of relating. They had more to tell: what Mr. Y had formerly described as a minor problem with alcohol now emerged as a serious addiction, whilst Mrs. Y revealed that she was bulimic. Each of them had felt for a long time that alcohol and food were more dependable than human partners, particularly each other. Instead, they relied on an unconscious agreement, almost a contract, that each would let the other down just when it mattered most, so proving the point for each of them that their closest objects were absolutely not to be depended on, or, more accurately, could be trusted to betray them. Mrs. Y often binged and then made herself vomit directly after therapy sessions, especially after sessions that she had experienced as unusually helpful.

The couple themselves quickly perceived that Mr. Y's addictive behaviour was similar. He, too, drank secretly; his alcoholic indulgence made him, too, vomit; and, just as his wife's bulimic activity could be provoked by a "good," nourishing session, Mr. Y told how, in his secret drinking, he would excitedly imagine getting on particularly well with me, whether in sessions or in imagined coincidental encounters outside of the therapy. These quasi-daydreams were characteristically followed by vomiting. His feeling of triumphant well-being was invariably short-lived, followed quickly by guilt, depression, and resentment.

Thus the Ys were able to expose, after the opening weeks of therapy, a much more disturbed, perverse, and paranoid realm, in which each played roles of being cruel, rejecting objects, or the one who was cruelly betrayed. The couple had surrendered to the grip of their psychotic relationship. They felt excited by these destructive activities, and, when "enjoying" them, felt superior to me and my "boring therapy" and to their own "boring" lives as parents, workers, money-earners, etc. Nevertheless, before matters had gone too far in a mutually destructive direction, they had been able to turn to a third party, a therapist, for a realistic, non-psychotic intervention. Like Mrs. X, and unlike Mr. X, they were each able slowly to develop a capacity to step outside their psychotic capsule and to begin to observe their dangerous predicament more accurately.

They began to worry how they were affecting their children, describing how each would start to "slag off" the other spouse to the children. I interpreted that I was to feel defeated and slagged off myself by these "developments," and I also spoke of my impotence to stop them carrying out this abusive practice. The couple responded by becoming more aware of their anxiety about their own relative impotence to inhibit their growing addiction to this sadomasochistic area. They began to struggle to give these addictions up in favour of trying to move the central marital relationship towards a more complementary collaboration of valuing and depending on each other and working to create a constructive, rather than destructive, family life. Many times each would report in tones of fairly undisguised triumph that the other had let them down, had betrayed them yet again – and the victory was, of course, over the therapist as well as over the spouse. But, differently from Mr. and Mrs. X, the Ys showed signs of being quite determined to persevere in their joint attempt to transform the core of their marital relationship from primarily aggressive and perverse sadomasochistic dynamics to a predominantly collaborative, developmental, and loving partnership.

Mr. and Mrs. Y provided the therapist with the genuine satisfaction of working with a couple who, over time, developed their shared capacity for insight. The work was aided by the couple's appropriate anxiety about the damaging effect their jointly enacted destructive phantasies were having on each other and their young family, an instance of how the presence of children will sometimes help to alert a couple who are stuck and submerged in a psychotic swamp to become aware of the passage of time, its developmental demands, and the terrible consequences if these are ignored. They began to set up more humane and realistic ideals. Amongst these, forgiveness no longer felt like an impossible, persecutory ideal, but attained a grittier, less idealistic, everyday quality. Real development was now possible. One had a sense with this couple that, broadly speaking, they had managed to move out of their threatened, shared psychotic enclave, and were now claiming their rightful position in "developmental time," in which their ideals became more oriented toward reality, and in which they experienced more ordinary oscillations between the paranoid-schizoid and depressive positions, with an underlying sense of forward movement.

Conclusion

Both couples initially presented as if they were ordinarily rational – at a deeper level they were actually living in a virtually psychotic universe, their joint couple psyche consisting of an agglomeration of two people who were stripped of their differences, individuality and separateness, functioning virtually entirely on massive joint projection. Time effectively stood still or was meaningless: the couples were triumphantly forcing a continual re-enactment of a phantasised past in the present. This usurping of the potential of the developmental present expressed a psychotic hatred of developmental reality, a hatred that had the couple in its grip (see Freud, 1911; Bion, 1957).

A crucial component in work with couples where betrayal is a major factor is the quality of each of the partners' superego, and therefore of their joint superego. Mr. and Mrs. X's superegos were excessively moralistic and punitive. They used to join in a virtual orgy of self-righteous, mutual condemnation, aimed not at development but simply beating each other into submission, and at enjoying the sadomasochistic gratifications of the beating. Development was the enemy of this psychotic superego relationship. For Mr. X, this never changed. For Mrs. X, there was a sea change when she began to perceive the fundamentals of their relationship differently. Mr. and Mrs. Y had to negotiate a similar move. It rocked Mrs. Y to perceive that the superior certainty she cultivated delivered only superficial conviction, and, ironically, was more likely to lead to the very betrayal she feared. It required real courage for her to risk searching for a different kind of moral compass in which there were far fewer absolutes, and in which she had to renounce her superior position in order to join her husband on an equal level in being implicated in their joint imperfections and problems.

Both couples struggled with betrayal of their unconscious ideals. Definitions of betrayal came to differ substantially, as did their sense of what might be forgivable. The paranoid-schizoid kind of forgiveness (exemplified by what Mr. X was prepared to offer his wife) seemed absolute, with a kind of psychotically dogmatic certainty as to what constituted an offence; whereas depressive forgiveness (exemplified by what Mr. and Mrs. Y were eventually able to offer each other) seemed deeper, though, almost ironically, never quite offering the same quality of absolute assurance.

One might envision many a couple's developmental journey as consisting of the transition from a primarily projective system (particularly involving mania and denial) to a more mature, combined state of mind in which each partner projects less, so that the self becomes less confused with a partner, the boundary between self and partner becoming more conscious, as well as between the couple and others, e.g. children. In line with this process, the couple's overall ideals, recognising each other's difference and separateness, need to become more humane and tolerant. Simultaneously, the couple will experience the quality of their relationship less as unchanging, living in an eternal present, moving to becoming much more aware of shifts and changes in their feelings towards each other over time. If the couple is able to accept this process as inevitably realistic and in itself dynamic and interesting, they are far more likely to reap the fruits of an ongoing, developmentally benign overall atmosphere within the totality of their relationship.

References

Bell, D. (2006). Existence in time: Development or catastrophe. *Psychoanlaytic Quarterly*, 75: 783–805.
Bion, W. (1957). Differentiation of the psychotic from the non-psychotic personalities. In *Second thoughts* (pp. 43–64). London: Karnac.
Britton, R. (1989). The missing link: Parental sexuality in the Oedipus complex. In J. Steiner (Ed.), *The Oedipus complex today: Clinical implications* (pp. 83–101). London: Karnac.
Freud, S. (1911). Formulations on the two principles of mental functioning. In J. Strachey (Ed. & Trans.), *The standard edition of the complete psychological works of Sigmund Freud* (Volume 12, pp. 213–226). London: Hogarth Press.
Freud, S. (1917). Introductory lectures on psycho-analysis. In J. Strachey (Ed. & Trans.), *The standard edition of the complete psychological works of Sigmund Freud* (Volume 16). London: Hogarth Press.
Freud, S. (1930). Civilization and its discontents. In J. Strachey (Ed. & Trans.), *The standard edition of the complete psychological works of Sigmund Freud* (Volume 21, pp. 57–146). London: Hogarth Press.
Jaques, E. (1965). Death and the mid-life crisis. *International Journal of Psychoanalysis*, 46: 502–514.
Klein, M. (1952). Some theoretical conclusions regarding the emotional life of the infant. In *Envy and Gratitude* (pp. 61–93). London: Karnac.
Money-Kyrle, R. (1971). The aim of psychoanlaysis. In D. Meltzer (Ed.), *The collected papers of Roger Money-Kyrle* (pp. 443–444). London: Clunie Press.
Morgan, M. (2005). On being able to be a couple. In F. Grier (Ed.), *Oedipus and the couple* (pp. 9–30). London: Karnac.
Rosenfeld, H. (1987). Destructive narcissism and the death instinct. In *Impasse and interpretation* (pp. 105–132). London: Routledge.
Ruszczynski, S. (2005). Reflective space in the intimate couple relationship: The "marital triangle." In F. Grier (Ed.), *Oedipus and the couple* (pp. 31–48). London: Karnac.

Chapter 9

Discussion of "Psychotic and depressive processes in couple functioning"

Julie Friend

I would like to thank Francis Grier, not only for the thought-provoking chapter, but also for his intriguing and singular contributions to psychoanalytic thinking about couples over the years. As both an editor and a writer, he has explored the impediments to creative couple life. Grier has imaginatively mined the Oedipus myth to enrich our understanding of couple dynamics, unfolding the familiar story to highlight aspects of couple relating as represented by the three different couples in the story: Oedipus' parents, Laius and Jocasta, who "cannot cope with a threesome" (with difference, guilt, exclusion, jealousy, and other intense emotions); Oedipus and Jocasta, who illustrate the desire to turn a blind eye to truths that are felt to be unbearable; and the king and queen of Corinth, an apparently more well-functioning couple who seem able to live generatively within a more realistically perceived world.

In his influential paper "No Sex Couples, Catastrophic Change, and the Primal Scene," Grier (2005) builds on Britton's thinking and addresses the central importance for couple life of coming to some terms with Oedipal reality, and of navigating triadic relating. In his paper "Lively and Deathly Intercourse," he enlists Bion's conception of L, H, and K links, representing loving, hating, and the need for knowledge, as vital and vitalizing elements in psychological and couple life. I have long admired Grier's finely tuned ear for the thematic tensions inherent in couple life and for the countervailing internal forces we all struggle with, and to have the chance to discuss his work.

The two couples he talks about in "Psychotic and Depressive Functioning in Couples" – one more rigidly sunk in a paranoid-schizoid world than the other – no doubt sound familiar to couple therapists. We hear them in our offices lamenting, "What happened to us?" or angrily declaring, "You weren't like this before!" Paradoxically, although they are trying to retain what Grier terms an "ideal solution," we can see them relentlessly maintaining a torturous engagement with each other. Their rigid ideal of harmony, as Grier beautifully puts it, ironically feeds a claustrophobic, rigid, controlling atmosphere in the room. A manic, driven, insistent manner of speaking to each other can make thoughtful engagement a challenge at best. There is a pressure in these couples to see things the same way, and they can show surprising cruelty, bullying, and provocation at a hint of difference, as we hear in Mr. and Mrs. X. Things must be as they think they *should* be, not as they actually are. Even couples who are more realistically engaged with one another have moments like the ones Grier has chosen as his focus. As clinicians, we can find it hard to think; our interventions seem to go nowhere. Or, if there seems to be a slight shift and opening up of thinking, one member of the couple will invariably provoke an interaction that will, in a millisecond, set things right back to where they were. At such moments it is clear that change and development are being experienced as terrifying by the couple and are to be avoided at all costs.

Grier's thinking builds on that of Klein and Britton, both of whom stress the centrality for psychological development of facing Oedipal reality, emphasizing "that the Oedipal complex develops hand-in-hand with the developments that make up the depressive position ... (and) ... the working through of one entails the working through of the other" (Britton, 1995). Morgan (2005) and Ruszczynski (2005), as Grier mentions, have explored the link between the capacity for couple relating with some traversing of Oedipal realities – specifically, the capacity to recognize triadic reality is essential for the capacity to hold a "third position" in a couple. This capacity includes the ability to understand and accept another's point of view without losing one's own. The working through, of course, is easier said than done, and is never completed for any of us. Since Oedipal development means letting go, to some degree, of the phantasy of being in complete possession of one's primary object, it requires a capacity to bear loss, guilt, and envy, which, "if not tolerated, may become a sense of grievance or self-denigration" (Britton, 1989). Superego expectations can then become quite harsh, as Grier describes, as unbearable feelings and perceptions are projected in an effort to avoid psychic pain. Grier focuses in this chapter on how these conflicts appear in the arenas of couple ideals and in the couple's difficulty with the experience of the passage of time. He illustrates his thinking through the close discussion of his work with two couples, Mr. and Mrs. X and Mr. and Mrs. Y, the latter with more capacity for development than the former.

Couple ideals, idealization, and ideologies

Grier notes that we very frequently hear about ideals from the couples who come to see us. I agree and think that ideals can usefully be thought of from various angles. For example, couples typically share values and future goals, which can also be thought of as ideals. Perhaps they were lucky enough to have experienced the heady idealization (Kernberg, 1995) that accompanies falling in love and had imagined a more ideal future self in connection with a life with this particular partner. Healthier couples are able, over time, to become more realistic about each other, weathering inevitable disillusionments, and hopefully developing a deeper love for the unique capacities of – and a tolerance for the incapacities in – the other. But even in better functioning couples, we will glimpse hints of an unconscious, idealized view of a couple when we hear things such as, "We're doing pretty well, but we had a fight this week," showing the wishful ideal that a couple can and should avoid disagreement and discord, and always be perfectly in tune.

In the couples Grier takes as his focus in this chapter, the couple ideals function predominantly defensively, and might more accurately be described as ideologies, because they operate as fixed, doctrinaire rules for relating that must be adhered to and that have a fundamentalist feel. There is little thoughtfulness or curiosity about why one's partner behaved in a way that departed from expectations, but only harsh recrimination and a sense of betrayal. The emotional stakes are so high that there is little reflectiveness about experiences of disappointment and no mourning of the lost idealized view. Separateness cannot be accepted in these couples. Grier notes that without help, "the couple will remain in the orbit of narcissistic, paranoid-schizoid functioning, in which the reality and the consequence of difference … of the partners will not be tolerated" (p. 124). It is also useful to consider ideals as the more conscious representations of the *unconscious* ideas that we all hold about what a couple is (Morgan, 2001, 2010). These internal, unconscious ideas are built from, and part of, one's Oedipal experience, and may include unconscious ideas regarding how couples function, what men are, what women are, what couples do together and to each other, and of inclusion and exclusion. This internal image can also include phantasies about what it means to bring people, parts of people, and ideas or parts of the self together. Couples who are very frightened of making such links can have great difficulty moving forward in their lives and making joint decisions, such as deciding whether or not to have children. All of this holds true, by the way, regardless of the genders of the couple.

In thinking about Grier's chapter, it is also important to consider the idea that individuals choose partners in whom they unconsciously perceive a receptivity for projected parts of the self, or who may represent disowned aspects of oneself. Choice of partner represents *both* a developmental and a defensive arrangement. Here is Ruszczynski (1993) on the subject:

> By making such a choice, by creating a marital fit, the couple may be making an unconscious contract for the purposes of development *and* defense. Developmentally, the attraction … is toward knowing more about the repudiated parts of the self as located in the other, and in doing so becoming more integrated. Defensively, the attraction … may be an unconscious shared collusion to retain certain splits and projections in a shared defense against shared anxieties.
>
> (p. 204)

If the couple fit is based too much on a defensive agreement, as with the couples Grier brings us, development in one partner can, in fact, evoke enormous anxiety in the other because change or growth in one partner can mean a change in the arrangement of projections of unbearable parts of the self. The feeling of betrayal about changed or lost ideals that Grier brings our attention to in this chapter is more understandable in this light, since change in one partner *is* a sort of breach of contract regarding the management of anxiety and feared unconscious ideas. The partner's development may signal that they are no longer available, for example, to continue to hold a projected experience of the other in the way they used to. It is not surprising from this vantage point that change in one partner may be met with great resistance and hostility, to the degree that they feel ill-equipped to encounter the psychological challenge they now, unwillingly, face.

The consequences of chronometric time

Grier also shows us ways that the difficulties couples can have facing parts of reality are revealed in the couple's relationship to time. Time is a complex and rich subject in psychoanalysis, and there is much that can be thought about in regard to couple functioning and couple psychotherapy. I applaud Grier for continuing to develop this avenue in our thinking about couples. He eloquently tells us that a couple's rigid "ideal of perfect harmony goes hand in hand with attempting to live in a ... timeless zone, where nothing changes ... since all should be perfect" (p. 127). Couples in states like this not only attempt to control separate space and individuality, but their strong fear of development can also affect their experience of chronometric time, showing a phantasy of omnipotent control over perhaps the most immutable, unavoidable, element of reality: the fact that time passes.

Coming to some terms with the reality of time is an enormous psychological accomplishment of central consequence to the development of psychic structure. In Kleinian terms, the recognition of the reality of chronometric time is an integral element of depressive position functioning. Bion notes that "The non-psychotic personality must be capable of ... frustration, and hence awareness of temporality" (1992, p. 1). Lombardi (2003), in writing about the experience of time in primitive mental states, explores the recognition of time as a central element in the ability to distinguish between subjective and objective reality. Awareness of chronometric time is a part of the ability to tell phantasy from reality; to bear frustration and disappointment; to distinguish between what one wishes and what is actually so.

We can commonly hear couples express their current experience of time. For example, when their language is peppered with anguished or angry accusations of "He always" or "She never," we hear a collapsed experience of time and are probably in the presence of a paranoid-schizoid frame of mind. There is no past, no future. This sort of language alerts us to a high level of emotional distress, a communication of the feeling that the upset feels infinite, and overwhelming. We may in such moments be seeing the experience of timelessness that accompanies trauma or an emergency (Davoine & Gaudulliere, 2004). Fisher (2009 and this volume) describes proleptic thinking, a rigidly absolute certainty about the future that can show itself in couples in ritualized interactions that have a closed feeling and a quality of inevitability. Or in another sort of difficulty with time, we might witness one partner say something brutally hurtful to the other, then lightly apologize and go on as if nothing happened, as if time could be erased and you could have "do-overs" in a relationship, a denial of the actual impact one person has on another in real, irreversible time.

In his chapter, Grier is talking about couples with a more profound and global problem with time. He says their "hatred of development ... had a psychotic quality in its utter refusal to recognize and make realistic accommodation" (p. 131) to life. In speaking of Mr. and Mrs. X, he tells us that they

> continue to enact [an] ... archaic, enmeshed relationship, in which each spouse almost perfectly fitted the projective identifications of the other ... Mrs. X was to be dominated and never ... respected as an ... adult woman. Mr. X, too, would never grow psychologically into an adult male, but would retain the gratification of ... remaining a boy controlling his (wife's/mother's) sexuality.
>
> (p. 131)

I have some questions about this section of the chapter, both regarding terminology and theoretical orientation. On the one hand, Grier is suggesting that early, conflictual Oedipal experiences are at work here. The implication with Mr. and Mrs. X is that they are reconstructing a wished for and feared relationship to early objects. Grier outlines this beautifully, describing for us Mrs. X's "investment in keeping her primary identification as daughter rather than woman" (p. 131). In this model, development and change in the relationship would mean taking back and working with previously projected parts of the self, facing painful loss of phantasized control over an object, re-evaluating identifications, becoming conscious of guilt about Oedipal triumph, and, of course, mourning. Indeed, this is how we hear Mrs. X proceed with Grier's help, and this formulation makes great sense.

On the other hand, Grier also says the couple was:

> Living in a virtually psychotic universe ... functioning virtually entirely on massive joint projection. Time effectively stood still or was meaningless: the couples were *triumphantly* forcing a continual re-enactment of a phantasised past in the present. This usurping of

the potential of the developmental present *expressed a psychotic hatred of developmental reality.*

(p. 139, italics added)

I agree with Grier that this couple has intense "joint anxieties about developing psychologically and sexually" (p. 131). I am not sure, though, how to make sense of his thinking of the couple's difficulty as showing a "psychotic hatred of development," or of his use of language that emphasizes "triumphant destructiveness" in the couple. It is not clear what the word "psychotic" is meant to describe here; I would like to understand what Grier means when he describes the couple's motivations in this way. Does Grier feel destructiveness was a primary motivator for these couples? Perhaps he is emphasizing the pull of perverse elements of organization in the couple over the conflictual ones that he carefully describes in the chapter. I'm also curious to understand more clearly how he sees the elements of conflict and of sadomasochism interweaving. What would he see as the motivation for such hatred of development, if not a fear of pain or anxiety? Does he believe there is an absence of a drive to develop in these cases? How would he think about this theoretically?

I also have questions regarding Grier's use of diagnostic language. In describing the couples, he uses a number of terms interchangeably. For example, he has described the couple dynamics as "borderline psychotic," "psychotic narcissism," "narcissistic, paranoid-schizoid," "psychotic triumphant immaturity," and as "psychotic anti-reality, anti-developmental." These descriptive classifications – related, to be sure – are clinically distinct. Greater precision regarding these terms, and what Grier means by enlisting one versus another, would be very useful.

Finally, I have a specific concern regarding the clinical implications of the term "anti-developmental." On the one hand, it certainly evokes the desperate dread about development and facing aspects of reality that are felt to be unbearable, and also conveys the aggressive intensity with which pain is avoided. On the other hand, the implications of this language are troublesome. The term implies a polarization and opposition between an "anti-developmental" patient and a presumably "pro-developmental" clinician. While we operate with developmental goals in mind in our clinical work, I am wary of language that could imply a "for and against" framework, and prefer instead an emphasis on fostering an arena in which profound anxieties can be thought about empathically.

This is consistent with a central goal of helping couples build a relationship that can, hopefully, function as a psychological container for them both.

The history of Mr. and Mrs. X

I appreciate the level of detail that Grier provides in the clinical material, which I found rich and interesting. I will touch on two areas: the element of time, which raises technical considerations about difficulties facing this aspect of reality, and Grier's work with the Xs.

Grier's use of history in working with these couples represents a way of bringing the reality of linear, chronometric time into the room in a lived, experiential way. He does not tell us whether he actively pursued their histories, but he makes great use of what the couples have lived through to construct his ideas about what constitutes the problem between them. I imagine in his attention to their histories the couple might have felt he was saying to them, "There is time, and you are living in it. You have a past. We can think together about this past, and how it affects your present, so that you might imagine a future with different possibilities."

With couples such as these, asking about history can interrupt or pierce the fantasy of "no time," and contribute to a thoughtful atmosphere in which meaning, causality, and consequence can begin to form. Bringing in the fact of chronometric time in the form of history is in itself a powerful interpretation. This is consistent with Bion's idea, stated here by Lombardi (2003), that "promoting the awareness of temporality is equivalent to that aspect of the work on K (Knowledge) that facilitates tolerance to frustration and acts as a catalyst for the functioning and growth of the non-psychotic part of the personality" (p. 1534). Along these lines, attention to history, including asking about history, might be seen as a "structuring interpretation" (P. Goldberg, personal communication, 2010), one that in this case introduces an aspect of reality that is being denied or ignored. In thinking about this chapter, I realize that I often elicit history with a couple precisely at those moments when a couple seems caught in a repetitive, stuck interaction in my office. Rather than simply trying to change the channel, I have been responding to the experience of collapsed time between them. Curiosity about history is a way of trying to open up space to think about and develop perspective regarding what is going on inside and between them.

I will turn now to Mr. and Mrs. X, who Grier so evocatively describes as "living in each other's pockets" in "a psychotically eternal present." We can feel the claustrophobic, controlling atmosphere within which this couple lives when Grier tells us about Mr. X's relentless need to control his wife, and about Mrs. X's ease in subjugating herself, her individuality only finding expression in her compulsive flirtatiousness with other men. We also see that Grier's interest in understanding the impact of their histories on their present indeed had a positive effect, at least on Mrs. X, who "began to experience herself as a person with a past, a present, and a future" (p. 132).

There is a crucial moment in the work with the Xs when things seem to shift. In response to Mrs. X's flirtatiousness and servile quality of relating to him, Grier comments to her that he was "apparently meant to find this flattering or seductive," at which point he says, "she started to wake up to what she was doing, and then began to find a freer, more autonomous relationship to me" (p. 132). Grier's powerful interpretation seems so straightforward and naturally voiced, and at the same time it is layered, complex, and addresses many levels at once. First, in bringing her attention to the flirtatious behavior that was probably automatic and barely conscious to her, Grier was effectively saying, "Mrs. X, look at yourself; what are you meaning to do? How are you thinking of yourself, and of me?" Through his simple but pointed confrontation he invites her to reflect and to think. Second, by remaining thoughtful, he was demonstrating that he was separate from her fantasy of him; he does not yield to what she might have imagined as a seduction, but instead remains in possession of his thinking capacities and deals with her in a caring, non-punitive, developmentally encouraging manner. Additionally, by communicating *his* ability to think and observe, Grier operates out of a third position, an achievement born out of some capacity to face Oedipal reality, thereby bringing into the experience in the room the possibility that one can survive facing the realities of desire, separateness, and exclusion. The revolutionary implication of Grier's intervention is that there are other possibilities, that there can be three-dimensional space, that there is more to who Mrs. X is than she is consciously aware of, and that chronometric time exists.

Grier also tells us that "Mrs. X's developmental drive was not able to trigger a corresponding effect in her husband" (p. 132). Why might that be? We would have to take into account Mr. X's intense conflicts about development and his rigid insistence on keeping things organized as they have been. At the same time, though, I wonder if there may be an additional way to understand Mr. X's inability to move forward. Let's look again. In describing this moment in the treatment, Grier tells us: "when I had interpreted how I was apparently meant to find this flattering and seductive, she *started to wake up* to what she was doing, and then began to find a freer, more autonomous relationship to me" (p. 132, italics added). When I first read this, my associations went to *Sleeping Beauty*, with Grier as Prince Charming, awakening the lovely princess and rescuing her from the cruel, evil witch. What else might be happening here? Who is who right now in the consulting room? My association alerted me to attend to the transferences in the room, and to think about the particular triangular configurations that might have been operating.

Perhaps, alongside Mrs. X's developmental response to Grier, she also experienced his interest in her as another opportunity to link herself with a father and exclude a disempowered mother, this time in the form of her husband. Mr. X might have felt he was plunged into living his nightmare, having lost control of his wife, and had to avoid his awareness of this by maintaining, and even strengthening, his omnipotent, disparaging, and dismissive stance. I don't imagine he had a way of including a useful father in his mind, and perhaps this was an element in his inability to link up with Grier in a developmental way.

I think Grier, too, played a part here. It is unavoidable that we as couple therapists will become part of the shifting configurations in the room, as the emotionally intense worlds that couples inhabit come alive in our offices. I agree with Morgan (2010) when she reminds us that it is informative and important "to maintain our own curiosity ... about ... our countertransference, and the way in which we can get caught up in enactments with the couple" (p. 53). Grier notices something amiss in his difficulty in maintaining an analytic stance with the Xs, and endeavors to correct this by being more empathic to Mr. X. However, it is also vital to consider how a particular countertransference difficulty reflects, and is instructive regarding, the specific dynamics operating in the couple.

It seems to me Grier may have been caught in an enactment in which his involvement with helping Mrs. X also excluded her husband, whom Grier struggled to relate to. In the consulting room, as in Mr. and Mrs. X's early histories, dyads again exist at the expense of the primary couple. This is important clinically because it is a central element contributing to this couple's difficulty in establishing their relationship as a "reflective space" (Ruszczynski, 2005) for their individual and joint functioning and development. It might have been useful for Grier to speak to the couple openly about this specific, triangulated dynamic in the same direct fashion in which he addressed Mrs. X regarding his concerns about her flirtatiousness toward him. It may have been a way of reaching out to Mr. X and helping the couple see how powerfully their internal object worlds were actively shaping their relationship in the present. It might also have been a way to awaken in *Mr. X* a greater ability to consider his part in the couple's difficulties, and helped him access what was being offered to him in the therapy.

Early in his chapter Grier tells us, "It is the mark of a developmental moment when a couple can start to bring their ideals to consciousness and subject them to critical scrutiny" (p. 126). He goes on to say that this is easier said than done. I agree, and as is the case with Mr. X, we are not always able to help a couple face their profound anxieties. Grier's exploration of couples' ideals and of their difficulty with the experience of the passage of time has given us another way to think more deeply about the complexity of couple life, and about what an emotionally difficult task development is. I want to thank Grier for the way that he privileges the importance of tolerating, even welcoming, change and uncertainty in couple relationships.

References

Bion, W. (1992). *Cogitations*. London: Karnac.
Britton, R. (1989). The missing link: Parental sexuality in the Oedipus complex. In J. Steiner (Ed.), *The Oedipus complex today: Clinical implications* (pp. 83–101). London: Karnac.
Britton, R. (1995). Foreword. In S. Ruszczynski & J. Fisher (Eds.), *Intrusiveness and intimacy in the couple* (pp. xi–xiii). London: Karnac.
Davoine, F. & Gaudulliere, J. (2004). The coordinates of time when time stands still. In *History beyond trauma* (pp. 163–207). New York: Other Press.
Fisher, J. (2009). Macbeth in the consulting room: Proleptic imagination and the couple. *fort da*, 15(2): 33–55.
Grier, F. (2005). No sex couples, catastrophic change, and the primal scene. In F. Grier (Ed.), *Oedipus and the couple* (pp. 200–219). London: Karnac Books.
Grier, F. (2009). Lively and deathly intercourse. In F. Grier, (Ed.), *Sex, attachment and couple psychotherapy* (pp. 45–62). London: Karnac.
Kernberg, O. (1995). *Love relations: Normality and pathology*. New Haven: Yale University Press.

Lombardi, R. (2003). Knowledge and experience of time in primitive mental states. *International Journal of Psycho-Analysis*, 84: 1531–1549.

Morgan, M. (2001). First contacts: The therapist's "couple state of mind" as a factor in containment of couples seen for consultations. In F. Grier (Ed.), *Brief encounters with couples* (pp. 17–32). London: Karnac.

Morgan, M. (2005). On being able to be a couple: The importance of a "creative couple" in psychic life. In F. Grier (Ed.), *Oedipus and the couple* (pp. 9–30). London: Karnac.

Morgan, M. (2010). Unconscious beliefs about being a couple. *fort da*, 16(1): 36–55.

Ruszczynski, S. (1993). Thinking about and working with couples. In S. Ruszczynski, (Ed.), *Psychotherapy with couples* (pp. 197–217). London: Karnac.

Ruszczynski, S. (2005). Reflective space in the intimate couple relationship: The "marital triangle." In F. Grier (Ed.), *Oedipus and the couple* (pp. 31–48). London: Karnac.

Chapter 10

Romantic bonds, binds, and ruptures
Couples on the brink

Virginia Goldner

"Bill and Jane," a couple I saw many years ago, are placeholders for all the anguished, angry, exhausting, and poignant partners who have made their mark on my work as a clinician and theorist. They inspired and defeated me in equal measure, and they ground this essay, which attempts to bring together many of the theories I have fallen in love with over the years. Psychoanalysis, feminist theory, and systems theory, of course, but also developmental and attachment theory, Fonagy's work on mentalization, the strategic family therapies, and containing all of these, the relational turn. I have tried to capture the intellectual synergy of putting all these discourses to work, and to have them work on each other, all of which is necessary when treating couples on the brink.

Any couple therapist knows the drill. Two partners who politely introduce themselves, tolerating the necessary small talk and business details with appropriate compliance, but clearly itching for the moment when, having now placed themselves in your esteemed professional hands, they can finally let loose and leave the mess to you. Of course it's too early to be forced into the position of containing the extreme states and dangerous ways of people you don't know from Adam. But whether too early in the treatment, or too late in your day, these people will have their way with you.

As you probe for some history and context for the emotion-drenched enactment that will wait no longer, the ferocity and volatility of the couple's initial presentation can often feel ramped up for the benefit of the therapist, evoking one's experience of patients labeled borderline, who tend to conflate showing with being, feeling with influencing. The borderline analogy is meant to be suggestive, but it is also technical. Most of the partners in our office practices do not have severe personality disorders, but "pathology" is, of course, context dependent. No one is immune from the contagion of reactivity, and few amongst us can resist the siren call of a fight (sometimes to the death) over who gets to inhabit the victim position – the pleasure in that pain being that the other gets branded the perpetrator.

Couples on the brink are trapped in a particularly toxic strain of that process, one that can overwhelm and envelop everyone in their wake, often causing couple therapists to experience the kind of secondary trauma that Gabbard (1986), in describing the treatment of borderlines, called a "physiological countertransference" – pounding heart, dry mouth, trembling limbs. (Indeed, I will soon argue that the circumstance of severe couple conflict is, in line with thinking in current attachment theory, truly borderline-ogenic.)

In the face of that raw intensity, one's ordinary working state cycles between hot and defensively cold, between anxious, hyperattentive caregiving (regulating, soothing, comforting, all hard-wired responses to distress in those we love), and the private abdication of that caregiving ("I've had it with you two"). The heat, the threat, the confusion, and finally the sheer clinical exhaustion can ignite a defensive withdrawal in even the most devoted clinician. Instead of allowing oneself to receive, contain, and ultimately metabolize the couple's traumatic states, the therapist thinks ironic thoughts. One of my favorite phrases from the heyday of family therapy captures this mind set: "The Situation is Desperate, but not Serious."

Yet despite the intensity of arousal, which is of course contagious, the therapist needs to be able to self-regulate, to calm down – without shutting down. More than likely, these people have hit a nerve. Literally. Being in the presence of people who may be winners in life but are now losers in love – who are often in a state of disbelief, shock, and shame over having been brought so low ... This is a trigger. In treating couples on the brink, we are constantly being re-exposed to intensely disruptive trauma states – preconscious sense memories of our own untidy, shameful history of romantic loss and failure. Each new couple is iconic before they become unique, and it is here, at the outset, that we are already warding off all traces of that Pathetic Me that knows their experience all too well.

The performance of our duties as a clinical interviewer can serve to keep such identifications at bay because our diagnostic ambitions constitute the couple as objects of our scientific gaze, rather than as people who just happen to be "Not-Me (*now*)." But the identificatory pain such couples activate always threatens to resurface, as they sink into their version of the Paul Simon lyric – "Losing love is like a window in your heart. Everyone sees you're blown apart, everyone sees the wind blow."

Couples in crisis may present in many different ways, content issues and personality styles run the gamut – but whether theatrically voiced or floating in the ether, something is always the same – the shock, the fear of collapse, the profound confusion over what is going on – a situation that incites extreme reactivity, paranoia, hypersensitivity, the feeling of "carrying my guts in a bag," as one man said.

When the one you love keeps hurting you, when the one who hurts you doesn't try to make it better, when the one you need abandons or frightens you, when the one you know becomes impenetrable or unknown to you, when the one who knows you no longer recognizes you – these are the ubiquitous traumas of love lost. This is the shock of omnipotence shattered.

It's every country and western song: your lover can torture you, make you desperate for air, reduce you to abject extremes of begging and collapse or drive you to extremes of destructive aggression – and s/he can make it all go away in the blink of an eye. If only my partner softened, welcomed me back into the familiarity of our relational space, my ordinary world would click into place *in a nanosecond*. If only my good mother would come back to me, I'll never do those bad things again.

Yes, think precisely in terms of an attachment crisis – think of the toddler's angry protest, his worry and despair, his joy and relief when reunited with his one and only. Attachment is romantic, and romantic love is, in both the formal and evocative sense, an attachment process. That is why derailments of romantic bonds – loss, injury, deadlock – constitute what trauma theorists consider "relational 't' trauma." Everyone sees you're blown apart.

You know the feeling of a sudden fight with someone you love, that aspect of it where you can't believe this is really happening, the escalation as you try to clobber the other into recognition. This is the moment when "anger as protest," which Bowlby (1973) called the anger of hope, curdles into anger as retaliation, the "anger of despair." It is also the moment when your partner has become the living embodiment of Fairbairn's "tantalizing object"; there, but now not there for you – and unlike that toddler, no appeal, no protest brings them back.

Attachment: "from the cradle to the grave" (Bowlby, 1973)

There is now a long-standing, interdisciplinary consensus that the same mechanisms that regulate the mother–infant bond, which grow the brain and co-create the mind, also mediate attachment bonds throughout the lifespan (Zeifman & Hazan, 1999). Sue Johnson, the co-originator of Emotionally Focused Therapy (Greenberg & Johnson, 1988), argued early that romantic relationships were "bonds, not bargains" (Johnson, 1986), a perspective empirically validated by many subsequent investigators, including Beatrice Beebe, whose research comparing adult and infant nonverbal communication patterns led her to conclude that "romantic love is an attachment process" (Beebe & McCrorie, 2010).

Indeed, if you have been living and sleeping with your partner for two years (it should be no surprise that we only attach to those we touch), you are now bonded, wound around each other, nervous system to nervous system, and your psychic state is now joint property. You may not be happy, it may not be good, but despite ourselves, it is our human nature, to paraphrase Crosby, Stills and Nash, to "love the one we're with."

We are, in fact, biologically connected to those with whom we have close relationships, a truism Judith and Allan Schore (2008) distilled in one far-reaching sentence: "At the psychobiological core of the intersubjective field between intimates is the attachment bond of right brain/mind/body states" (p. 15). Brain researchers Stuss and Alexander (2000) captured the process in a single image: "Attachment is affectively burnt into the brain" – an insight echoed by Philip Bromberg (2010), who took to italics to proclaim that "it is not just the mind, *but the brain itself that is intrinsically relational*" (p. 21).

A.N. Schore (2012) now talks about attachment as the evolutionary mechanism through which intersubjectivity comes on line, evolves, and complicates, while Fonagy (2001) described attachment as "the motive force" behind the mutual state regulation that occurs between relational partners. It is this regulatory process, he maintained, that potentiates or shuts down the capacity to mentalize: the ability to hold other minds (including one's own) in mind. Mutual recognition between persons (I–thou relations), which is the cornerstone of the relational ideal (Benjamin, 1995), cannot proceed without mentalization.

Attachment alarm/borderline relating

"Proximity to a loved one tranquilizes the nervous system," Allan Schore (2005, p. 19) told us, in one of his memorable rhetorical turns, but Solomon and Tatkin (2011), his former students, reminded us that romantic bonds can also be very risky. Under stress, such bonds can be dangerously amplified or reduced, causing an extreme psycho-biological shift in a couple's immediate experience. As a result, communication degrades, and is now "by impact, right brain to right brain, not one mind to another" (Schore & Schore, 2008). This is a moment known all too well by couple therapists, who are forever asking partners "what just happened?"

In this heightened state of arousal and dys-regulation, the symbolic register in which therapy is primarily conducted in the early stages – questions, answers, commentary – can feel like an empty add-on, language itself a desiccated, pseudo-mature form of compliance. People flush, the blood drains, eyes avert or glare, a woman gasps for breath after lashing out at her husband in a sudden, lacerating one-liner. And it's only 10 minutes into the session.

A patient of mine, channeling Dan Stern's construct of "now" moments, has taken to calling these cascades "whoosh" moments. Like the dream's sudden discontinuous shifts, these ferocious escalations can erupt out of a clear blue sky, as someone gets insulted or injured – reacts, attacks, counterattacks, "the right brain communicating its unconscious states to another right brain tuned to receive its frequency" (A.N. Schore, 2005, p. 18).

The intersubjective neurobiology of such "runaways" (the systems term) can be traced back to the right brain's split-second, preconscious assessment of danger and fright, that moment when the attachment system switches on (see also Slade, 2014). But it is important to emphasize, as Lyons-Ruth (2003) explained, that the hard-wired, intersubjective machinery of attachment reactivity is activated *only under conditions of fearful, relational distress*. Attachment arousal is *off*-line until relational danger is triggered, which is one of the reasons couples on the brink ignite our skepticism. One minute they are falling to the ground, the next they are scrolling on their smartphone and ordering from the online grocer. (When my partner *stops* scaring me, my ordinary world *does* click into place in a nanosecond.)

But now consider that, once activated, the threat-related mobilization of the attachment system also *de*-activates our capacity to mentalize by evoking overwhelming negative affect. As a result, chronic negative misconstrual between partners becomes the norm, as we continuously conflate effect with intent ("s/he is hurting me" becoming "s/he is *trying* to hurt me"). In the mind blindness of these right-brain, doer–done to escalations, mentalization becomes partial and temporary. Bateman and Fonagy (2006), writing about the treatment of borderlines, connected this collapse to "attachment trauma," especially to finding a spoiled or malevolent self in the mind of the caregiver. Relational alienation between romantic partners creates just such borderline conditions, since both experience the other as negating their essential goodness. Neither can hold the other in mind because their own mind is now in such a state. As Benjamin (1995) explicated, "What cannot be worked through and dissolved with the outside other is transposed into a drama of internal objects" (p. 40).

What is lost in the demise of the two-person perspective is what the early systems theorists called "double description" (Bateson, 1979), that "spiral of reciprocal perspectives," of "view upon alternative view" (Laing, 1965/1976) that we have come to consider the bedrock of intersubjectivity. As Benjamin (2004a) later discussed, this default to a one-person setting collapses relational thirdness; the mental space that is potentiated by the conjoined view. The resulting vacuum leaves the dyad un-minded, unheld, and unsafe, and the couple eventually loses faith in the lawfulness of relational processes, which can ultimately lead to a loss of lawfulness itself.

The clashing of wills, the inevitable personal corruption and self-betrayals, the shock of not being understood and of being cast as malevolent, the disbelief one experiences at encountering the faithlessness of the partner, all this leads to a state of collapse – and a desperate call to a couple therapist.

Relational (small "t") trauma

An angry yearning for the lost relational home drives the downward spiral of alienation in such failing couples. Each apparent escalation reflects the unremitting effort of one partner to master the unresolved trauma of the other's nonrecognition (and the trauma history that is triggered by that refusal). Trauma theorists have taught us that it is not necessarily a specific event that is traumatic so much as it is the failure of the relationship that permitted that event to occur, allowing its impact upon the victim to go unrecognized, unacknowledged, and without amends. In distressed relationships, each partner can only see themselves as the other's victim, as the hurt one, not as the one being hurtful. But now consider that *even the state of being hurt makes you the bad one*, because your pain is now aversive, driving the partner to misconstrue, psychically abandon, disbelieve, even attack.

This is especially true of romantic relationships, which constitute a particularly unique form of attachment. The person who is one's "safe haven" and "secure base," the one who heals/regulates and cares for you, is *also* the one who can hurt and frighten you. Unlike parent–child relations (or therapist–patient relations), which are meant to be asymmetrical, in the sense that the caregiver privileges the care-seeker's needs, love relations are *bi*-directional, in that each partner is both the one who needs and the one who is needed.

In the parent–child situation, the parents' caregiving is not directly affected by the child's behavior, except at the extremes, because the parent's attachment security is not dependent on the child's state of mind. But in romantic love, the caregiving partner is also in the vulnerable position of being the care-seeking child, whose needs will be met only if the caregiver is "of a mind" to meet them (which may not be possible if he or she has just suffered an attachment injury at the other's behest).

Thus, no matter the particulars or pathology, *everyone's romantic partner can be a source of comfort but also of danger, the cause and solution to our pain* (Hesse & Main, 2000). When one person's need ignites the other's unresolved trauma, a catastrophic attachment paradox occurs, producing a cycle of continuous rupture. The one you need keeps hurting you; the only one who can make it better is making it worse.

Relationships that have fallen into this degree of disrepair are not simply "insecure" in the technical sense. Insecure attachments actually exemplify somewhat successful defensive strategies for managing the fear and anguish caused by a parent or partner's inconstancy. By contrast, truly failing relationships are not only painful and unsafe, they can be actually toxic, exemplifying the agony characteristic of relational trauma. In the formal lexicon of attachment theory, these are bonds that would be considered "disorganized."

Disorganized attachment is alarming and disturbing. The mothers of children classified as disorganized have been found to parent in a frightened and frightening manner. Their unnerving behavior (which can be quite subtle) engenders contradictory responses in the child, who is caught in an approach/avoidance conflict. Fear of the mother activates the attachment system, so the child feels compelled to seek proximity and comfort from her, but proximity-seeking increases a child's fear (getting too close to this currently frightening figure), so s/he contradicts her approach (freezing, falling to the ground, running backward, etc.). Hesse and Main (2000) labeled this predicament "fright without solution," a tormenting experience, as anyone who's ever watched those haunting videotapes can attest.

Attachment researchers have established that frightened or frightening caregivers are those whose current mental state regarding attachment is characterized by a lack of resolution regarding loss or trauma. If a caregiver has not experienced comfort and soothing in relation to his or her own early fear-evoking experiences, the other's pain and fear will evoke unresolved fearful affects, including sense memories of his or her own helplessness as a child in obtaining comfort. Couples on the brink are caught in the vice-grip of this same paradox, except that one partner's unresolved state of mind does not necessarily have to hearken back to originary childhood traumas, although there is always that aspect. Sue Johnson wrote that wounds to attachment relationships that result from a partner's emotional unresponsiveness in times of intense need may be equated to trauma with a small "t" (Johnson, Makinen, & Millikin, 2001). Sense memories of such injuries can erupt like a traumatic flashback, overwhelming the partners and their process. People speak in life-and-death terms, and a "Never again" gauntlet hangs in the air.

Mordecai (1995), using the related concept of "ambient trauma," described how such family histories can mark their victims with negativism and despair. This deathly legacy is compounded by the fact that being unresolved around trauma can lead to an inability to *absorb* repair, which appears to be more significant than attunement or rupture itself to the life and fate of relationships (Lewis, 2000). The injured party needs *too* much recognition, so that the very work of repair triggers a new "old" injury, and thus a moment of healing turns into just another breach.

Romantic attachment: danger and safety

Our culture of individualism, with its phobic dread of dependency, has severed romance from attachment, aligning eros with danger and agentic masculinity ("libido"), while attachment is consigned to childhood, weakness, and femininity. These cultural divisions are also reflected in our clinical theories. While the attachment perspective puts the search for safety and security above all other motivations, the psychoanalytic tradition has historically privileged desire. Although this split was theoretically resolved by Fairbairn's move ("libido is object seeking"), these gendered dichotomies still persist, despite years of research showing that secure attachment *thrives* in a climate of relational rigor, rather than in the ministrations of an omni-available mother, completely identified with the child's needs.

Psychoanalytic theory has followed culture in erecting a firewall between eros and attachment, the action and legacy of the incest taboo, perhaps. We still want to keep "the environment mother in the kitchen and the object mother in the dungeon" (Goldner, 2006, p. 634). This binary is convenient since, in sexual relations, we are typically just play-acting the diabolical, and will soon want mommy back, even if it is now in the form of watching the news, side by side. By splitting sexuality off from the need for safety and security, we are deploying sex (in theory as well as in life) as a manic defense.

Even Stephen Mitchell (2002), writing about romantic love, defaulted to these habits. He positioned attachment as "the great enemy of erotism," writing that:

> we learn to love in the context of the contrived and necessary safety of early childhood, and we continue to seek out the kind of safety that screens out [the very elements that fuel the erotic:] the unknown, the fantastic, the dangerous.
>
> (p. 46)

But the problem with Mitchell's astute critique is that he ultimately conflated safety, a two-person relational achievement, with "safety-*operations*" a one-person defensive maneuver. Relational safety is not necessarily deadening or antisexual. In fact, staying in love with the one you love is possible *only in a context of safety* – not the flaccid safety of tepid cohabitation, but a dynamic safety, whose robustness is established via the couples' lived history of risk-taking and its resolution – the never-ending cycles of "winning and losing" (Davies, 2004), separation and reunion, and of rupture and repair (think of Seinfeld's "make-up sex") (Goldner, 2004a, 2006).

Romantic vitality and inhibition are not driven simply by the excitement of danger (vitality) or by the fear of risk (inhibition), as Mitchell argued, but by the variety of ways *the partners make that danger safe*, and also by whether they are able to make good on their promise to keep loving, despite the hurt they inevitably cause each other. In this sense, Mitchell was both right *and* wrong. The issue is not a one-person *conflict* (danger *vs.* safety), but a two-person *dialectic* (danger *and* safety).

Gender makes its claim

The allure of romantic love is that its inherent action is mutative and healing. But the truth is that the family, hardly that "haven in a heartless world," is actually our most violent institution outside of the military at war (J. Gilligan, 1997). Moreover, although 50 years have elapsed since the publication of *The Feminine Mystique*, gender inequality is still the norm in domestic life (Esmiol, Knudson-Martin, & Delgado, 2012).

Gender continues to tie a Gordian knot around the heart, and in very troubled heterosexual relationships it remains an open question whether romantic love can be made safer for women and less threatening to men. A young Anglo man, for example, reflecting on the sudden intensity of his explosive outbursts, came to this insight. "One thing I realize every time I hit her, is that I *need* her. And when I *need* her, I'm gonna get her, I'm gonna get her – no matter what." And from a Hispanic woman who could not be persuaded to remove herself from the escalating conflicts she was having with her volatile partner:

> Even if he hits me, he isn't threatening to me, because he showed me his weaknesses. At home, I was just a decoration trotted out for company. I was not needed. So how can he be a threat? I'm crucial to him.
> (Goldner, 2004b; Goldner, Penn., Sheinberg, & Walker, 1990; see also Rachel Snyder's, 2013, chilling piece on domestic homicide in *The New Yorker*)

Gender inequality reproduces itself one mind at a time, via the gendered premises that constitute hetero-normative masculinity and femininity (see also Sheinberg & Penn, 1991). For every abusive man operating with the premise, "Once I'm angry, I'm not responsible for what I do," there is an abused woman starting with the premise, "I'm responsible for everything in this relationship." And for a man driven by the axiom, "If I don't win, I lose," there is a woman organized by the belief, "A bad man is really a hurt child who needs a good woman to take care of him" (Goldner, 1991, 2004b; Goldner et al., 1990).

Such gendered mandates dictate terms that require compliance but also provoke resistance, which is one of the reasons romantic relationships can take on a peculiar paradoxical cast. For example, this was the message one man felt his mother was sending: "Be strong like your father, so that you can protect women like me from men like him." And in another, the message from father to daughter read like this: "Listen to your mother who is the vehicle through which I speak, although she disagrees with me."

Consider how, in that first example, for the boy to follow his mother's injunction, he would have to identify with his father, or at least with his father's phallic narcissism, which would mean repudiating his femininity, and his identification with his mother. Thus, in being a loyal son to mother, he would have become a traitor to her cause. Now imagine that grown man falling in love with the woman in the second example, whose loyalty to her father required that she identify with her mother, a woman whom he knew had privately repudiated him.

Speaking truth to power

The inherently charged nature of couple work derives from a synergy of past and present relational emergencies. The conjoint interview is, in itself, a therapeutic scene of address that activates our developmentally charged sense of urgency around naming and fixing disturbed processes within and between those who matter most to us. Indeed, a couple session should be seen as a contemporary, fraught iteration of what developmentalists call a "joint attentional scene" (Tomasello, Carpenter, Call, Behne, & Mol, 2005). This is the circumstance where a child attends conjointly with an adult to a third object of interest, purposefully drawing the other's attention to it, and engaging in emotional commentary about it. ("Look at this!" gestures the child. "How should I feel about it?").

This complex form of social referencing, which is initially expressed preverbally, via pointing, can be pleasurable, but it can also be distressed

("Did you *see that*???"). This is the schema that is reactivated in the charged atmosphere of couple therapy, which by its very nature, re-evokes the child's experience of trying to fix things by speaking truth to power. Such a bid is inherently risky, since it is always possible that the child will be disconfirmed, or that nothing will be done. Worse still, the whistle-blower might be blamed for what is wrong, or just for pointing out that there is, in fact, something wrong.

In couple work, each partner is like that alarmed child, seeking an authority's confirmation for what he or she is seeing, clear as day. But in the present circumstance, the adult's eyewitness testimony is being contested by another eyewitness, the partner's very own love object. Since psychic reality is only granted the status of externality if it is consensually validated, the collision of these competitive narratives can become psychically catastrophic. The issue is now not simply a matter of who is right but of whether or not someone is crazy.

There is no room for complexity at this stage in the downward spiral. If someone is a little bit right, then someone else must be totally wrong. The couple's history of relational incompetence and bad faith will make anything less than absolute validation feel as if one is being thrown to the wolves. As long as the couple is caught in a do-or-die competition, any expression of need or desire by one partner will constitute a danger signal for the other, and is thus a potential trigger for both. As a result, despite the therapist's best efforts, the ordinary caring conditions of psychotherapy can become a high-stakes torment for couples, each interaction a test of who will be chosen and who will be blamed.

Some thoughts on the initial phase of treatment

Couple treatment is a Petri dish on impasse, stalemate, and deadlock. However our patients present, *this* is their presenting problem. The clinical challenge is to co-construct a way out while allowing oneself to be pulled in. The work must be conducted on a knife edge – too much order results in pseudo-mature resolutions that don't last the night, too little – a bloodbath.

At the outset, the therapy is there to serve as a safe haven from a dangerous "All Bets Are Off" state of emergency. The therapist who presents with an ordinary air of confidence and stance of fairness begins as the voice of God, the parent/judge of last resort. The first task is to reassert lawfulness, initially via being the purveyor of rules – how things are done around here – turn taking, no interrupting, no outbursts, and so on. It is the restoration of these conditions and principles, which Benjamin (2004a) labeled the "moral third" (similar to Carol Gilligan's, 1989, "ethic of justice"), that makes the reemergence of empathy and attunement possible. (This is Benjamin's "nascent third," which Gilligan called an "ethic of care.")

The containing, regulating, soothing, educative, ethically instructive aspects of good-enough psychotherapy, traditionally back-grounded in individual treatment, are here foregrounded to the relief of all the parties. As Greenberg and Goldman (2008) elucidated, these tasks are critical to the work of healing because relational distress is ultimately caused by breakdowns in other and self regulation of affect (especially anger, sadness, fear, and shame). Bearing and working through these states in the presence of the partner is at the crux of the work. Indeed, there is often immediate relief and a sense of redress when disturbed ways of being with others are rectified in the here and now – where misfires can miraculously get a do-over, affects can be calmed, affect tolerances enhanced, complex messages translated, ruptures painstakingly repaired, and the emotional consequences of attachment injuries worked through among the principals, rather than being reported to a third party, such as an individual therapist, who can do very little with one person's one-sided picture. (Individual therapy is, after all, an "only child" treatment.)

Couple work is conducted in the rough and tumble of the relational here and now, where we are constantly witnessing micro-violations that must be made right. Of course, we will sometimes fail in our role as rescuer, becoming an indifferent bystander, an unseeing, neglectful, or unfair parent. But unlike the back-against-the-wall real parent, who, under ordinary circumstances, will call it like s/he sees it ("You go to your room/You say you're sorry"), couple therapists are trained to evade that other shoe dropping by reaching for one of those "too-smart-by half" interventions the family therapy field is known for. Such moves can, however, come across as the weak response of a timid parent who cannot depart from some variant of "I love you both the same," when what might be called for is "Listen you two, I have reached my limit!"

We feel too guilty when we cannot – or do not wish to – identify with the hurt part of the badly behaved person, because their meanness or aggression or defensive narcissism is hurting the partner or is destructive to the treatment. Justice or care? Too often, we flip/flop between them, an ambivalence that can be reflective of the "hostile/helpless" state of mind seen in mothers of disorganized children who cannot handle them, a harshness alternating with a helpless "giving up" that leaves the child (or patient) in a state (Lyons-Ruth, 2003).

Such failures are, of course, a portal into many couple treatments since, like these overwhelmed mothers, couple therapists are often being asked to function at the outer edge of their capacities. Indeed, distressed couples' rage-proneness, sadism, and despair are so common that secondary trauma and compassion fatigue are commonplace aspects of a long working day.

Mentalization and negation

We can also expect very little help from our patients at this early stage. They are often operating from the stance Fonagy, Gergely, Jurist, and Target (2002) called "psychic equivalence," a mind-set in which one's psychic reality is conflated with external reality ("My reality = Reality"). Unlike mentalization, which allows us to *play* with reality because we know it to be perspectival, psychic equivalence dictates that there can be only one accurate way of seeing things: *my way.* Moreover, mental states can fluctuate, in part as a function of the state of the mind with whom we are engaged. One may, for example, begin a relational sequence with one's habits of mentalization intact, but if that other mind is operating from a stance of psychic equivalence, one's paranoid fortress will start to beckon and we will eventually fall off the wagon and default to our one-person truth as well.

This is the point of no return in many failed couple treatments, since the conjoint enterprise depends upon what the early family therapist Boszormenyi-Nagy and Spark (1981) called "multipartiality" – the capacity to know one's truth is partial by being able to hold other perspectives in mind. In Aron's (2000) terms, this means being able to hold the tension between seeing oneself from both inside and outside, as both subject and object. We depend on our patients being able to work with numerous versions of the question "Can you see how, from her point of view, you ...?" To which the patient too often replies, "Yeah, and can't you see what s/he is doing right now??"

Sharing a mind with a mind operating in psychic equivalence is not possible if one attempts to complicate, or to propose an alternative way of seeing too quickly – or too instrumentally. This will be perceived as suspect, perhaps even as an attempt to drive the thinker crazy. "(Are you telling me ...) the world is flat?? That shoe is an apple??" In the world of psychic equivalence, "complexity" comes across as a ploy, the parent's regulatory reminder that the other child has a point too.

In such moments, a clinical default to empathy fails too. "I can see this is very hard for you ...," "Yeah, and how would you feel if your wife/husband was constantly lying?" The patient (correctly) feels s/he is being fobbed off by the therapist's technical performance of "Empathy," since soothing without highly specific recognition is patronizing – to children and adults alike. The comfort that agitated, aggrieved partners seek is the link to Externality – Reality. If the question is "Don't you *see* that???" the answer cannot be "I see you are very upset."

Holding complexity

If we are to do a therapy that goes beyond the premature expectation that the embattled partners adopt a two-person view, we must allow, indeed facilitate, their descent into their uniquely distraught psychic idiom, with all its vilifications of the partner seated next to them. For the work to proceed deeply, everyone must understand that couple treatment (like analytic work) *is conducted in transitional, as well as transactional space*. This is a workplace where one's internal objects collide, in real time, with the implacable "otherness" of the Other (who must, for the moment, tolerate being Other to him- or herself). This is the therapeutic paradox at the fulcrum of conjoint treatment, which can be borne only if the partners trust in the ultimate fairness of the process over time. "I will suffer your momentary negation of me (in favor of your interiority), because you will be asked to recognize *me*, in all *my* extremes, before too long."

Positioning the couple to hold to such a stance requires ongoing, unwavering acts of containment and recognition, analogous to what happens when parents peel apart two brawling siblings who are still trying to land one more punch. First we get between them, then we comfort each of them, helping them to calm down. *Then* we ask, "What just happened?"

What is needed in these circumstances is not necessarily an insight, so much as a way of speaking to that moment *in* the moment. Not the psychotherapy 101 of "I can see you are feeling mad/sad," although none of us ever do enough of that. Rather, what is called for is an accurate rendering of the shared reality of the moment, one that captures the immediacy of the relational event. "She *really* startled you there." "That look on your face is saying, 'Uh Oh, I know what's coming now.'" "Looks like you're asking yourself, 'How could he *say* that?'" "Whew, its *chilly/hot/scary* in here." All variants of the kind of quick, accurate mentalizing that "mind-minded" mothers (Meins et al., 2002) display when tracking their children's play.

We now know that getting psychic reality straight – moment by moment – is uniquely central to the development of secure attachment, and is actually more important to its ongoing maintenance than maternal sensitivity alone. In other words, the parent (or therapist) who can say, "I *do* see what's going on around here!" (Levenson, 1972) produces stronger relational security than the one who just intones, "Oh, poor baby." Not surprisingly, Meins et al. (2002) have shown that the most secure children are those raised by mothers who are both mind-minded *and* kind-hearted.

Double binds

Work with borderlines and with children scored as disorganized on attachment has shown that lies, deceptions, and systematic distortions in family communication are commonplace (Liotti, 1999). Such families are deformed by "mystification," Laing's (1965/1976) term for the pathogenic process where the child (or partner) is labeled mad or bad for accurately perceiving what is going on – "You can disconfirm me, but I cannot disconfirm you."

We now know that mystification does not "cause" schizophrenia, as the original double bind theorists reasoned, but it does seem to constitute the "universal pathogenic situation" that Jay Haley went on to describe (Sluzki & Verón, 1971). Under these toxic conditions, psychic equivalence is not necessarily a mental handicap. It could, in fact, be understood as a defiant act of mental freedom. ("You *cannot* disconfirm me if my reality *is* reality").

Couples caught in the most severe impasses are usually operating in this way, since each partner has reason to fear that the other will try to bend the truth to serve their interests, just as their parents did. Distortions and absolutism, combined with a history of crazy making parents, a family culture of double-dealing, double binds, and of overt and covert scapegoating, all conspire to leave each partner hunkered down. In a ruthless "I win/you lose" economy, owning one's own part is just a stupid mistake.

In such a context, even a good interpretation of a patient's resistance to the therapist's more complex view can get sucked into the meat-grinder of suspicion. Tx: "I wonder if you are skittish when I offer a different perspective because you were blamed for seeing things accurately when you were a kid?" Pt: "This is not about my past – this is about what is going on right now!!"

At such points, the couple is caught in a life-and-death struggle over who is hurting whom, but more important, *over who is causing what*. In Davies' (2004) framework, the couple is embroiled in a debate over reality and truth that is laced with blame and badness. As she has memorably discussed, the dogged attempt by each person to avoid being the bad one reproduces a parent–child relationship in which something toxic is being forced into the other while being denied in the self. The two are caught between love and sanity, a gauntlet that can now derail their love relations and defeat their treatment.

As one of my patients explained, once he was able to reflect on why he had never been able to tolerate my attempt at being balanced (which he saw as my "Being Balanced," a puerile couple therapy technique):

> It's never worked for us. It gives her a pass. And she's right, I have hardened toward her. In the past, I would make peace and let her blame me for the fact that *she* is in a chronic, roiling state of turbulence, because I needed sex or a feeling of having my home intact. But now that I am in analysis, I am not going to give up so easily!

Putting it all together

I'm going to use aspects of my treatment with this couple (whom I shall call Bill and Jane), to illustrate how disqualification can be driven by the need to be understood on one's own terms, and to have the other acknowledge the validity of one's perception.

I can't say they didn't give me fair warning. Bill opened the initial session with "We are in peril," Jane adding, with a dead-on stare, "Can you handle us? You are our last stop." I managed to parley their one-two punch with some serviceable response (no longer available to me), but as I looked into their darkened ominous faces, I wondered if I had the strength, and already sensed that I didn't have the will, to provide them with the "safe, but not too safe" (Bromberg, 2010) situation they so clearly would require.

Bill and Jane's relationship was a theater of enactment, the pervasive shadow of trauma darkening even the manic defense of romanticism. There was a false brightness and a palpable sadness to the best of times, as they held their breath, waiting for the moment when they would be traumatized by another rupture that would not yield to words, to therapeutic soft sounds, to reason or caution.

They had similar kinds of trauma histories, which potentiated their mutual and multiple identifications, but those commonalities also meant that they could often trigger each other's worst fears. Bill's parents divorced when he was a young child, leaving him the angry child of parents who appeared to be kind and organized in public but were frightening and incompetent in private. Jane's father died when she was in her teens, leaving her the noisily unhappy daughter of a narcissistic and duplicitous mother, who punished her for seeing things too clearly. The couple's romantic relationship was constituted as a safe-house for these two lost children, bonded like Hansel and Gretel, making their way through the dangerously unsettled forest of their conjoined minds. But this reparative fantasy was ultimately coercive: "If you don't keep me safe, *I* will be dangerous."

Indeed, despite their hunger for mothering, Jane and Bill's anger around not getting it would make them both very hard to soothe and regulate. Jane would resist my therapeutic ministrations, taking comfort only from Bill, who could snap at any moment, the poignant lost boy shoved aside by a raging feral creature. "Soothe *me*," Jane would wail, taking the measure of her momentarily orphaned state. But when Bill would comply, ineptly, she would be triggered, since she could always detect the one false note that would infect his expressions of concern.

This was because Bill, given his trauma history, could not be comforting and protective unless he was stepping into a pure attachment scene – Jane as a little bird shaking in the nest, not Jane, the sullen tweener. Since

Bill could never tolerate her dark moods, he would coercively try to get her to shift her state, which would, of course, only make things worse. His double message of care and blame was a confusing, triggering communication that never ended well. ("You are bad when you are hurt, because your being hurt hurts me.") Jane's attempts at comforting Bill when he needed care were equally barbed. Neither could see how their performance of soothing did not soothe. It confused and inflamed.

In these cycles of repair-as-rupture, they could never rest in the other's care. Each one's bid for TLC triggered the other's painful history of deprivation and scapegoating, which led them to respond to each other with a hollow protection, often laced with criticism and blame. As a result, each one was both the "cause and solution" to the other's pain.

Moreover, once they were triggered, conflict could rarely be processed, held, or mediated. Accusations just ricocheted between them in a tit-for-tat escalation. (*You* are the bad one, No *you* are! *I* am the victim, No *I* am!) In their never-ending battle over who was the perpetrator and who was the victim (see also Seligman, 1999, on intersubjective projective identification), the couple was reproducing the "kill-or-be killed" relationship each had with their mothers. Either they became the bad/sick one in return for keeping their mother close, or they named the game and were forever exiled – a Hobson's choice that could never be resolved. (See the exchange between Davies, 2004, and Benjamin, 2004b, on relational bad objects.)

Therapy was a major point of contention between them. Jane felt that Bill's commitment to his analysis had marginalized her as his confidante and psychic mentor, while Bill felt that Jane's refusal to go into individual treatment made it impossible for him to get her to address her issues. For Jane, therapy was always suspect (her father was a psychiatrist), and she tolerated the couple work only because it was a venue to connect with Bill, who found her distrust of treatment self-serving and reminiscent of *his* mother's evasions.

Here is a segment from the end of a session that circled, endlessly, around these themes. Had you been behind the one-way mirror, you would have seen me running the gamut with this couple – tracking, soothing, holding/containing, softening, interpreting, coaching/coaxing – the whole nine yards. But Bill and Jane were having none of it, and I eventually decided to back off and let them find their own way. Bill began by talking about an incident that was casting a long shadow.

B: (softly, anxiously) We had problems over the weekend. Jane's anxiety problems are constant. Suddenly she just darkened after a beautiful morning – and it made me mad.... We eventually had a long talk and we both felt better.

J: I didn't feel any of that! It was a two-hour, exhausting conversation. I felt no better at the end than at the beginning. We have spent all this time and money and he still thinks he can diagnose me! **Jane has "anxiety problems"!!??**

B: But I *said* I could see what she was saying.... Jesus, if I say anything about her, she thinks I think I am blameless. And then she can go off on me for that and we *never* get to the thing I am trying to point out! ... (gets soft) I have been in retreat (makes a gesture of helplessness and Jane rolls her eyes).

J: He's representing himself as the victim – but *he's* the one who fights *me*! And then he has the nerve to represent himself as the righteous one!

VG: I see how you are afraid, Bill, that Jane is going to get me off track. (He nods.) And Jane, I see how you're afraid I'm going to be taken in by Bill. (She looks up warily.)

J: (Despite herself, softening) I can't work on my long-term issues when you jump all over me, it's not safe to do it! I *do* have anxiety issues, but you shouldn't be so hard on me! I have loved you all these years, and I never shamed you around your issues ...

VG: Jane, that's a good first step, acknowledging that anxiety *is* a "long-term issue" for you. But Bill, she added something very important – that she can't really work on the problem in a "you are the sick one" environment.

B: (Having none of it) But *I can never say how destructive – how painful these moments are!* I can never get that far! **I can't really talk in here. You don't want to hear it, and she'll just wriggle out of it *again*!**

VG: Bill, she did just start to give you a big acknowledgment – and you are still all riled up. What's going on?

B: Because I'm remembering the end of the fight. After my careful, loving wrap-up – after we had gotten through it all, she gets up in a huff and says, "Well, I have to load the dishwasher now," huff, huff, huff.

J: I always load the dishwasher! And I *did* acknowledge my part. What I said wasn't the mature thing to say, it was nasty. But I was exhausted, and I didn't think the discussion was good at all, and now it was two hours later and I didn't get any sleep – but I *did*, I acknowledged it right away –

B: (Sudden, bellowing outburst) **Are there going to be any rules here at all? Am I just supposed to sit back and** ...

(What? – my head is spinning)

VG: Bill, why are you interrupting her?? – She just said "what I did was bad."

B: **Because she *didn't* say it right away! I had to beg for it, go nuts to get it!**

VG: OK, I get it – so this must be making you feel that you have to go nuts right here, right now. You don't think she's *really* acknowledging her destructiveness, which is making you feel like you have to flip out here in order to get me to see what's really going on (just as you had to do with your father, who always appeared so well put-together).

J: What's the point?? It's always about him! Like I don't know what I did is bad? So he had to browbeat me for two hours to get me to see that?? **I was fighting, so I didn't acknowledge it right away. I was *still fighting*! I *did* see, but I didn't care – yes, I was being reckless! I didn't care, I was still fighting!**

VG: I can see that when that switch is flipped there is no overriding it until you feel spent.

J: **Look I am fighting for my life with him!**

VG: Bill, when she is scared – like now, she feels the way you do – like she's fighting for her life – that's why, even here, she can't – she *won't* give up. She wouldn't be standing here – nor would you – if you weren't both like that. But you don't see her underlying fear – I often don't see it either – and Jane, you don't see the impact you have. You feel you are just fighting your way out like a cornered animal, but you don't see that for him you are like a freight train barreling down.

J: **He holds his hands up like that poor little boy – but don't be fooled!! He pulled the phone out of the wall!!**

At this point, my temptation is the "Listen, you two, I have reached my limit" intervention.

This is what I *did* say:

VG: *Listen, you two* – I can't take this much longer. One of you will have to come out and help me. I am going to be tapped out if I am left alone out here without any support much longer. I think I have about another minute in me. I can feel that I'm almost at my limit.

While neither Bill nor Jane literally "came out to help me," both of them helped me by not saying anything more. We all sat quietly for a few minutes until the hour drew to a close.

The intervention, though startling, seemed to create the necessary quiet to settle things down. I allowed myself to say it because I knew the couple would understand that my "collapse," even if it had occurred, would have been partial and temporary – that I would have recovered my powers, my well-being, and my commitment to the work. Otherwise, I could not have spoken as I did. But I also believe that the Kleinian specter of damaging, exhausting, and ominously weakening me served to shock the couple into an awareness of their destructiveness in a way that nothing else had done.

With the breach of my omnipotence, the chill of reality's indifference to their plaints soaked into our collective consciousness, shifting something in the ethos – permanently. While the couple continued to be hyper-reactive and "on alert" as the work continued, there were also times when I could see them reaching for an approximation of the depressive position, even if it was fitful and fragile.

Moreover, it seemed that the more *I* accepted my limits, the more my stamina and understanding seemed to grow. In a later session, for example, when the couple started to careen into another all-or-nothing battle over who was the true victim in the relationship, I caught myself working too hard to save them from themselves. This time, I was able to pull back and capture our collective state of arousal with a clarity I did not have before. This is roughly what I said:

I see I'm not getting through to either one of you. You hear me, but you don't *want* to listen, because you don't *want* to calm down. You want to tear yourself away from me so you can keep on fighting. You'll fight till you drop. You are like Gladiators – nothing but Death will stop you.

In this instance, while I was not explicitly sounding an alarm about myself, as I had done in the earlier session, I was, once again, challenging the couple to take more responsibility for their reactivity and dysregulation. The effect was the same – a quieting of arousal. Here I believe it was my recognition, *and acceptance*, of the ferocity and drivenness of their reactivity that produced that oddly calming effect. Perhaps we all felt something of the stillness of surrender, even though the Third to which we were yielding was one of destructiveness.

By giving us all permission to "accept the things we could not change" (the AA Serenity Prayer), I was, without planning it, deploying a variant of the old family therapy technique of "prescribing the symptom" the couple had come to change (their endless, exhausting arguments). Like the family therapy strategists of the 1980s, who were often faced with impossible cases, I found myself telling Bill and Jane that I could not help them be more peaceful, because their addiction to fighting was apparently necessary in the larger scheme of things. (Gladiators are not free agents.)

The intervention was also a clinical paradox in that I was explicitly telling them that I accepted therapeutic defeat, while I was, of course, continuing to treat them. My interpretation – that they were doomed Gladiators without a cause – was clearly sobering. Moreover, by truly accepting (with no irony or sarcasm) that at least for now, I could not, and perhaps should not, try to encourage them to take a softer, more reflective stance, I shifted the terms of our power struggle, leaving them with nothing to fight *against*. In line with the old theory, the only way they could continue to resist my therapeutic efforts was, paradoxically, *to calm down*.

In the months that followed, Bill and Jane did grow better able to see how their "fights to the death" over Truth and Reality were actually killing them. In the heat of battle, the endorphins of borderline arousal blind us to the fact that we are actually drawing blood, and that bodies do bleed out. Over time the couple became more willing to dial things back, in part because they were developing the capacity to wait, to trust in the ultimate fairness of the process over the long term.

We terminated before a summer break some years ago. I am sure they are still together. They really love each other. And as with all couples, it is Bill and Jane who ultimately must decide how much change is possible, how much compromise is tolerable, and whether separation can be borne.

While I was probably only a small part of their big story, Bill and Jane made a lasting impact on mine. They forced me to work through the very hard ideas in this chapter and they come back into focus, in all their poignant intensity, every time I teach them.

References

Aron, L. (2000). Self-reflexivity and the therapeutic action of psychoanalysis. *Psychoanalytic Psychology, 17*, 667–689.

Bateman, A. & Fonagy, P. (2006). *Mentalization based treatment for borderline personality disorder*. New York, NY: Oxford University Press.

Bateson, G. (1979). *Mind and nature: A necessary unity*. New York, NY: E.P. Dutton.

Beebe, B. & McCrorie, E. (2010). The optimum midrange: Infant research, literature, and romantic attachment. *Attachment: New Directions in Psychotherapy and Relational Psychoanalysis, 4*, 39–58.

Benjamin, J. (1995). *Like subjects, love objects*. New Haven, CT: Yale University Press.

Benjamin, J. (2004a). Beyond doer and done-to: An intersubjective view of thirdness. *Psychoanalytic Quarterly, 73*, 5–76.

Benjamin, J. (2004b). Escape from the hall of mirrors: Commentary on paper by Jody Messler Davies. *Psychoanalytic Dialogues, 14*, 743–753.

Boszormenyi-Nagy, I. & Spark, G.M. (1973). *Invisible loyalties: Reciprocity in intergenerational family therapy*. Oxford, UK: Harper & Row.

Bowlby, J. (1973). *Attachment and loss: Volume two*. New York, NY: Basic Books.

Bromberg, P. (2010). *Awakening the dreamer*. New York, NY: Taylor & Francis.

Davies, J.M. (2004). Whose bad objects are we anyway?: Repetition and our elusive love affair with evil. *Psychoanalytic Dialogues, 14*, 711–732.

Esmiol, E., Knudson-Martin, C. & Delgado, S. (2012). Developing a contextual consciousness: Learning to address gender, societal power, and culture in clinical practice. *Journal of Marriage and Family Therapy, 38*, 573–588.

Fonagy, P. (2001). *Attachment theory and psychoanalysis*. New York, NY: Other Press.

Fonagy, P., Gergely, G., Jurist, E. & Target, M. (2002). *Affect regulation, mentalization and the development of the self*. New York, NY: Other Press.

Gabbard, G.O. (1986). The treatment of the "special" patient in a psychoanalytic hospital. *International Review of Psycho-Analysis, 13*, 333–347.

Gilligan, C. (1989). *Mapping the moral domain: A contribution of women's thinking to psychological theory and education*. Cambridge, MA: Harvard University Press.

Gilligan, J. (1997). *Violence: Reflections on a national epidemic*. New York, NY: Vintage.

Goldner, V. (1991). Toward a critical relational theory of gender. *Psychoanalytic Dialogues, 1*, 249–272.

Goldner, V. (2004a). Review essay: Attachment and eros: Opposed or synergistic? *Psychoanalytic Dialogues, 14*, 381–396.

Goldner, V. (2004b). When love hurts: Treating abusive relationships. *Psychoanalytic Inquiry, 24*, 346–372.

Goldner, V. (2006). Let's do it again: Further reflections on eros and attachment. *Psychoanalytic Dialogues, 16*, 619–637.

Goldner, V., Penn., P., Sheinberg, M. & Walker, G. (1990). Love and violence: Gender paradoxes in volatile attachments. *Family Process, 29*, 343–364.

Greenberg, L. & Goldman, R. (2008). *Emotion focused couples therapy*. Washington, DC: APA Publishing.

Greenberg, L.S. & Johnson, S.M. (1988). *Emotionally focused therapy for couples*. New York, NY: Guilford.

Hesse, E. & Main, M. (2000). Disorganized infant, child and adult attachment: Collapse in behavioral and attentional strategies. *Journal of the American Psychoanalytic Association, 48*, 1097–1127.

Johnson, S. (1986). Bonds or bargains: Relationship paradigms and their significance. *Journal of Marriage and Family Therapy, 12*, 259–267.

Johnson, S., Makinen, J. & Millikin, J. (2001). Attachment injuries in couples relationships: A new perspective on impasses in couples therapy. *Journal of Marriage and Family Therapy, 27*, 145–155.

Laing, R.D. (1965/1976). Mystification, confusion & conflict. In C. Sluski & D. Ransom (Eds.), *Beyond the double bind* (pp. 129–219). New York, NY: Grune & Stratton.

Levenson, E. (1972). *The fallacy of understanding*. New York, NY: Basic Books.

Lewis, J. (2000). Repairing the bond in important relationships. *American Journal of Psychiatry, 157*, 1375–1378.

Liotti, G. (1999). Disorganization of attachment as a model for understanding dissociative psychopathology. In J. Solomon & C. George (Eds.), *Attachment disorganization* (pp. 291–317). New York, NY: Guilford.

Lyons-Ruth, K. (2003). The two-person construction of defenses: Disorganized attachment strategies, unintegrated mental states, and hostile/helpless relational processes. *Journal of Infant, Child, and Adolescent Psychotherapy, 2*, 105–125.

Meins, E., Fernyhough, C., Wainwright, R., Das Gupta, M., Fradley, E. & Tuckey, M. (2002). Maternal mind-mindedness and attachment security as predictors of theory of mind understanding. *Child Development, 73*, 1715–1726.

Mitchell, S. (2002). *Can love last: The fate of romance over time*. New York, NY: Norton.

Mordecai, E. (1995). Negative therapeutic reactions: Developing a new stance. *Psychoanalytic Psychology, 12*, 483–493.

Schore, A.N. (2005). Psychoanalytic research: Progress and process notes from Allan Schore's groups in developmental affective neuroscience and clinical practice. *Psychologist-Psychoanalyst, 25*, 18–19.

Schore, A.N. (2012). *The science of the art of psychotherapy*. New York, NY: Norton.

Schore, J.N. & Schore, A.N. (2008). Modern attachment theory: The central role of affect regulation in development and treatment. *Clinical Social Work Journal, 20*, 9–20.

Seligman, S. (1999). Integrating Kleinian theory and intersubjective infant research: Observing projective identification. *Psychoanalytic Dialogues, 9*, 129–159.

Sheinberg, M. & Penn, P. (1991). Gender dilemmas, gender questions and the gender mantra. *Journal of Marriage and Family Therapy, 17*, 33–44.

Slade, A. (2014). Imagining fear: Attachment, threat, and psychic experience. *Psychoanalytic Dialogues, 24*, 253–266.

Sluzki, C. & Verón, E. (1971). The double bind as a universal pathogenic situation. *Family Process, 10*, 397–410.

Snyder, R. (2013, July 22). A raised hand: Can a new approach curb domestic homicide? *The New Yorker*. Available at www.newyorker.com/reporting/2013/07/22/130722fa_fact_snyder.

Solomon, M. & Tatkin, S. (2011). *Love and war in intimate relationships*. New York, NY: Norton.

Stuss, D. & Alexander, M. (2000). Executive functions and the frontal lobes: A conceptual view. *Psychological Research, 63*, 289–298.

Tomasello, M., Carpenter, M., Call, J., Behne, T. & Mol, H. (2005). Understanding and sharing intentions: The origins of cultural cognition. *Behavioral and Brain Sciences, 28*, 675–691.

Zeifman, D. & Hazan, C. (1999). Pair bonds as attachments: Re-evaluating the evidence. In J. Cassidy & P. Shaver (Eds.), *Handbook of attachment* (pp. 436–456). New York, NY: Guilford.

Chapter 11

Discussion of "Romantic bonds, binds, and ruptures: couples on the brink"

Rachael Peltz

I'd like to begin with a quote from a favorite writer of fiction and essays, David Grossman (2008):

> If we observe those around us, we will find that even between couples who have lived together for decades – who have lived more or less happily, and who love each other and can function well as parents and as a family – there can often be, almost instinctively and unwittingly, a complex unspoken agreement (whose application, incidentally, requires a most sophisticated and nuanced form of collaboration!), the main tenet of which is that it is best not to know one's partner through and through. Not to be exposed to all that happens within him. And not to recognize these "occurrences" or name them explicitly, because they have no place within the framework of the couple's relationship, and they might even tear the relationship apart from the inside and bring it crashing down, something neither partner desires.
>
> (p. 32)

Later on he notes:

> We human beings are uneasy about what truly occurs deep inside the Other, even if that Other is someone we love. And perhaps it is more than unease; perhaps it is an actual fear of the mysterious, nonverbal, unprocessed core, that which cannot be subjected to any social tamping, to any refinement, politeness, or tact; that which is instinctive, wild and chaotic, not at all politically correct. It is dreamlike and nightmarish, radical and exposed, sexual and unbridled, at least according to the social-order definitions that prevail among "civilized" people (whatever that term may mean). It is mad and

sometimes cruel, often animalistic, for good or for bad. It is, if you will, the magma, the primordial, blazing material that bubbles inside every person simply because he is human, simply because he is an intersection of so many forces, instincts, longings and urges.

(p. 35)

Grossman adds that a powerful motivation for his writing is that it allows him "*to know the Other from within him.* To be able to touch, if only for a moment, the blaze that burns within another human being" (p. 36). With this in mind, I shift to a quote about Bion, by South African analyst Duncan Cartwright (2010):

For Bion, a real human connection is like an emotional storm caused by the coming together of minds that crave and resist each other.... The task becomes finding ways of tolerating the emotional storm for long enough so that it can be thought about and given particular personal meaning.

(p. 3)

I open with these quotes, appreciating the challenges we all encounter in our efforts to form intimate relationships in couples – deeply craving and mysteriously resisting. The desire to be fully known, loved, and accepted is second only to the impossibility of ever being fully known, loved, or accepted and likewise of fully knowing, loving, and accepting one's partner. It is only in accepting that a gap exists between the most intimate of partners that any intimacy can be truly experienced. The clamoring we hear about wanting to be known, or feeling shut out, is often about something else, which can direct us to the collapsed state of couples present in the cases Virginia Goldner describes in her chapter "Romantic bonds, binds, and ruptures: couples on the brink."

We must ask ourselves, "What are we striving for in our work with couples?" Realistically, I believe we try to help couples expand what they can experience, feel, and think about separately and together as they move through life. Whatever binds them must serve the greater good, providing a source of inspiration in the face of adversity from within, between, or outside of the relationship. Mary Morgan (2001) refers to that internal capacity as the "couple state of mind" that is the "third" entity, larger than either individual, which stands to hold, contain, and thereby comfort each member when they feel vulnerable or expansive. It is what couples rely on without knowing it, when they turn to each other in the hope that otherwise overwhelming, unbearable, and even beautiful experiences can find a place between them, leading to growth – pollination (Grossman, 2008, p. 32) – of the couple and each of its members. I have often referred to it as a delicate plant that needs tending. It also reminds me of my mother's sage words, "Rachaela, in a marriage you have to take the good with the bad" – her version of the necessity of holding multiple perspectives of your partner in mind. Of course, even in the most spacious of couples, certain traumatic experiences exceed their capacity to contain them (Nathans, 2012).

While every couple forms a dynamic system, composed of conscious and unconscious elements of each member, not every couple shares a couple state of mind. This is where we couple therapists enter into the picture. Morgan (2001) of the Tavistock group refers to the "couple state of mind" as that position assigned to us as therapists, as the ones who must keep not only each member but also the relationship in mind. However, creating psychic space in the therapy of couples on the brink is more than half the battle.

What enables some couples to attain this precious capacity while so many others cannot? Is there something unique to the couples in perpetual crisis whom Goldner describes that obstructs their development of this capacity? These couples are missing the couple state of mind, leaving them without the sense of commitment, security, or flexibility that this capacity can provide. Goldner suggests that their "emotion-drenched histories" send them plummeting into attachment patterns that they have no recourse other than to repeat. They are not able to rely on each other to hold the needs of the relationship in mind, or help them process difficult emotional experiences as a consequence of being trapped in a cycle of withdrawal or reactivity. Depending on your model, one could say they are too busy defending or warding off aspects of themselves to fully bond with the other. Or, in keeping with the repetition compulsion that is wired into the circuitry of disorganized attachment patterns, as Goldner suggests, they keep trying to extract from their partners what they were unable to receive as children, only to rewrite the old, tired story, which ends in collapse.

For couples ensnared in this way, returning to the volcanic metaphor, it is as if each partner's magma chamber is touched off by the other in our consulting rooms. They feel respectively attacked, betrayed, controlled, misrecognized, and certainly blocked from drawing on each other's containing capacities. As one patient recently put it, "I feel trapped in a version of myself with him."

Of course, no one could sustain the ability to be receptive, interested, or thoughtful in such an emotionally torrential environment. To an outsider it appears these couples foment crisis, though I have been surprised by how they can mobilize when there is an actual crisis. At those junctures they are freer to work together. It seems that the call to mobilize as a result of a crisis outside of themselves binds the unconscious anxieties otherwise released in the course of everyday life. But, once it subsides, I have been equally surprised by the quick reinstatement of the hair-trigger emotional maelstrom. The perpetual crisis settles in as the fantasies each had about the other begin to erode, releasing tremendously shattering disappointment, anger, anxiety, and dread, which serves to fuel each person's insistence on "saying it again, one more time" – the experience they feel has not been properly understood by their partner – only to feel rebuffed, refused, rejected. "Why can't you hear me?" "Why won't you listen?" Why must each partner cling so desperately to his or her own version of reality? What is at stake here?

What is at stake here is none other than one's integrity as a person in desperate search for recognition. However, given what I understand about disorganized attachments from Goldner and Kaplan (personal communication, October 2012), it is precisely the hunger for safety and recognition that signals danger and destruction for the children born into these complex systems. When they partner in couples, they are captured by the ghost of these attachments whereby every love object automatically vacillates between savior or traitor. This generates equally compelling inner conflicts about feeling they must rescue or risk betrayal. I am reminded of the literature on the transmission of generational trauma in which similar discoveries have been made. In her now famous book *The Telescoping of Generations*, Haydee Faimberg (2005) describes the development of alienated identifications with disavowed aspects of parents' histories, locking the child in the impossible position of incorporating what has been disavowed and experiencing the threat of betrayal should they avow their own separate identities, thus breaking with unconsciously transmitted parental needs.

Against this complex familial dynamic backdrop, couples find each other unconsciously searching for a partner who will rescue them from an internal conflict they have yet to even identify – so raw and unprocessed are these experiences. The dissolution of this desperate rescue fantasy releases Katrina-like storms of emotion we are challenged to quiet, in order to begin the work of cleanup and reconstruction, if we can make our way in.

One large caveat before continuing: The opportunity to write this chapter is a kind of homecoming for me in that I began my clinical work as a couple and family therapist at a time when psychoanalysis and family systems theory were themselves highly polarized, so much so that they were largely irrelevant to each other – two closed systems, despite many family systems theorists having begun their training as psychoanalysts. Though I understood this schism, I remember the frustration and relish this opportunity of bridging these long divided schools.

In fact, the interweaving of dynamic systems, attachment, and neuropsychological theories present in Goldner's chapter is itself an example of sustainable bridge-building, using composites of the natural substances contained in each theory to demonstrate the depth of the reverberation of couple dynamics on every human system, from our neural pathways, to unconscious (often highly disorganized and insecure) attachment patterns. This interweaving ultimately helps us to understand what each member can tolerate of his or her experiences, emotion, and capacities for representational thought, in relationship to themselves and their partners. I would add to this rich synthetic matrix Bion's (1962) theory of the psychic apparatus – or waking dream thoughts – which I'll briefly sketch out.

Bion and more contemporary collaborators, notably Ogden (2005), Ferro (2002), Civitarese (2013), and proponents of field theory, have generated a sea change in thinking about the role of dynamic unconsciousness in psychic life and relationships and how it can be accessed in the therapeutic encounter, which includes analytic work with couples. For Bion, the dream represents a proto-thought in which aspects of unconscious life appear in order to be linked together. So, the dream is itself a construction and a communication with unconscious guideposts on the royal road to conscious discovery and thought. Think of fragments of emotion, images, scenes, sensations, stories bubbling up – as opposed to the dream that must be excavated in order to reveal its unconscious meanings. The destination on the Freudian map leads to the cavernous location of the unconscious with the undoing of dreamwork as the guide. Bion's destination is well above ground, in the analytic field, where the reverberating unconscious elements generated by both patient and analyst have a hope of coming together in the construction of a meaningful narrative. Once constructed, this narrative figure becomes the ground that shifts to form new images and narrations, and so on (Peltz, 2012).

The role of dynamic unconsciousness in the psychic lives of couples functions in similar ways. The transformation of emotional life that takes place within couples' relationships is based on the strength and quality of the bond, and each person's respective capacities to respond to the dynamic unconscious present in the field between them. This allows unassimilated, often disturbing, mental states to be made more tolerable. In the best of circumstances, as tumultuous emotional experiences surface in one member of the couple, the other member comes forward in a manner that "detoxifies" them. This emotional and mental connection occurs at different levels of experience – sensory, unconscious, preconscious – allowing disturbing emotional experiences to be processed and understood, implicitly or explicitly. In whatever ways each couple divines for themselves – holding, comforting, talking, eating, playing, having sex, doing things – the couple creates a safe atmosphere that can potentially expand what can be felt and thought about together; or, on the contrary, something will trigger a defensive response and the psychic space between the couple rapidly constricts, in accordance with the equally unconscious phantasies of the couple and both partners. Working with couples one always wonders what can this couple share and process together and what must be kept out of the field between them? Are there secrets? What are the rules and "operating procedures" around here? This leads us to establishing the existence and location of the containing function in this couple. When does it fail? What is taking place when one partner hears the other's plea for help as an accusation, or an unbearable reminder of feelings they cannot tolerate in themselves? Or as an abandonment? Sticking with the storm metaphor, in couples, the possibilities for triggering storm patterns are endless.

The goals of therapy in couple work are not that different from individual work in that we try to mobilize the unconscious life of the couple and make that system known. But first we must weather the initial storms and establish a "calm enough" atmosphere in which safety can be assured, the safety required for any kind of psychological work to take place. Here is where we all become child therapists, entering the world of careful, though spontaneous, calibrations, attuning ourselves to what can be heard, taken in, and used by both members. What's happening in the field, right in front of us, is the question we take up whenever possible – "What's going on here?" – which helps us in our efforts to first notice, and then attend to, the shared experiences between us.

Where we all converge in dynamic systems, attachment theory, neuropsychology, field theory, and Bion's concept of dynamic unconsciousness is around the pivotal notion that the mind functions as a "self-organizing, non-linear system" in which experiences of all kinds are filtered out of awareness, schematized, stored, and utilized. And that dynamic system is fortunately an open one, highly influenced by subjective and inter-subjective emotional experiences. A change in one sphere can reverberate at different levels, each having non-linear influences on the other. As therapists we then become partners in the co-creation of those critical, transformative, inter-subjective experiences, which then expand what can be felt in each other's presence, generating new experiences and meanings and shifting the ways our systems function in the hopes of rebooting the complex circuitry of our mental capacities and emotional responses.

Let's now turn to Bill and Jane, the couple in Goldner's chapter, and ask "What's going on here – what do we notice in this field?" The following is the beginning of the vignette:

B: (softly, anxiously) We had problems over the weekend. Jane's anxiety problems are constant. Suddenly she just darkened after a beautiful morning – and it made me mad.... We eventually had a long talk and we both felt better.

J: I didn't feel any of that! It was a two-hour, exhausting conversation. I felt no better at the end than at the beginning. We spent all this time and money and he still thinks he can diagnose me! **Jane has "anxiety problems"!!??**

B: But I *said* I could see what she was saying.... Jesus, if I say anything about her, she thinks I think I am blameless. And then she can go off on me for that and we *never* get to the thing I am trying to point out! ... (gets soft) I have been in retreat (makes a gesture of helplessness and Jane rolls her eyes).

J: He's representing himself as the victim – but *he's* the one who fights *me*! And then he has the nerve to represent himself as the righteous one!

VG: I see how you are afraid, Bill, that Jane is going to get me off track. (He nods.) And Jane, I see how you're afraid I'm going to be taken in by Bill. (She looks up warily.)

(p. 173)

Let's stop here. What do we observe from our position outside of this powerful couple's force field? Goldner's description of Bill's opening words – "softly, anxiously" – stuck with me. His comments seem to seesaw between softness – vulnerability, surprise, mournfulness, "we had problems" – and anxiety escalating into attack – "Jane's anxiety problems were constant."

Jane's experience is one of exhaustion, bitterness, and the utter certainty about being attacked and blamed for their problems, leaving Bill as the victim. Goldner's intervention speaks to their mistrust that the therapist will be able to keep them both in her mind, also reflecting their feeling of being dropped in the mind of each other. Instead of opening anything up – as it might have in other circumstances or couples, Jane became more inflamed, reiterating her experience more emphatically.

In the remainder of the session the same pattern repeats itself, only the roles shift depending on who Goldner hears taking momentary responsibility for their emotional state of mind. Each effort Goldner makes to expand the field by interjecting her take on what has been said has the opposite effect, adding fuel – experienced as blame – to the already burning fire in the room. The therapist as third can only be experienced as a judge, approving or disapproving, with a verdict in hand, confirming one's goodness or badness. This is evidence of a binary system – for me or against me; victim or perpetrator. There is a sharp division, in Bion's terms, between the container and the contained. The therapist has been inducted into the system in which any love object is once again viewed as either rescuing or betraying one from the unrelenting indictment of blame. Each member of the couple experiences the other's bid as an accusation. Whatever is being triggered far exceeds their capacity to hold the other in mind as a potential source of comfort. Instead they feel they must defend themselves by out-sourcing blame and attack, another way of thinking about a complex web of persecutory projections. Each one is using the other to get rid of unwanted internal experiences – at the expense of the relationship.

One has the sense that there is a very hot potato in this room being tossed back and forth – suggesting something about the unconscious phantasy of this couple. No one can afford to touch something, but what? In keeping with what continues to surface in the field of this couple, it must have to do with the mix of self-blame and fear associated with each of their experiences of vulnerability in their primary attachments. Neither of these people can tolerate any approximation of hurting or betraying the objects they depend on and consequently ward off that possibility by invoking it in the other. Under these conditions the therapist is experienced, by definition, as "taking sides."

Goldner speaks of an unconscious symmetry in these couples whom she understands are looking for a "relational home," and who are seeking to gain mastery over the unresolved trauma of the other's non-recognition. I fully agree that there is an unconscious symmetry in these couples. Each partner is held captive by an unnamed and unprocessed set of painful experiences they carry into the relationship. Each wants the other to protect him/herself from feelings they both find unbearable. When that doesn't happen, they lash out and we're back in the storm. Or, put another way, when one person feels upset in some way and conveys this to the other, he or she cannot tolerate the unpredictability of the other's response, based on the fact that they are separate people with their own set of vulnerabilities and triggers. One gets the impression that behind the splitting and intense warding off of the other's communications in the session is a terrible experience that both Bill and Jane share in separate ways. I imagine that they sensed this about each other early on. That is to say, it is conceivable that they share a pain they locate in the other that they can't know about and that the unconscious phantasy of the couple is found somewhere in this territory: you must protect me from feeling badly, hurtful, damaging; that is our pact.

Unfortunately their worse fears have landed squarely between them. The ghosts in the nurseries have returned to haunt the couple. Bill and Jane are not free to calm each other's fears because each of their efforts turns into a massive trigger for the other one. One trigger ignites another and another and any containing function is lost. Perhaps in the early stages of the relationship they could offer each other comfort and safety through some implicit understanding – a resonance that contained them, or a more mysterious bond of love that compelled them (Friend, 2013). But, systems change over time, as do life circumstances, which can shift or intensify, taxing already fragile systems. If this is true, it helps us understand the experience of the hot potato in the room. The pain that binds them paradoxically also repels them. Then, when the therapist voices anything that can be viewed as support for one member of the couple, this intolerable experience of being fundamentally at fault, shamed, and humiliated is invoked big-time in the other.

How one masters a trauma of non-recognition becomes a moot point in these instances as a consequence of the degree of raw, unprocessed, and overwhelming experiences being warded off. We are also living in the land of part-objects at such junctures, in a frantic struggle to keep unwanted aspects of oneself out. That can account for the experience Jane describes as "fighting for her life." Viewing one's partner as a separate person, each one deserving of recognition, is not an option in these confounding and crowding dynamics. Instead we are witness to the complementary bombardment of projective misrecognitions. Something inside her and inside him feels deadly and must be kept out by blaming the other – as if he or she could protect them but is simply holding out.

One further point. Some of the literature on clinical impasses suggests that a symbiosis is created between therapist and patient in response to the unconscious pressure to keep certain key experiences out of the field (Ferro, 2002). What is initially needed to insure the patient a bond of safety becomes a roadblock to further development later in the process. Once again, a tie that binds can become one that later repels. In apparatus terms, the container of the analytic couple has become rigidified. It won't let in certain emotional experiences. This extruded dimension must be brought back into the field. But how?

How do we quiet the storm long enough to safely identify any of the raw emotion present in the field of this couple's therapy? My honest response is: take whatever you can get and work with it. By this I mean to direct our attention to the minutest of perceptions that catch our attention in ourselves and the field of the couple – fleeting occurrences that surface, as if in a dream, and help register unconscious dimensions of the relationship.

I agree with Goldner that our initial goal with couples is to capture the immediacy of experience that bubbles up in the field. These fleeting encounters introduce us to elements of what neither member has words to describe. These elements can then begin to take form in the therapist's mind and are tentatively introduced to the couple in a form we hope they can use. This sets the stage for establishing a safe setting for shared experiences, which provides the building blocks for future exploration, although it is not always in the consulting room that one is visited by such fleeting encounters.

We think about our patients in ways we are not aware of all of the time. So, though Jane and Bill are not my patients, during the time I was writing this chapter, one day while driving I found myself humming, "Try a Little Tenderness." It took me a while to make anything of it, until I thought, the antidote to self-blame and humiliation would certainly be tenderness. Then I imagined Goldner singing Bill and Jane a lullaby, in a soft and gentle voice. How could we think about this if we are to take it seriously, as a reverie that might offer guidance to what this couple can hear? I imagined saying to them,

> You are both tired, sad, in need of comfort. Can you imagine letting down for just a bit? I think you are both so worried about being bad, to blame, full of shame, that any hint you hear from the other sends you into a panic that it is the truth – that all of your fears about yourselves as bad and shameful are simply true. You are both so hungry for comfort and recognition of what is good in you.

Of course, this could fall on deaf ears. But, if we are tuned into what comes next, the couple will offer us supervision by way of the emotional quality of their response to what we say. I am not offering this as a suggestion for every couple, by no means, but more as an example of the ways our experiences with and of the couples enter the inner sanctum of our psychic lives – which can then direct us, if we are receptive and attentive to these visitations.

We are also especially challenged by the limits of our own personalities in conjunction with those of the couples we see. What comes naturally for one person, a little tenderness, is a terrific challenge for another. I think of some of the couples I have worked with who struggle in very similar ways as Bill and Jane, and I am filled with remorse over my own difficulties locating a little tenderness amidst the steady stream of assaults on each other and the treatment. On the other hand, our strengths as personalities offer our best hope for making contact with the people we see – offering them what Bion (1963) referred to as "passionate" connections. Bringing ourselves into the exchanges we encounter offers an essential part of the containing function in that it allows the patients to engage with us – witnessing in us the emotions evoked in the process of containing and expanding what can be experienced and rendered meaningful. Passion is that ability to emotionally and mentally engage and survive the engagement of the Other.

In closing, I would like to return to Grossman's (2008) earlier quote about the exquisite and mutual balance we are challenged to achieve between the intense craving to know and not to know one's partner. Knowing that Grossman is an Israeli writer reminds me of the quality of the backdrop of all couple relationships – that is, the society in which they live and hopefully thrive. Thinking about this dimension of couples' lives only intensifies our appreciation of the number of forces that shape and act upon the couple at any given moment in history. It has been nearly 40 years since Christopher Lasch (1979) published his famous *Haven in a Heartless World*. In that book he underscored how expectations for self-fulfillment, thwarted in so many other realms of life at this time, land squarely in the domain of the family, as other forms of public and communal life diminish. Due to this intensification, what we are led to believe is our haven has become our hothouse. While what we think of as family has surely expanded for the better – including many more configurations of pairings outside of the old patriarchal heterosexual unit – nonetheless, the pressures on every configuration of partnership has only intensified in those 40 years. Keeping this in mind adds another layer of compassion for ourselves and the couples we see.

References

Bion, W.R. (1962). *Learning from experience*. London: Heinemann.
Bion, W.R. (1963). *Elements of psychoanalysis*. London: Heinemann.
Cartwright, D. (2010). *Containing states of mind: Exploring Bion's "Container Model" in psychoanalytic psychotherapy*. London: Routledge.
Civitarese, G. (2013). *The violence of emotions: Bion and post-Bionian psychoanalysis*. London: Routledge.
Faimberg, H. (2005). *The telescoping of generations: Listening to the narcissistic links between generations*. London: Routledge.
Ferro, A. (2002). *In the analyst's consulting room*. New York: NY: Brunner-Routledge.
Friend, J. (2013). Love as creative illusion and its place in psychoanalytic couple psychotherapy. *Couple and Family Psychoanalysis* (3)1, 3–14.
Grossman, D. (2008). *Writing in the dark: Essays on literature and politics*. New York, NY: Farrar, Straus and Giroux.
Lasch, C. (1979). *Haven in a heartless world*. New York, NY: Norton.

Morgan, M. (2001). First contacts: The therapist's "couple state of mind" as a factor in the containment of couples seen for consultations. In Francis Grier (Ed.), *Brief encounters with couples*. London: Karnac Books.

Nathans, S. (2012). Infidelity as a manic defense. *Couple and Family Psychoanalysis* (2)2, 165–180.

Ogden, T. (2005). *This art of psychoanalysis: Dreaming underarm dreams and interrupted cries*. London: Routledge.

Peltz, R. (2012). Ways of hearing: Getting inside psychoanalysis. *Psychoanalytic Dialogues* (22)3, 279–290.

Chapter 12

How was it for you?
Attachment, sexuality and mirroring in couple relationships

Christopher Clulow

In 2009 a party was held to launch a book I edited, entitled *Sex, Attachment and Couple Psychotherapy* (2009). At the event there was a lively discussion about the nature of sexual desire between men and women. A few days afterwards I received a note from the wife of a well-known cartoonist in the UK with whom I'd got into conversation at the party. She enclosed a copy of one of her husband's cartoons from his "Home Truths" series. The cartoon depicts a post-coital couple lying in bed together. The rather smug-looking man asks the woman "How was it for you?" to which he gets the tetchy response, "How was what?"

What "Home Truths" might we take from this? For me, part of the humour of Mel Calman's cartoon lies in the relationship it depicts – not just the "put down" following the "put up", but an image of supposed post-coital intimacy failing to conceal an ocean of difference in the partners' experience of what has gone on between them. The "home truth" I want to explore is the proposition that sexual feelings, which I'm distinguishing from sexual behaviour, are discovered through relationships. The question "How was it for you?" implies not only curiosity (more often anxiety) about another person's experience, but also a questioning of one's own experience, containing the thought that the experience of the enquirer is dependent upon the experience of their partner. Sexuality, and the feelings surrounding it, then become intersubjective phenomena, something that is generated by what goes on between people as much as what goes on within them.

Men and women do sometimes find themselves unable to comprehend their own and each other's sexuality, making it difficult for them to talk about their feelings together and entertain the kind of curiosity that allows the questions, "How was it for you?" and "How was it for me?" to be asked. Worryingly, this lack of comprehension might go for therapists, too. I was more than a little shocked by the assertion that psychoanalytically informed couple therapists have a tendency to shy away from exploring sex with the couples they see, preferring not to ask how it was for them (Kahr, 2009). When you come to think about it, this is extraordinary, given that sex is arguably the key factor distinguishing adult couple/romantic relationships from other sorts of relating.

Yet, I suppose it also makes some kind of sense, given the focus of psychoanalysis on understanding the emotional and developmental roots of adult behaviour (including sexual behaviour) and the knowledge that presenting complaints often indicate other relationship difficulties and developmental disorders. So I hope I'm not avoiding sex by exploring its developmental roots. Nor, by adopting a relational approach to thinking about this affective dimension of sexuality, am I intending to behave like one of the apocryphal group of psychotherapists who, upon passing beyond the portals of this life, come across a signpost pointing in one direction to "The Garden of Eden" and in the other to "The Lecture on the Garden of Eden" and nervously opt for the latter! The child psychotherapist Adam Phillips' wry comment that "all our stories about the madness of love are stories of impossible conflict" (2005, p. 128) is an appropriate caution against tidying up into any one explanation something as inherently disorderly as sex.

Sex and attachment

Sexuality faces us with conceptual dilemmas. For example, on what basis might we choose between narratives that seek to explain the phenomenon of sexual desire – and its absence – in dyadic or triangular relational terms? On the one hand, psychoanalysts have developed Winnicott's (1967) essentially dyadic ideas about maternal mirroring and applied them to understanding the psychogenesis of sexual desire. Their approach, which I will summarise later, highlights the significance of an absence in maternal mirroring that may be pivotal in motivating desire. Here, we might question whether focusing on the experience of infant sensuality and the responses it evokes is adequate to explaining the different ways adults develop as sexual beings. On the other hand we have narratives that focus on the relevance of Oedipal dynamics, the dynamics of relationship triangles – both internal and external – to the development of adult sexuality. These narratives will feature in what follows, although my primary focus will be on the relationship between attachment and sexuality, and the relevance of Winnicott's concept of maternal mirroring to understanding sexual desire.

So, a proposition: desire exercises its hold on us through confronting us with a sense of absence. We long for someone, something, or some outcome to relieve the tension generated by this absence and to make us feel replete and complete. The sense of longing – desire – motivates us to take action, to seek out the object of our desire. Sexual desire combines aggression and receptivity to this end, resulting in a melting and merging with another into something resembling a borderline state. We might make a link between this combination and biochemical processes involved in generating desire when we consider the roles played by testosterone, oxytocin and vasopressin, neuropeptides that are involved in the neural control of sexuality through driving aggression and social bonding in both men and women (Panksepp, 1998).

But absence can also trigger fear, especially in infancy, when the presence and responses of a parental figure are vital to the vulnerable child's developing sense of security. Fear matches desire as a powerful emotion driving behaviour. We act to protect ourselves, to avoid anxiety, either fighting our way out of or taking flight from threatening situations. Fear provides the motivation either to cling to others or to separate ourselves from them, in the hope that this will protect us from the risks we anticipate will result from involvement.

Problems with sexual feelings can be linked with the conflict between desire and fear, between feelings of love and hate towards the same person, between the comfort of the familiar and the excitement of the unknown. What Glasser (1979) described as the "core complex" – an inter-related set of feelings, ideas and attitudes that he applied to understanding perverse relating – is a central part of the "impossible conflict" that Adam Phillips was referring to. It is a phenomenon that Boerma and I (2009) applied in a more ubiquitous fashion when trying to understand disorders of desire in ordinary couple relationships: namely, the conflict between allure and threat associated with merging and separating from others who are important to us. The "impossible conflict" is also contained in what some assert to be a fundamental incompatibility between sexual and attachment systems of behaviour (see, for example, Eagle, 2007).

Both classical psychoanalytic and contemporary attachment theories attempt to explain such conflicts in relational as well as biological terms.

For Freud, sexual desire was an aspect of what he described as "libido" – an innate, instinctual form of energy that was channelled through ducts determined by anatomy and the developing body, and whose expression was shaped by social influence. His reworking of the Oedipus myth proposed that the first object of sexual desire for both boys and girls was the parent of the opposite sex. For him, adulthood and maturity were associated with relinquishing this primary and forbidden object. The mechanism that enabled boys to withdraw their libidinal cathexis of their mothers was the paternal threat of castration, combined with an acceptance of their inadequacy to the task of displacing father. For girls it was the belief that they had already lost their penis and that this could only be compensated for by carrying their father's baby, which would enable them to recover the lost penis through a process of symbolic equation. To be fair, Freud did see the trigger for converting desire into affection for parents as a less sadistic business for girls than for boys, and concluded that his understanding of developmental processes for girls was "unsatisfactory, incomplete and vague" (1924, p. 179).

Freud's model was essentially phallocentric, in that the psycho-sexual development of boys was his primary focus and the lens through which he understood developmental processes as a whole. This perspective led him to view the split between love and desire in men as having resulted from attachment to mother being placed in conflict with sexual rivalry with father (Freud, 1912). If this conflict was not resolved through relinquishing mother as a sexual object, the need to protect her (and subsequent loved objects) from incestuous wishes resulted in a state he described as "psychical impotence", with the consequence that "where they [men] love they do not desire and where they desire they cannot love" (p. 183). The splitting of love from sexual desire was thus associated with having failed to clear a fundamental developmental hurdle, an achievement that implied the capacity to mourn and accept the loss of the fantasy of sexually possessing the opposite sex parent and being central to an exclusive pair relationship. Mourning this loss was the precondition for enjoying a broader network of relating, where being part of a triangle neither triggered the need to divide and rule by intruding on or excluding others, nor elicited overwhelming anxiety in the self about being intruded upon or excluded by others.

Attachment theory, essentially a dyadic relational theory, offers us a different perspective on the genesis and expression of sexual desire.

While acknowledging the place of biology in the dynamics of desire, it emphasises the significance of the mother-infant rather than the parental couple in shaping and channelling its expression (although Klein [1928/1975] also located the Oedipal conflict in the nursing couple relationship between mother and infant). Attachment, caregiving and sexuality are considered from an attachment perspective to be different but inter-linked systems of behaviour that are essential components of romantic love (Mikulincer & Goodman, 2006). But they are not necessarily compatible with each other. Attachment behaviour is motivated by the need for comfort and reassurance in the face of a perceived threat. When activated it overrides curiosity, the wish to explore, the desire to share with and the capacity to care for others. What's needed in this context to deal with a sense of threat does not sit easily with the relaxed sensuality that makes for a satisfying sexual encounter.

A further problem is that attachment, caregiving and sexual behaviour can look like and become confused with each other. Each implies a certain level of intimacy, and it may be that the heightened arousal of affect associated with intimate encounters decreases the capacity to read our own motivations and those of others accurately. In these circumstances sex may be used in the service of meeting attachment needs or for providing a caring response: discerning between the wish for a reassuring hug and a sexual invitation may then be difficult to gauge.

In contrast to Freud, attachment theorists understand the split between love and desire not in terms of unresolved incestuous wishes, but as the failure to integrate and distinguish between attachment and sexual systems of behaviour that can be at odds with each other. Eagle (2007, p. 34) writes:

> One needs one's spouse or romantic partner, as one's attachment figure, to be familiar, predictable, and available. Yet there is a good deal of evidence that predictability, familiarity and availability frequently dampen the intensity of sexual interest and excitement. Thus, I am suggesting that, apart from any consideration of incest wishes, the antagonism between the attachment and sexual systems goes some way toward accounting for the split between love and desire, which, I propose, is essentially a split between attachment and sexuality.

Attachment theory is rooted in closely observed studies of mothers and infants. This focus on the earliest dyadic relationship provides a basis for the proposition that the relationship between mother and infant forms the prototype for thinking about couple intimacy, including sexual intimacy, in adult life. The parallels are not difficult to draw. The importance of eye contact and the special gaze is characteristic of nursing and erotic relationships alike, as is the "baby-talk" that denotes a special and exclusive kind of intimate connection. The close, physical, skin-to-skin contact between a mother and her baby is replicated by the entwined bodies of lovers. And the reciprocal sensitivity to mood that creates encounters in which interpersonal boundaries can dissolve and reform travels across both relationship domains.

So, it has been argued, if a child grows up with the experience of being securely attached to his or her primary parent, there will be room for the pleasurable anticipation of ultimate gratification, even if this is delayed (Messler-Davies, 2005). Having confidence in someone who can be relied upon to be both available and responsive creates room for feelings of sexual desire. For lovers, as for infants and their parents, we might extend the argument and suggest that the security they feel within themselves and in their relationship allows time for desire to be kindled together and developed between them, while also affording protection against any accompanying feelings of anxiety or apprehension about becoming lost in each other. The delays, disruptions and separations that are a part of emotional and erotic encounters do not threaten rejection or a frustrating withdrawal but add an enticing frisson to the experience of desire, there being confidence about eventual sexual consummation and the relief of tension associated with it. In an erotic context this has been described as the "sexuality of hope", and contrasted with the "sexuality of despair" (Laschinger, Purnell, Schwartz, White, & Wingfield, 2004), applying to the sexual relationship Bowlby's (1973) distinction between "the anger of hope" and the "anger of despair" (hopeful protest engaging the parent, despairing protest entrenching resentment about repeated failures to do so). The "sexuality of hope" is built on cycles of arousal and soothing during infancy that create confidence that intense need states will be satisfied, allowing pleasure to be extracted from the frustration associated with arousal through the anticipation of eventual relief.

This contrasts with the child or adult who has grown up insecurely attached. Here there is not the same level of confidence about how available and responsive others will be. Consequently the young child, and later adult, will develop strategies for managing the arousal of his or her need states, and the feelings that accompany them, in ways that aim to protect against the disappointment, frustration and rejection that is predicted to follow. And if relational experiences have been sufficiently traumatic to hamper the development of an organised strategy for managing attachment conflicts, it may be particularly difficult to know about, never mind give expression to, such arousal. Abstinence, promiscuity, one-night stands, sexual coercion and cybersex are behaviours that can all be understood in terms of attachment-related anxieties. Mikulincer and Shaver (2007), in their wide-ranging review of attachment in adulthood, provide empirical support for the relevance of attachment conflicts to behaviour in the sexual arena. While attachment security allows freedom to play with, explore and co-create sexual experiences within a relationship, they found attachment insecurity to be associated with both confusing and rigidifying the boundary between sex and attachment: anxious attachment assimilating sexual desire within, and avoidant attachment disconnecting it from, the hunger for love, acceptance and security.

Behavioural differences associated with insecure attachment have been linked with "pretend" and "psychic equivalence" states of mind (Fonagy & Target, 1997). Both these modes are concerned with the relationship between inner and outer realities, and describe processes in which there is no or very limited capacity either to distinguish or test the difference between the two. Pretend functioning, associated with avoidance, denotes a retreat from engaging with the world by defining involvement in terms of relationships of detached control. In this state of mind the world is how *I* choose to define it. Psychic-equivalence functioning, associated with anxious-ambivalence, denotes a tendency to equate internal and external realities as if they are one and the same. In this state of mind outer realities are infused with internal states that may be experienced as outside the self: the world may then come to seem how *you* choose to define it. We might expect that the psychic equivalence mode of relating makes people susceptible to being incorporated into the sexual behaviour and fantasies of others who are important to them, making them vulnerable, whereas "pretend" modes of relating may set the rules of play in order to create a sense of invulnerability. Each mode can be distinguished from the capacity to "mentalize" (Fonagy, Gergely, Jurist, & Target,

2002): to know about and draw distinctions between different emotional realities inside and outside the self, and to reflect upon connections between them.

Neither "pretend" nor "psychic equivalence" modes of relating are pathological in themselves. Imaginative games in childhood – and their adult expression in, for example, the performing arts – are accepted as potentially healthy ways of fostering development through playing with reality. Wright (2009) argues that throughout life we turn to art, religion and theatre to mirror and give form to our emotional experience – we search, as do infants, for experiences outside ourselves that resonate with our own. Through these channels we engage with our own internal worlds of fantasy relationships, and we enter into those of others. Only when the boundary between internal and external realities is rigidified or removed does playful relating convert into defensive non-interacting. Attachment security is highly relevant to bounding these modes of relating.

An illustration

Frédéric Fonteyne's film *Une Liaison Pornographique* (Fonteyne, 1999) illuminates the tension between physical desire and emotional involvement – between sex and attachment – through depicting the relationship between two characters called, simply, "Elle" and "Lui". The film opens with Elle speaking retrospectively to an off-camera interviewer (therapist?) about placing an advert in a "lad's" magazine for someone with whom she could enact her sexual fantasy. We then see Lui showing this advert to the same unseen interviewer (at a separate meeting), which he would have the interviewer believe he has kept less as a souvenir of the relationship than as a trophy of sexual conquest.

The film moves into showing how their relationship started and developed, using a voice-over device that allows the audience access to what each partner is thinking as well as saying to the other. She describes her first impression of him: "He was smiling. He has a lovely smile. His eyes crinkle up and his whole face seems to smile." For him there was a similar but less detailed account of his initial attraction to her: "Her expression had something special." She finishes her coffee and tells him she has booked a room in a nearby hotel. He's disconcerted, and orders a brandy. She asks if he's OK. He queries whether she's thinking he might be ill. She says she's asking if he likes her. He doesn't answer, instead trying to assert his position by asking if she's done this kind of thing before. She makes a humorous digression about having gone with an Italian and feeling cheated because she'd wanted a hairy man and he was smooth. She playfully asks where he's from and is he hairy. Spain, he answers, and, yes, he has hair on his body. He gets the bill, and they go to the hotel where he checks in and pays for them both.

As with every first encounter negotiations are going on at multiple levels. There are implicit communications contained in their facial expressions accounting for their unthought initial attraction to each other, a certain amount of skirmishing around whether it was safe to express this attraction between them and who was to take the risk of doing so, her parrying his anxiety that she might be predatory by reassuring him with humour about her interest in the externals of hair (and not the internals of heart?). And then there is his use of withholding information and taking financial control to establish a balance of power between them in which he can feel in charge. Preceding these implicit negotiations is the explicit understanding that their relationship is to be purely sexual and kept in a compartment quite separate from the rest of their lives. It is to exist only within a tightly circumscribed time and place. This is their implicit contract, their "pretend" relationship, designed, perhaps, as a defence against their shared fear of becoming emotionally involved.

Cutting back to the interview, and following their first sexual experience of each other, Elle is asked, in effect, "how was it for you?". She thinks for a moment before saying "very, very, very good". Asked about what they did together she refuses to say, making clear her reason is not to do with prudishness but because this was something private between them: "an affair of the heart". Asked the same question Lui is less sure about how it was, but says it was OK. He, too, declines to go into detail. What is striking is how different they appear as they look back on their relationship in comparison to how they appeared at the time it was taking place: her hair has changed from being very fair with him to dark, almost black, as she recalls the experience. From being facially hairless when they were together, Lui now sports a trimmed moustache and beard. Perhaps hair was, after all, an important litmus test of how much they brought of themselves to their relationship, and what they took from each other. Which, we are tempted to ask, is the real Elle and Lui?

When the couple next meets he suggests they go for a drink and have dinner together. This they do, and her voice-over describes her wonder at sensing she has known him for ever, finding how easy it is for her to open herself up to him. She recasts the story of Adam and Eve as they talk together: two people discovering each other, naked, in the snow. Eve falls over on her back and her rump becomes red and raw. He rubs her body to warm her up and in doing so becomes sexually aroused, which leads to them having sex. The story is like a dream sequence, and can be seen as being about the two of them, a dream that introduces warmth as the precursor to sex, not the other way round. The terms of their contract is shifting: their relationship was supposed to be restricted to sex, the implicit rule was that there should be "no mention of our lives". She proposes they go to the hotel and start over as if for the first time. Afterwards he offers her a lift home. She pauses, clearly tempted to accept, but then says she thinks a taxi best. Once again they part, merging into the anonymity of the crowd. As she reminisces with the interviewer she recalls "getting used to him: his face, his body, his voice", and there is a sadness as she tells him that the relationship lasted only three to four months. For Lui, the estimate was six months, but he discloses nothing about how he feels about this.

At their next meeting and over dinner she proposes going to the hotel, asking: "What if we made love?". "Have sex", he queries? "No", she replies, "made love normally". He gets caught up with whether she is talking about the missionary position, and she says she wants to be on top. This time they are more exposed in their vulnerability. She needs to orgasm under the sheets so he doesn't see the uncontrolled "grimace" of ecstasy in her face. He is surprised and anxious about the excitement generated for her by being "on top". For her the sex is perfect and mutual. For him there is anxiety; her excitement triggers something in his performance that he apologises for – whether premature ejaculation or inhibited orgasm is left unclear to the viewer. For her it doesn't matter. She is emotional, but her tears disconcert him. She can't explain them, saying only that she feels lost, not knowing where she is with herself.

When they next meet he is very late and she tetchy, being on the verge of leaving their café meeting point. He is brusque with her about why she left him the way she did. They have angry sex, and each is non-committal about the next meeting. But as she leaves him to descend the subway he apprehends losing her and races after her, knowing he has no contact details or way of reaching her if she decides not to show up in the future. He fails to find her.

Attachment, sexuality and mirroring 203

When they next meet he's early and she's late. Both are anxious, and passionately engage with each other. They are interrupted by an old man trying to get into their room, claiming it belongs to him. Lui redirects him down the hotel corridor and are about to resume making love when they hear a noise outside their room and find the man slumped on the floor. The emergency services are summoned, and while they wait with him he is desperate to convey that he doesn't want his wife contacted. He says he has been killing her for 40 years, that he can't stand her, but doesn't want her to know of his plight. He takes his wedding ring off and gives it to Lui. They follow the ambulance to the hospital and discover the medical orderlies have found his wife's contact details and been in touch with her. This woman, who has a name, Madame Lignaux, comes to the hospital in distress, telling them she has been left by her husband for other women many times. "I don't need his presence", she says to them, "only to know he's alive". For all his running after others she knows he ultimately comes back to her, but this time she fears she might irretrievably lose him. She says she would not survive that; she would kill herself, because she couldn't live without him.

Elle and Lui leave the hospital. He offers her a lift, but she declines. He reassures her that Madame Lignaux won't kill herself, but at their next meeting she is reading the paper announcing her suicide. Elle tells him she doesn't want to go to the hotel this time but just have his company. As they talk she risks declaring her love for him. He is moved to tears, but can't reciprocate. They go to the hotel and share a bath. There is warmth and intimacy between them as they face the question: "What will happen to us?"

Their next meeting is a visual master class in portraying how attachment insecurity creates the conditions for catastrophic misunderstanding, as each partner fatally misreads the other's desire. From their voice-overs we learn that they both have accepted inside themselves that they love each other and want to be together. They gaze into each other's eyes for signs of how this message will be received. They have both decided to stay together, but when Elle momentarily breaks eye contact Lui misinterprets this to mean she wants to break off their relationship but is having difficulty telling him. We "hear" him thinking: "I was in love ... and then I knew. She didn't want to. She wanted to stop. She hadn't said anything but it was obvious. I could read her face." So he decides to help her and says: "Between the two of us ... it won't work." "No", she replies, almost without registering what he is saying, and he reinforces the message he thinks she wants to hear, which is that they will only end up hating each other. We then are made privy to her thoughts:

> I had decided to stay with him. But when he said the two of us wouldn't work it seemed obvious. He was right. We had to split up. I could see that he wanted to stop it. So I wanted that too.

How far they had come from "pretending" through sex to finding themselves in a state that might best be described as mutual "psychic equivalence"!

In his reflections about the film, Sabbadini (2009) considers three themes of psychoanalytic interest: the relationships between erotic and loving feelings, the Oedipal dynamics in every passionate couple relationship that contains an implicit, if not explicit, unconscious fantasy of excluding a "third" and the narcissistically idealised and fused relationship state that accompanies falling in love. For my purposes I am most interested in the second of these: his observation that the viewer of the film is the excluded third, tantalised by the nature of the sexual fantasy and what goes on in the hotel bedroom but denied access to both. He comments: "... much as the film excludes its audience from their secret, Lui and Elle deliberately deprive each other of those fragments of identity (name, age, marital status, job) which, as they rightly suspect, could only interfere with their fantasies" (p. 1445). This absence, he comments, may have been a necessary ingredient of their sexual desire.

Mirroring and sexuality

It is to the significance of absence in the mirroring of sexual desire that I now want to focus attention. While Fonteyne's film allows us to hear something of how Elle and Lui represent their relationship, it provides us with no information about their developmental histories. We can only observe their behaviour, listen to their thoughts and speculate about the significance of the real world through their responses to the intrusion of a less than idealised depiction of a married future upon their fantasy relationship. We might infer the attachment status of the two partners and how this influenced their way of being as a couple, but we cannot chart the developmental processes that might explain how their state of mind in relation to attachment came about.

For this we need developmental theory. I have been drawn to the construct Winnicott (1967) offered in describing the "mirror" role parents and caregivers play for infants and its relevance to the therapeutic process (Clulow, 2014), and now want to consider what relevance this might have for the generation and expression of desire. Winnicott proposed that infants discover their own emotional experience in their mother's face because what she looks like is related to what she sees in her infant's face. Not only does the mother provide her infant with physical, bodily holding, she also "holds" her infant's affective experience, and so contributes to shaping her infant's existential sense of self: "When I look I am seen, therefore I exist" (ibid., p. 114).

Mirroring is a less-than-perfect term for what goes on in this process except, perhaps, in its pathological form. It captures insufficiently the two-way co-construction of the mirroring process and implies that the mother offers an exact, if reverse, reflection of the infant's expression. It restricts the medium of holding and reflecting experience to facial expression when tracking changes in excitement and arousal, something that Stern (1985) amongst others has extended to include other pre-verbal forms of communication – for example, the earliest language of "motherese". It also overlooks the importance of touch, and the tactile sense of holding and being held – an experience from infancy that is recovered in adult life in couple relationships, especially through sex. Nevertheless, Winnicott's perspective offers a window on how early relationships shape the mind. What the mother does, in the best of all worlds, is to read accurately the cues of her baby and to respond in ways that are in tune with the baby's internal state, but not in ways that replicate it. When her responses are in tune with the infant's gestures they are said to be "contingent" (attuned), but what she also does is to "mark" (differentiate) her responses, so that a distinction is drawn between what belongs to her and what belongs to her baby (Gergely & Watson, 1996). Her success (or otherwise) in accurately reading and appropriately bounding that experience has been associated with different patterns of attachment: secure attachment is associated with contingent and marked mirroring; insecure avoidant attachment with low contingency and high marking; insecure anxious-ambivalent attachment with high contingency and low marking.

If mirroring is a vital conduit through which infants come to know their own feelings and mind (as Winnicott proposed and many child development studies would affirm), it is reasonable to assume that it is highly relevant to laying the foundations for integrating sexual feelings within the self. This is territory that Target (2007) and Fonagy (2008) have explored. They note that signs of genital arousal are visible in boys from infancy, and even prenatally, but that it is unlikely that the infant's experience is what adults would describe as sexual desire. Their feelings are more likely to be ones of pleasurable sensuality. However, they may evoke reactions from parents that imply that what they are seeing in the genital arousal of their offspring is sexual arousal. Target and Fonagy note that, while most mothers are aware of genital arousal in their infants, especially in boys, they are likely to ignore or turn away from it. This turning away is in marked contrast to how they respond to other emotional states they perceive in their infants. Their evidence is drawn from a survey of mothers' responses to the expression of emotions from infants aged 3–6 months, and, more generally, from the absence of references to sexual arousal in infant observation studies.

What Winnicott highlighted as an important process in the psychogenesis of disorders was that when mirroring is inaccurate or unmarked, or both, the infant sees in the mother's response, and subsequently internalises as part of the developing self, not his or her own experience but a mismatched or amplified mental state belonging to the mother. Sensual excitement, when associated with genital arousal for the parent, may become associated in the infant's mind with a sense of loss and absence if the parent turns away. The experience of absence becomes what is internalised instead of an accurately mirrored sensuality. Sexual desire and absence become interlocked with each other, and the quest becomes one of finding that lost experience in others. The recovery of sensual-cum-sexual feelings through evoking desire in others is then the means through which these feelings become recognised and integrated into the self.

There is a brief passage in Fonteyne's film that might be viewed as illustrating this process. In one sequence we hear, through her voice-over, Elle's wonderment at how awareness of her partner's sexual desire for her arouses her own desire: "a man looking at you, you feel his desire, and then – the strangest thing – you feel desire for him". Whether we understand this as identifying with her partner's emotional state, as projective identification of the partner's feeling elicited in her or as an empathic response triggered by the firing of mirror neurones is something to debate, but what we are clearly observing is an intersubjective phenomenon.

I am intrigued yet unsure about Fonagy and Target's extrapolation of Winnicott's ideas to psycho-sexual development, although my hesitation raises a challenging question: why should I exclude this part of emotional development from a theory that, for me, passes the test of clinical utility in relation to other areas of emotional development? My doubt comes from an impression that in clinical situations we are more likely to see the consequences of intrusion, not absence, in the mirroring of infant sensuality. If parents sexualise the early sensuous experiences of their infants (i.e., fail to "mark" or distinguish the infant's state from their own) and respond with excessive interest, fear or disgust about their bodily indications of sensory excitement (the opposite to turning away), the infant may then internalise not their own experience but the unprocessed sexuality of their parents, an alien object that needs defending against.

How might infants be protected from the enigma of "unconscious maternal seduction" (Laplanche, 1995)? Diamond and Yeomans (2007) suggest that the parental couple may affect mirroring processes from the outset of life, returning us to the relevance of the Oedipal triangle for psycho-sexual developmental outcomes. They refer to research that shows that, as pregnancy develops, a mother's representation of the foetus is associated with her representation of her partner. They argue that fathers, or other "third parties", have an impact from the outset of an infant's life through being in the mother's mind. This has relevance to thinking about mirroring processes: if there is no "third" presence in the mother's mind, might she be more vulnerable to unconsciously seducing her infant by mirroring her own experience rather than that of her infant? The modulating presence of a partner might allow enough separation between mother and infant for the infant to develop his own sensual imagination, providing that the separation is not so extreme as to impoverish the infant through removing the mother's attuned responsiveness. In adult life sensual impoverishment or over-stimulus may have the effect of inhibiting or enacting the expression of feelings of sexual desire.

Lichtenberg (2007) helps mark the distinction between infantile sensuality and sexuality by focusing attention on the earliest experiences of body-to-body contact – sucking, touching, holding, stroking and so on – that are essentially sensual experiences for the infant. These, he argues, form the platform upon which later sexuality can be developed. Adult sexuality then rests on the bed of infant sensuality and not, as Freud postulated, on resolving Oedipal conflicts surrounding an innate sexual impulse. His attention is on the role shame plays in socialising infants, curbing the expression of their sensuous excitement within bounds that are parentally and culturally defined. Shame down-regulates affective experience by signalling disapproval. Disapproval labels the infant's experience, and if prohibitions are not handled sensitively can convert pleasurable experiences into something wilful, naughty, disgusting or humiliating. The platform of sensuality on which sexuality is subsequently built is then compromised, distorted and incomplete.

There is some empirical (as distinct from clinical) evidence linking tactile caregiving with sexual relating. A Canadian study investigating the interrelationship of attachment, caregiving and sexual systems in adulthood found that couples at ease with each other in a tactile sense were more likely than others to be satisfied with their sexual relationship (Péloquin, Brassard, Lafontaine, & Shaver, 2014). Examining four dimensions of caregiving (proximity, sensitivity, control and compulsive caregiving) in both community and clinical samples they singled out the mediating role of proximity for all three behavioural systems, concluding "a caregiver's willingness to be close helps satisfy a partner's attachment needs for closeness … Physical proximity in the context of couple relationships also seems to foster emotional closeness and sexual interest, contact and intimacy in partners" (p. 573). Of course, the direction of flow might run in the opposite direction (sexual fulfilment supporting caregiving proximity), but it is likely that there will be mutuality, not uni-directionality, in the processes that link the expression of sensuality and sexuality.

Implications for therapy

What might all this mean for couple therapists working with sexual problems from a psychoanalytic perspective? In this chapter I have explored intersubjective aspects of sexuality, and particularly the developmental significance of close relationships for coming to identify and integrate emotional experience within the self. In working with couples I have been influenced by Winnicott's (1967) description of the therapeutic process, which is very much in terms of the therapist's role in mirroring affective experience:

This glimpse of the baby's and child's seeing the self in the mother's face, and afterwards in a mirror, gives a way of looking at analysis and at the psychotherapeutic task. Psychotherapy is not making clever and apt interpretations; by and large it is a long term giving back what the patient brings. It is a complex derivative of the face that reflects what is there to be seen.

(p. 117)

But how relevant is this to working with sexual problems?

Winnicott's description alerts us to how important the therapist's responses are for positive therapeutic outcomes, especially their capacity to cue into implicit, non-verbal communications. Psychoanalytic psychotherapy relies heavily on language to convey emotional attunement and to delineate experience, and this is often very effective (Shedler, 2010). But communication does not rely solely on language but on an array of signals conveyed through behaviour, body language, eye contact and so on. There are times when the language of interpretation can be inadequate to the task of addressing some conditions, perhaps not least disorders of sexual desire. Is this because we turn away from sexuality in mirroring the experience of our patients? While parents need to be attuned to the sensual experiences of their infants and not convert them into sexuality, maybe we, in managing this dilemma prefer, in Colman's (2009) terms, to interpret away from sexuality and towards sensuality? Perhaps we need to recalibrate our sensitivity to sexual feelings in the consulting room, and to reconnect bodies and minds in our therapeutic techniques for addressing sexual problems as sensate focus techniques attempt to do (Pacey, 2014)?

Attachment theory was conceived in the cradle of infant–parent relationships. It has extended its application to couple relationships. The challenge is now to mine the rich seam of theory and research it has generated to inform therapeutic practice with couples, especially in connection with their unique bond of sexuality. The implications for doing this are unlikely to require a new mode of practice; they are more likely to involve making adjustments of degree than of kind to existing practices. With this in mind I conclude with some broad pointers for therapeutic practice, not new in themselves, but offered in the spirit of refreshing the ways we already think about how to involve ourselves with couples:

- The first task of any therapy is to build the therapeutic alliance – in attachment terms, to build the therapeutic relationship as both a safe haven and secure base from which partners might explore their own and each other's experiences. This involves balancing support and challenge in the way interventions are made to maintain optimal levels of anxiety – high enough to evoke curiosity, but not so high as to raise attachment anxieties that close down the capacity to reflect on experience.
- We are never free agents in this, as therapy is always an experience that is co-created by couples and therapists.
- For couple therapy an important aim is to increase the capacity of the couple relationship to act as a safe haven and secure base for the partners, containing their anxieties and enabling them to weather the storms of life and learn from them. The therapist's task is then to work with the psychological skin around the couple, making their relationship, rather than either of the partners, the principal focus of attention and the site for change.
- Success in doing this provides a platform for exploring how partners' represent their relationships, the shared unconscious phantasies and beliefs that drive these representations, and the function they serve in regulating emotions. In this process the therapist strives to become attuned to the key emotional communications of the couple, not least in the context of the transference, and to offer something back that mirrors their reality.
- The mirroring role of the therapist involves providing something related to but separate from the couple's experience ("contingent" and "marked"), creating room for that experience to be engaged with, reworked and ultimately re-presented. This also applies to how therapists work with partners to help them mirror (in both contingent and marked ways) their separate experiences.
- Eliciting and testing the ways partners represent their relationship, and themselves in it, is an important part of the work. These narratives signal their identity and contain the unconscious assumptions that shape their interactions with each other. They also have a significant role in regulating affect. As representations change, so will the feelings associated with them, creating pathways for the affective life of the couple to change.
- Sometimes language may be insufficient in this process, and embodied enactments may be needed to generate different experiences. Sex

is a somatic part of the couple relationship that can be resistant to "top-down" cortical processing, requiring instead (or as well as) "bottom-up" techniques that allow couples literally to "come to their senses", learning about themselves through increasing sensory awareness in their bodies (Le Doux, 1996).

- Embodied therapeutic enactments are most likely to be effective when a context of trust and meaning has been established, taking us back full circle to the secure base function of the therapy and couple relationships, where affect can both be experienced and thought about.

References

Bowlby, J. (1973). *Attachment and Loss: Separation*. London: Hogarth Press.

Clulow, C. (2014). Attachment, affect regulation and couple psychotherapy. In D. Scharff & J. Savege Scharff (Eds.) *Psychoanalytic Couple Therapy: Foundations of Theory and Practice*. London: Karnac.

Clulow, C. & Boerma, M. (2009). Dynamics and disorders of sexual desire. In C. Clulow (Ed.) *Sex, Attachment and Couple Psychotherapy*. London: Karnac.

Colman, W. (2009). What do we mean by "sex"? In C. Clulow (Ed.) *Sex, Attachment and Couple Psychotherapy*. London: Karnac.

Diamond, D. & Yeoman, F. (2007). Oedipal love and conflict in the transference/countertransference matrix: Its impact on attachment security and mentalization. In D. Diamond, S. Blatt & J. Lichtenberg (Eds.) *Attachment and Sexuality*. New York, Analytic Press.

Eagle, M. (2007). Attachment and sexuality. In D. Diamond, S. Blatt and J. Lichtenberg (Eds.) *Attachment and Sexuality*. New York, Analytic Press.

Fonagy, P. (2008). A genuinely developmental theory of sexual enjoyment and its implications for psychoanalytic technique. *Journal of the American Psychoanalytic Association*, 56: 11–36.

Fonagy, P. & Target, M. (1997). Attachment and reflective function: Their role in self-organisation. *Development and Psychopathology*, 9: 679–700.

Fonagy, P., Gergely, G., Jurist, E. & Target, M. (2002). *Affect Regulation, Mentalization, and the Development of the Self*. New York: Other Press.

Fonteyne, F. (Director). (1999). *Une Liaison Pornographique* [Film]. France: Artemis Productions.

Freud, S. (1912). *On the Universal Tendency to Debasement in the Sphere of Love*. SE, 11 (pp. 177–190). London: Hogarth Press.

Freud, S. (1924). *The Dissolution of the Oedipus Complex*. SE, 19 (pp. 173–182). London: Hogarth Press.

Gergely, G. & Watson, J. (1996). The social bio-feedback theory of parental affect-mirroring. *International Journal of Psycho-Analysis*, 77: 181–212.

Glasser, M. (1979). Aggression and sadism in the perversions. In I. Rosen (Ed.) *Sexual Deviation*. London: Oxford University Press.

Kahr, B. (2009). Psychoanalysis and sexpertise. In C. Clulow (Ed.) *Sex, Attachment and Couple Psychotherapy*. London: Karnac.

Klein, M. (1928). Early stages of the Oedipus conflict. *International Journal of Psycho-Analysis*, 9: 167–180. [Reprinted in *Love, Guilt and Reparation*. London: Hogarth Press, 1975].

Laplanche, J. (1995). Seduction, persecution, revelation. *International Journal of Psycho-Analysis*, 49: 1–19.

Laschinger, B., Purnell, C., Schwartz, J., White, K. & Wingfield, R. (2004). Sexuality and attachment from a clinical point of view. *Attachment and Human Development*, 6: 151–164.

Le Doux, J. (1996). *The Emotional Brain: The Mysterious Underpinnings of Emotional Life*. New York: Simon and Schuster.

Lichtenberg, J. (2007). *Sensuality and Sexuality across the Divide of Shame*. London: Karnac.

Messler-Davies, J. (2005). The times we sizzle and the times we sigh: The multiple erotics of arousal, anticipation and release. In K. White (Ed.) *Attachment and Sexuality in Clinical Practice*. London: Karnac.

Mikulincer, M. & Goodman, G. (2006). *Dynamics of Romantic Love*. New York: Guilford.

Mikulincer, M. & Shaver, P. (2007). *Attachment in Adulthood. Structure, Dynamics and Change*. New York: Guilford Press.

Pacey, S. (2014). Personal communication.

Panksepp, J. (1998). *Affective Neuroscience, The Foundations of Human and Animal Emotions*. Oxford: Oxford University Press.

Péloquin, K., Brassard, A., Lafontaine, M. & Shaver, P. (2014). Sexuality examined through the lens of attachment theory: Attachment, caregiving, and sexual satisfaction. *Journal of Sex Research*, 51(5): 561–576.

Phillips, A. (2005). *Sane Sex*. London: Faber & Faber.

Sabbadini, A. (2009). Between physical desire and emotional involvement: Reflections on Frédéric Fonteyne's film *Une Liaison Pornographique*. *International Journal of Psycho-Analysis*, 90: 1441–1447.

Shedler, J. (2010). The efficacy of psychodynamic psychotherapy. *American Psychologist*, 65(2): 98–109.

Stern, D. (1985). *The Interpersonal World of the Infant. A View from Psychoanalysis and Developmental Psychology*. New York, Basic Books.

Target, M. (2007). Is our sexuality our own? A developmental model of sexuality based on early affect mirroring. *British Journal of Psychotherapy*, 23(4): 517–530.

Winnicott, D. (1967). Mirror role of mother and family in child development. In D.W. Winnicott (1971). *Playing and Reality*. London: Tavistock.

Wright, K. (2009). *Mirroring and Attunement. Self-Realization in Psychoanalysis and Art*. London: Routledge.

Chapter 13

Discussion of "How was it for you? Attachment, sexuality and mirroring in couple relationships"

Leora Benioff

Christopher Clulow has done a wonderful job of highlighting some of the many technical dilemmas and poorly understood areas we face when contending with sexual difficulties in a couple. His chapter suggests that a split between safety and desire is at the base of some difficulties. In my discussion I am going to highlight some ways one might extend these ideas, as well as alternative ways of thinking that may shed light on the topic. Clulow also deftly illustrates some of the technical challenges we face when treating a couple functioning in the psychic equivalence position.

From Freud's (1925/1955) unanswered question – *What does a woman want?* – we have moved as couple therapists to asking, perhaps with the same puzzled frustration, *What do people want?* Do they want, Clulow asks, closeness, safety, reliability, and comfort? Or do they want danger, unpredictability, and excitement?

Are these mutually incompatible? Clulow implicitly reminds us of the essential notion that a couple who locates the lack of desire in one partner is often unconsciously fending off something as a couple. As we all so commonly experience clinically, in such couples rebirth of desire in the dormant partner often leads to loss of desire in the desiring but frustrated partner. Obviously, more is going on here than just difficulties with desire.

Desire and sexuality are unruly, capricious, resistant to conscious control, and always threaten to undermine our ideal views of ourselves and our partners. As individual and couple therapists, looking at excitement and desire plunges us into the worlds of unconscious phantasy, transgression, surprise, and enigma.

Clulow begins by using attachment theory to address the struggles with accessing desire in intimate relationships. He suggests a dichotomy between attachment behavior and sexual desire. Attachment behavior, since it is motivated by the fear of loss of the object, strives either to remain in contact or to defend against awareness of the impossibility of contact, and thus becomes antithetical to desire and sexual feelings. To desire means to become aware of absence. To tolerate desire you have to tolerate knowing you do not possess the object. In a way, lack of desire is a version of a defense against dependency, separateness, and envy. To desire means recognizing that (a) you are separate from the object of your desire, (b) you cannot control the object of your desire, and (c) you need something good outside of yourself.

Clulow is suggesting that some couples who are unable to manage desire in an intimate relationship may be unable to tolerate the underlying separateness and loss that desire involves being in contact with. Some people defend against this sense of loss by manically creating a sense that they do not need anything outside of themselves, manically denying separateness and the unknowability of one's partner, or by defensive deadening, as though too much feeling or contact with sensation is itself too disruptive to bear. This perhaps accounts for the retrospective idealization couples often fall prey to when thinking of the "easy sexuality" at the beginning of their relationships. In fact, early "untroubled" mutual desire may be a defense against the anxieties of not knowing each other, and of not yet being in true emotional contact.

This view holds something in common with Stephen Mitchell's ideas on this topic. In his 2002 book *Can Love Last?*, written to investigate this very question of why sexual desire is so apparently difficult to maintain in an intimate relationship, Mitchell suggests that the difficulty may be the opposite of how we conceive of it. Like Clulow, Mitchell emphasizes the primary importance of experiencing intimate relationships as safe and secure (p. 49). In order to feel safe, and not threatened by loss, people must come to believe that their relationships are known, predictable, and unsurprising. And, not surprisingly, such a stance deadens sexuality in many people. But what Mitchell argues is that this idea – that one's longtime partner is boring because they are so well known – is, in fact, an illusion, which might be punctured by sexual contact (p. 87). He points out that what we must all live with is the fact that our partners are never fully knowable – certainly to ourselves, or even to themselves – and that sex is inevitably full of ruptures, surprises, and otherness, as well as full of intimacy and knowing (pp. 43–45).

Thus, people defend against a scary sense of their partner's ultimate unknowability by deciding they are completely known and boring. This highlights a phenomenological component of sexual interactions that is rarely discussed. Much literature emphasizes the connected and intimate aspect of sexual contact with another. But there is a parallel level of experience: the fundamentally private nature of sexual experience, in terms of a private relationship with one's body that can never be shared. Sex is primarily non-verbal and relies heavily on projection, part-object relations, and internal unspoken phantasy (I suppose everything in life does, but sex even more so).

I once saw a couple where the woman complained of the expression on her partner's face during sex. It appeared that what bothered her was that he "became a different person; his face looked different." People do look different during sex because they are relating to bodily experiences and internal objects in a more physical and less mediated way. I think this woman's complaint highlighted the separateness and loneliness one has to tolerate to have sex. Possibly what she was overwhelmed by was this evidence that she and her partner did not share a mind, and that she did not really "know him inside and out."

Couples and individuals alike struggle with lack of desire and with desire: both remind people of sexuality's essentially unruly and not consciously controllable nature. Sexuality reminds us of the unconscious and unknowable aspects of ourselves, as it arises within us but appears outside of our will and conscious choice. No one can consciously change or create the objects or fantasies that excite or deaden. No couple experiences sexuality as a purely subject-to-subject encounter, devoid of part-object relations and unconscious excitations. To think about this a bit, and then extend its implications to couple work, it is useful to take a look at other visions of the genesis of sexual desire. Jean Laplanche, Ruth Stein, and Jessica Benjamin all grapple with the unruly and essential "otherness" of sexuality and desire.

Laplanche and Pontalis (1973) described an infant developing sexuality through contact with the enigmatic (unknown, unrepresented, and unconscious) sexuality of its parents, primarily the mother. Contact with the mother is infused with her sexuality and her unconscious desire. Not only is this unconscious for the mother, but adult sexuality is a world unknowable to the infant or young child. All they can experience is a sense of mystery and enigma that something is being transmitted to them that is far beyond their capacities for representation or knowing. This creates the excitement and otherness of sexuality: we live out our parents' unconscious desires, transmitted through our relationships to them.

Stein (1989) discusses sexuality in terms of excess, the unrepresented and unknown elements that create the poignancy and excitement of desire. There is always more coming toward the child than they can know or understand, but they swim in it and become imbued with it.

In attempting to understand and deconstruct what we have come to think of as "feminine passivity," Benjamin (2004) makes use of these ideas in ways that can help us understand Elle and Lui's abortive relationship. Benjamin reminds us that sexuality and the body are not only repositories for unmetabolized, unrepresented, and unmentalized experiences of self and other, but are actually developed into concrete and life-structuring foundations to contain excess that could not be symbolically represented or digested. She is particularly concerned with the experience of excess stimulation, originating in the inevitable developmental trajectory of being in contact with a parent's unconscious, but also in an interaction with an intrusive or overstimulating parent. Benjamin suggests that being the recipient of so much overstimulating "excess" leads the child to equate passivity with an uncontained and traumatized experience of receiving more than he or she can handle. In this, Benjamin moves away from Laplanche and Stein, who see excess deriving from parental unconscious erotic lives that infants "swim in" only as an inevitable, universal experience. Benjamin is concerned both with a universal type of excess and a more particular, troubling, *excess* of excess, so to speak.

Benjamin (2004) suggests that when a person experiences a fear of being overwhelmed by excess for which there is no external or internal help, they dissociate from and disavow it. There is no external containment because the excess appears to originate in the parent one would normally turn to for containment. This creates confusional states of excitement in the child, since "whose excitement" it is has become impossible to unravel. This lack of containment is associated with an extremely unpleasant, receptacle-like passivity, which becomes an experience of uncontained and overwhelming stimulation.

Benjamin suggests that in our culture, we can use gender polarity as an alternate register to manage otherwise unbearable unconscious tension. We develop a notion of feminine passivity and male activity to counterphobically disavow a fear of uncontained excess and psychically destructive over-stimulation. She suggests that:

> the feminine role is to embody the unwanted, primitively feared experience of helpless over-stimulation and to make of it an exciting invitation – one that, to the relief of both men and women, the phallus can act upon, control and structure.... [T]he catastrophe of being uncontained and overexcited – essentially unmothered – becomes gendered and signifies emasculation.... The template of femininity was constructed to hold unwanted experiences of vulnerability and helplessness and this occurs through the defensive splitting of activity and passivity.
>
> (p. 52)

It is possible that the breakdown of the relationship between Elle and Lui in the movie is unconsciously caused by their inability to tolerate a movement away from gender polarity. When he must risk vulnerability and reveal the fact that he needs something from her, which makes him passive and vulnerable, Lui constructs an idea that Elle is, in fact, not interested and rather than risk rejection by attempting to verify this, he states this as fact. This allows him to avoid the risk of rejection and also avoid any sense of the fear of excess – of the excess of stimulation that their relationship produced, despite their attempts to avoid it. To continue their relationship would have meant entering into a world of emotional excess, rather than a falsely compartmentalized and self-sufficient world.

Yet there is a hope that another way of relating to and experiencing sexuality exists. Though starting from different points, Mitchell, Laplanche, Stein, and Benjamin all describe essential unknowability, unruliness, mystery, and excess. One might then ask what it takes to bear this unknowability and enigma in a relationship. One level would involve a shared capacity to tolerate separateness without turning the other into merely a separate part-object to be used, but related to as a fully autonomous subject with its own unknowable fantasies and desires. Benjamin (2004) emphasizes the capacity to tolerate surrender and passivity, and to create a holding environment that "ensures that vulnerability will not plunge us into traumatic excess" (p. 54). But this can only occur through "awareness that strength derives not from denial but from acknowledging helplessness, damage and the overwhelming of the psyche by suffering" (p. 54).

A poorly attached or un-mirrored child (in the Winnicottian [1967] sense Clulow refers to) will not have a useful foundation built inside that would allow him or her to acknowledge or process psychic and emotional experience. Instead, the child will have to use constructions and defenses that rely on less authentic ways of being. One of these is counterphobic activity and dissociation, which is so beautifully portrayed by the cartoon couple at the beginning of Clulow's talk. The image is of a couple so dissociated from their own experience that they live only in a world of phantasy, part objects, and deadness. One partner believes he has had sex, without any apparent awareness of the actual other, who is also so separated from the experience that there is no recognition of what just happened to her own body. Neither person was actually in the bed.

Separating one's emotional and vulnerable self from one's sexual experience is a common dissociative defense against overwhelming anxiety about excess, as well as a defense against anxiety about confronting the separateness of the other. This is, in essence, one of the modern psychoanalytic ways to understand perversion. Fetishes, sexual rituals, repetitive or personally fixed masturbation or excitation fantasies are all ways we attempt to deny catastrophic anxieties, including the anxiety of excess.

Michael Parsons (2000) suggests that we consider something perverse if it is:

> anything which, first, places something between the person and the object so as to prevent a relationship based on respect for, and pleasure in, the otherness and personhood of the object, and which, second, turns that doing into an occasion for sexual excitement.
>
> (p. 46)

Yet, equally, no couple's sexuality exists that does not include the part object, the transgressive, and, thus, the slightly perverse. Separating one's emotional and vulnerable self from one's sexual experience is a common dissociative defense against overwhelming anxiety about excess, as we saw exemplified in the sad tale of Elle and Lui. They sought out anonymous sex in order to avoid the threat posed by excess and to avoid emotional contact infused with unconscious communication, but ultimately found themselves trapped by the impossibility of forging a relationship without true contact.

To summarize, we might extend attachment theory to include the unconscious world of object relations and phantasy in order to grasp the unruly, capricious nature of sexuality. Ideas about excess (normative and traumatic) and a non-idealized view of the complexities of connectivity and poignant loneliness that must be tolerated in intimate sexual contact can expand our work with couples who are trapped in sexual trouble not of their own making.

But clinical and academic words cannot capture the essence of this poignancy as well as poetry, and thus, *Misery and Splendor*, by Robert Hass (1989).

Misery and Splendor
Summoned by conscious recollection, she
would be smiling, they might be in a kitchen talking,
before or after dinner. But they are in this other room,
the window has many small panes, and they are on a couch
embracing. He holds her as tightly
as he can, she buries herself in his body.
Morning, maybe it is evening, light
is flowing through the room. Outside,
the day is slowly succeeded by night,
succeeded by day. The process wobbles wildly
and accelerates: weeks, months, years. The light in the room
does not change, so it is plain what is happening.
They are trying to become one creature,
and something will not have it. They are tender
with each other, afraid
their brief sharp cries will reconcile them to the moment
when they fall away again. So they rub against each other,
their mouths dry, then wet, then dry.
They feel themselves at the center of a powerful
and baffled will. They feel
they are an almost animal,
washed up on the shore of a world or
huddled against the gate of a garden to
which they can't admit they can never be admitted.

References

Benjamin, J. (2004). Deconstructing femininity: Understanding "passivity" and the daughter position. *Annals of Psychoanalysis*, 32: 45–57.

Freud, S. (1925/1955). Letter to Marie Bonaparte. In E. Jones, *Sigmund Freud: Life and work.* London: Hogarth Press.

Hass, R. (1989). Misery and splendor. In *Human wishes*. New York: The Ecco Press.

Laplanche, J. & Pontalis, J.B. (1973). *The language of psychoanalysis*. New York: W.W. Norton and Company.

Mitchell, S. (2002). *Can love last? The fate of romance over time.* New York: W.W. Norton and Company.

Parsons, M. (2000). Sexuality and perversion a hundred years on: Discovering what Freud discovered. *The International Journal of Psychoanalysis*, 81: 37–49.

Stein, R. (1998). The poignant, the excessive and the enigmatic in sexuality. *International Journal of Psycho-Analysis*, 79: 253–268.

Winnicott, D. (1971). Mirror role of other and family in child development. In *Playing and Reality*. London: Tavistock. (Original work published 1967.)

Chapter 14

Growing old together in mind and body

Andrew Balfour

People are living longer, our populations are aging, and many of us are now likely to reach an age that would have been considered very old a generation ago. Half of all of those born after 2007 can expect to live to over 100, and as one newspaper headline put it, "Those who are 60 now have the life of a 40-year-old from a century ago." There is no doubt that this extra time is a great opportunity; who has not looked at pictures of our parents or grandparents and said, "My goodness, they look ancient", when they were still at an age that would not now be considered old. However, as I shall discuss, this "bonus time" faces us more than ever with the truth of Freud's dictum that the "ego is first and foremost a body ego" (Freud, 1923, p. 27) and the economic and psychological consequences of this now confront us as a society and at the level of the individual, the couple, and the family on a scale never seen before. In Britain, for example, between 2010 and 2030, the number of people over 65 will increase by more than 50 per cent and the number of older people with disability or chronic illness by a similar proportion and, as a result, our National Health Service will face a huge shortfall in its annual budget (Ince, 2014).

The wish to extend life and defeat death may be, for the most part, a universal aspect of the human condition, faced as we are with the prospect of mortality. Medical science has been successful at pushing the limits of our lifespan, but the rate of human aging has not changed in thousands of years. In Greek mythology, the god Eos asked Zeus for the gift of immortality for her lover Tithonus, but, so the myth goes, she forgot to ask for eternal youth as well. Tithonus was immortal – but pretty soon he was no longer youthful and his years of immortality stretched out in endless aging. Without eternal youth, our increased longevity presents us with particular psychological challenges, such as how to tolerate the losses of our physical and mental functioning, to which we shall be increasingly exposed the longer our lives go on.

Of course, this situation is not entirely unique to our time. Freud himself was given a reprieve by life-saving surgery in 1923 and despite chronic pain made creative use of his extra years. The painter Matisse is another famous example: saved by surgery, his physical disablement gave birth to new development in his art in his last years. These men made good use of their "bonus time". Their extra years are now a commonplace experience for many of us. Given this, greater understanding of the psychological factors likely to enable us to continue engaging creatively is very important – what helps to allow us to sustain and inhabit our longer lives? What are the developmental and anti-developmental factors that we need to understand in order to navigate this landscape of later life?

To consider these questions, I will draw on a developmental model, in which early anxieties and defences, and the failures and achievements of our earliest years, are seen as very relevant to understanding how these challenges of later life will be negotiated. Of course, within psychoanalysis there are different ways of thinking about early life and its significance for our development. I shall draw particularly upon Klein's notion of "developmental positions" (1975), which captures how psychic development is not seen as static, never fully achieved, and that we oscillate between these positions throughout our lives, particularly under times of pressure, such as those that can present in old age. Klein's "paranoid-schizoid"[1] and "depressive"[2] positions are constellations of anxieties, defences, object relationships, and other feelings – and they provide a useful framework for considering how one position or another might be dominant for a couple at any particular time. As I shall discuss, for some couples and individuals, there may have been an equilibrium established earlier in their lives that doesn't hold under the weight of the difficulties of later life, in which early and more primitive anxieties may re-emerge and may expose vulnerabilities and fault lines that are the legacy of earlier times.

The resurgence of the body in old age

After a more silent period for many in younger adulthood, in old age the body asserts itself again and in later life this becomes inescapable. The novelist Penelope Lively (2014) writes from her own experience:

Doctors' surgeries and hospital waiting rooms are well stocked with those over 65; it is the old and the young who demand most attention. On a trip to (hospital) ... a couple of years ago my companions in the waiting room were seven elderly men and women, and three mothers with babies or toddlers, all of us supervised by a stern-faced security man in case we started causing trouble.... You get used to diminishment, to a body that is stalled, an impediment ... you have to come to terms with a different incarnation.

(pp. 38–39)

The facts of our limited time on earth face us, perhaps more than anything, through our experience of our bodies. The imprint of aging is on the physical body and the impact of this and its impingement upon the mind is signified by physical changes. Living longer, we are exposed more to the reality of physical aging, to age-related illness, and conditions such as dementia. Older couples are faced with aging in the mirror of their partner's physical changes and are confronted with the prospect of losing control over their bodies and with death, and these existential issues are signalled in the everyday difficulties the couple may start to face in their daily lives. How we adjust to this and find an acceptance that is enough in accord with reality is crucial. In the examples of some people, we can see a picture of hope – of later life as a time of development, of new riches, perhaps. Yet, for others, there can be a claustrophobic quality of being trapped or in flight from these pressing realities of age and what it augurs.

Awareness of death

How can we be aware of transience in a way that enhances our capacity to live, rather than filling us with despair or distancing us from immersing ourselves in life while we have it? Freud, recalling the old adage, "If you want peace get ready for war", suggests changing it to "If you want to be alive, get ready for death" (De Masi, 2004, p. 132). Yet, how difficult it is for us to be aware of this, of our existence in time, to be in a state of mind where knowledge of the fact of our death shapes our perception of time passing – this is a developmental achievement. But for some, the fact of mortality may be impossible to bear, and the anxieties of this stage of life can bring a more deadly state of depression or psychic retreat[3] from the reality of time passing into a timeless state – where death is effaced, leaving the person without internal good objects to support them and, therefore, without the resources for facing life or death. I shall return to this in the clinical case material that follows.

For Freud, the unconscious believes it is immortal – we cannot represent our non-existence in our minds, and if we imagine death, we are present as spectators at our own funeral. Yet, as Money-Kyrle (1971) points out, we are confronted in the everyday losses that make up our lives with the fact of our finitude, with the inevitability of the loss of our objects, and ourselves. These lines, from Wallace Stevens' (1954) poem "The Plain Sense of Things", to my mind convey something of the attempt to put into words our imagined non-existence:

> ... It is as if
> We had come to an end of the imagination ...
> Yet the absence of the imagination had
> Itself to be imagined. The great pond,
> The plain sense of it, without reflections, leaves,
> Mud, water like dirty glass, expressing silence ...
> (p. 503)

De Masi (2004) asks, how can we make death thinkable when it is both an unthinkable and yet also a disquieting presence in our minds? And here, I suggest, we need to include aging itself, the embodied experience of time passing, which is about loss and diminution of functioning – not only facing death, but the decline of functioning, which contains the prospect of death within it. Death is gradual, as one of my patients said, "... it isn't just switching off the light ... you see death in the little things you can't do anymore, that are lost".

Return of early anxieties

In many ways, the infant you once were you will always be, and this is as true of the older person at the end of life as it is of them in younger days – and this truth may be particularly heightened, as early anxieties can be rekindled at the end of life. T.S. Eliot (1944) wrote that in his beginning was his end (p. 13) – birth and death are coupled. In late life we may have a return of our most primitive anxieties of the dissolution or fragmentation of the self – the actual threats of old age, such as dementia, giving very real, external confirmation of such core underlying fears.

From a psychoanalytic point of view, whilst there are, of course, differences between schools, there is perhaps a consensus on the importance of the infant's early vulnerability and anxieties, and that the mother's response can have crucial long-term implications for development. For Klein, the infant is born with a terror of annihilation, whilst for Winnicott (1969), babies who experience significant environmental failure early on then carry within them through life the experience of "... the agony of disintegration. They know what it is like to be dropped, to fall forever ..." (pp. 259–260). In infancy, such terror of annihilation or disintegration was based on the infant's primitive state of physical and psychological vulnerability, and for some people late life can bring a new coinage of such anxieties. Whilst there are differences in these psychoanalytic approaches, perhaps what unites them is the understanding that what is important, in terms of the capacity of the mind to encompass this situation in old age, is how such anxieties were contained originally, in infancy. Where there have been early difficulties in dependency relationships, the threat of vulnerability and dependency in later life can be felt as a trauma to be avoided at all costs. The point here is that this is a trauma that has already happened in infancy, with the crucial difference that the infant is growing and developing with the potential for new experiences to repair things, whereas for the older person, the trajectory now is towards actual death. The question, then, is, what scope is there for development in late life? I shall return to this issue in the clinical discussions that follow.

Analysts such as Money-Kyrle (1971) and McDougall (1986) include aging and death as fundamental facts of life. As McDougall puts it: "How do we manage to bind the wounds to our narcissistic integrity caused by external realities such as the fact of aging and finally the inevitability of death?" She adds, "... most of us manage to make unstable adjustment to these realities but there is little doubt that ... in our unconscious fantasies we are all omnipotent ... externally young and immortal" (p. 9). The challenges of later life may elicit powerful infantile anxieties, and how these are experienced will depend on previously achieved developments. Here, again, I shall turn to Klein's notion of "depressive position" functioning, which crucially includes the capacity to mourn. Where such developmental achievement has been possible, and such states of mind are accessible, then there will be the possibility for more internal reparation,[4] for grieving of the losses the couple are faced with – although the limits of time remaining and the weight of loss that some have to bear in old age may test such capacities severely. Where paranoid-schizoid states dominate, then the prospect of facing death and the end of life may be predominantly persecutory, with a sense of failure, of isolation, and of being subject to demons. An example of this is Dickens's character of Scrooge, who, in his nightmares, gives us a picture of one's legacy being a torturing guilt and persecution, of Old Testament judgement and damnation.

Thinking again of the illnesses of old age, such as dementia, where there is the threat or actuality of fragmentation of the mind and body, this may be close to unconscious anxieties of fragmentation that have always been part of the internal world. The aged, declining body is a reality. We are all gripped by destructive drives, and when the body as an object of projection really is deteriorated and damaged, then inside and outside, inner phantasy and external reality may converge. This can cause particular problems, making mentalising, processing of feelings, and containment of destructiveness more difficult, and can be felt as a claustrophobic sense of being trapped with a damaged object – projected into the body – which one has attacked and damaged and which retaliates with persecuting punishment and threats to existence.

The following case examples convey how the experience of illness and deterioration of the body in old age affects the people concerned, whose varying capacities to contain their feelings and to mourn the losses they are faced with shape the way this phase of their lives unfolds. First, I will give an example of such a claustrophobic encounter for a couple with the reality of their mutual deterioration leading to a breaking down of their fragile equilibrium, increased cycles of projection, and the loss of capacity for containment in the psychiatric team around them.

Case example 1

This couple – and the problems of the psychiatric team trying to look after them – were brought to me for supervision. They had longstanding difficulties, but a more or less stable equilibrium had been maintained until the point at which there was physical deterioration and vulnerability in both of them. His brain operation and her operation and fitting of a stoma bag, which happened almost at the same time, led to an increased sense of claustrophobia at home. They showed great difficulty in tolerating close physical proximity and expressed hatred and disgust at the changes in the other partner. It seemed to be literally a case of "keep the shit away from me": Her intense humiliation and rage when, in the heat of one of their rows, which were escalating, he threw her stoma bag out of the window. They tried demarcation areas at home, creating separate domestic zones in the house – his space or hers, her kitchen, separate bathrooms – but this did not work. One was still felt to be invading the other's space: he comes into her kitchen; she invades his bathroom. It was a picture of increasingly volatile and escalating rows, an experience of claustrophobic invasion with aggression as a response, which further escalated the feeling of intrusion, takeover, and sense of dangerousness in the situation. Against this background, she put pressure on the team, demanding that the consultant should change her husband in this way or that way, and if he didn't prescribe the medication she wanted, she would ring up every day. It was very difficult for the psychiatric team to find any way of containment in the face of this barrage. As she felt more and more persecuted and out of control of her body and her mind, and as the disequilibrium between them and the cycle of projections intensified, the team felt increasingly controlled and unable to function with separate, thinking minds themselves. "We can't carry on like this", the psychiatrist said, and she could have been speaking the words of the wife, who said, "I can't live with him anymore", and began a campaign to have her husband admitted to a care home. Yet, he did not need looking after in a home, the team felt, and initially they resisted. However, the rows were escalating more and, eventually, the team decided that the best thing was to help them separate, as they saw it, by admitting him to a home.

As the physical problems had taken hold, the couple had intensified their projections into one another, trying to split off and deny these aspects of themselves by attempting to effect a physical separation from one another in his move to the home. But what was apparent was the instability of this solution, which was an attempted getaway from parts of themselves that could not be disposed of in this way. The situation of the couple was one of claustro-agoraphobia – of being trapped by bodies that were frighteningly fallible, deteriorating, and inescapable and which provoked hatred and projection – the need to get rid of these frightening, persecuting aspects of the self literally evacuated: the stoma thrown out of the window.

Opening a "window" of thought on such disturbing mental states is a difficult business, but containment – offering a receptive mind to try to take in and process such states of mind – can be very important in helping couples negotiate the challenges of late life. In this example, what is also evident in the struggle the psychiatric team experienced when faced with such powerful projections from this couple is how difficult this can be. Perhaps these two factors – the importance of containment and the difficulty of sustaining a containing mind when faced with states of physical and psychic fragmentation – are nowhere more apparent than in the emotional difficulties the couple may encounter when one partner has dementia.

Case example 2

Our awareness of the indivisibility of psyche and soma is thrown into relief by the threat of dementia, a condition where organic changes bring loss of mind. As our longevity increases, the incidence of dementia rises: one in five people over 80 develop it, and some predict that in due course 50 per cent of the population will develop dementia before they die. Statistically, the odds are very high that at least one partner in a couple may develop a dementia in late life.

What happens to such couples when one of the partners becomes ill with a deteriorating condition such as dementia? One pattern that can be observed is a "negative loop of withdrawal", where the person with dementia becomes more anxious about "getting it wrong", less able to keep up with verbal communication, and withdraws. The partner without dementia often takes over more and more, compounding the disablement of their partner, both partners becoming more emotionally out of contact with one another. There can also be the additional problem of the loss of the couple's social world, which can amplify the isolation and the claustrophobic anxieties of the couple, as they are thrown back more upon one another, with diminished external contacts. One woman described how, as the dementia progressed, they were shunned from the social life of friends.

> There is an unease and awkwardness about being with someone with Alzheimer's Disease and the people who come to visit with Martin and me has dwindled away to nothing.... People find it hard to

understand that I am strongly connected to him. ... Being wanted and supported as part of a couple is still relevant now – being recognised as linked. When I go out socially, people respond as though I am alone and don't recognise that I am part of this couple, that Martin is at home and that I have a bond with him.

Quinodoz (2014) describes the difficulty when such couples withdraw into psychic retreat, in refuge from paranoid-schizoid and depressive anxieties, and shut themselves away, no longer in communication with the outside, and emotional contact can also be lost between them. The claustrophobia of the situation can be palpable, and she writes of the need to open a window, to let air in from outside (p. 95). I would say that opening a window and "letting in air" is to express, and have a receptive mind available to take in, verbalised feelings as well as non-verbal projection, which, in the case of dementia, may increasingly replace language as the disease progresses. To hold onto communication and emotional meaning within the couple for as long as possible may help, though there are few psychological interventions available for such couples. This approach is the essence of Living Together with Dementia, an intervention that we are developing at the Tavistock Centre for Couple Relationships in London, which draws on psychoanalytic thinking and video-based approaches in order to pick up meaningful communications when they happen and to help the couple find meaning in everyday things, with the aim of increasing understanding and emotional contact between partners.

One woman with dementia vividly conveyed the strain of just managing – having to attend to ordinary, everyday things; to concentrate on not falling, on remembering, holding things together; constantly fighting against loss, fragmentation of experience, and encroaching disintegration. She told me how she has to work so hard day to day, moment by moment, to make sure she has everything and then finds that her back-up drive for her laptop is lost. She looks everywhere and then finds that her husband has found it and, worst of all, it is where it was supposed to have been. So the object is found, but she encounters her memory loss – the fragmentation of her mind, of her functioning – which is letting her down whilst she is working so hard to hold onto it. She feels rage at her husband when he is in any way felt to be critical of her, when he echoes the self-criticism that is there in her own mind. He feels he has to be very careful all of the time, walking on eggshells and, of course, he cannot maintain this. She feels shut out from the world of fast wit: increasingly, she is not part of that community of language in the same way anymore. At one session, she comments on a person on the train talking non-stop, and how she noticed the other person who was with them was shut out of the conversation. She feels shut out sometimes and also marvels at her husband's capacities; she says he seems to be doing things/thinking so fast. She told me that when he touches her softly, a physical contact that comforts her, it feels different. He was on his laptop at breakfast, typing fast, so she got out her laptop and, as she puts it, he got the message, shut his down, and pushed the lid down on her machine, touched her arm, and engaged with her. She tells me that she wonders what sort of connection animals or trees have physically with one another. Her displacement from the world of language is gradually happening more. For now, she can still express this and her awareness of her greater need for physical contact with him, for closeness.

There is a sense that they can be closer now – he says they have more intimacy than was possible when they were younger. He describes how they are together, how they hold each other physically more now. His care for her, in other intimate ways, feels to him to be a way they can be closer than they were in their youth – that he can make it up to her for his unavailability then. But things can also be more difficult between them. Some way into the work with them, he is able to talk about his aggression towards her when he is feeling most frustrated. And his experience of being able to talk about this and have his feelings taken in within the therapy seems linked to the increasing recovery of more intimacy between them.

What is interesting is the capacity of this couple, including the partner with dementia, to be in touch with loss and to find ways of thinking about and tolerating such painful feelings. What is evident is how much capacity they both brought into the situation, in terms of their ability to mourn and, hence, to stay in some emotional contact with themselves and with each other. To what extent, as the pressure of the illness increases and capacities are lost, more persecuted states of mind may begin to dominate is unclear, but my clinical impression is that, to some degree at least, this depends on how much containment can be offered by the partner without dementia. If we think of the original model of containment (Bion, 1962) for a moment, what is entailed is the taking in and processing of experience (in the original developmental model, the mother is doing this for the infant) and conveying back, in some way, that understanding – so that unmanageable experience is rendered more digestible, and can be taken back in, in a modified form. The psychoanalyst Margot Waddell (2007) points out how windows of clarity, of a briefly more integrated state, may be opened for the person with dementia when emotional contact is made through finding some way, in words or action, of conveying that understanding to them.

But this can be very difficult. It is important to recognise the tremendous challenge facing the carer and not to gloss over this or idealise what is possible. This draws our attention to the importance of the state of mind of the carer partner and their need for support and containment. They may have all kinds of feelings towards the individual with dementia in their care, apart from compassionate ones, such as resentment or hatred. These feelings might arouse tremendous guilt or anxiety and there may be a great need for help and containment with this. And yet, approaches to interventions generally do not address this more difficult area.

Changes in the couple's relationship

In a relatively healthy adult relationship, where projections are not too fixed but fluid, partners may be able to act as containers of difficult feeling for one another in a flexible way. In a relationship where one partner has a dementia, the burden will increasingly shift to the partner without dementia to act as container for their spouse. One man said, "She's always been so thoughtful ... now she shuts down – it used to be me who was the one who was more shut down ... now we are crossing over into opposite places."

But as the dementia progresses, it may not simply be that patterns get reversed or amplified, but instead that there may be a whole sea change. As the person with dementia becomes more deteriorated, not only are they unable any longer to offer containment for their partner as they may once have done, but they may also project something very persecuting into them. The carer partner may increasingly be needed to be the container in the relationship, but they are likely to be filled with their own feelings of loss, frustration, or rage, their own fears and anxieties – so it is very difficult for them to take in their partner's projections, their state of mind. One can see that the stage is set for a potentially difficult situation.

And so, as I have said, offering containment is very important. The presence of a third containing figure when things are so difficult for the couple – a therapist who is not going to judge but who will listen – can be very powerful. The model of our Living Together with Dementia project is akin to a Russian doll: the person with dementia contained by their partner, who is contained by the therapist, who has the containment of supervision. The important thing is containing the container, so to speak.

Those with personal experience of dementia may recognise the situation of coming up against concrete complaints that have a quality of perseveration – things are going missing or being taken or broken into – which, as they go on, can be wearing and feel meaningless. To return to the couple I described, the female partner complained in a repetitive way about losing what she called "her valuables", her jewellery, and her husband found the relentless perseveration of the same complaint extremely frustrating and tended to withdraw and disengage in response. Part of the work was to try to think about whether, alongside the real frustration of losing these actual objects, there may also be something else being communicated that perhaps centred around the theme of the losses they were facing together.

After some time there were shifts; for example, she started talking about the loss of her dreams: "I miss my dreams. Since the dementia, I don't remember my dreams any more. They used to be so vivid and often I would write them down … but now I can't catch hold of them." There was a lessening of the sense of her being so gripped by the more concrete, repetitive complaints and a shift to a poignant expression of her feelings about the precious things she was losing. "I can be feeling normal, and then I lose my jewellery … and it's like the dementia crashing in … it's the loss of my mind that I am seeing."

In parallel with this, he seemed to become more interested in thinking about what might be going on in his wife, to be curious about a possible meaning behind what could seem, on the face of it, to be meaningless accusations and complaints coming out of the blue. Whereas before these almost always provoked anger and frustration in him and a walling-off response – "I've just got to block it out", "… she's driving me mad" – he seemed to be able to have more space at times to take in her distress and to offer her reassurance. They began to cope with the complaints in various ways, setting a time limit in which they would look for the jewels together, which had a calming effect, and finding Perspex boxes to enable her to better see where her things were. There was also more transparent communication about the loss of her capacities and the losses within the relationship. He spoke more of what he couldn't hold onto in her: "She is the most precious thing to me and I'm frightened that soon I won't be able to find her again, even for short times." Being able to know about his own loss, and having someone talk to him about this, allowed him to be more available to her experience of loss, to contain it better. "I can't say it'll be all right, but I'll be alongside you. We'll go through it together", he said to her.

She responded, "… we are having a very open discussion now … this is the antithesis of the dementia, which makes me feel so hemmed in …". Interestingly, at this point in the work, I heard that she returned to reading novels – something she had not done since the diagnosis but which had always been important to her. Perhaps this example reflects the couple's difficulty with the loss of what is so precious, which is a sense of meaning to their actions, and conveys something of a recapturing of a meaningful narrative, if you like. In dementia, this may be fleeting and as the illness progresses, the person with dementia will be less able to do this. But if there can be kept alive a sense of the potential meaning behind behaviour or interactions, it is a reminder of the humanity of the other and helps to hold onto a sense of the person. This is important for the carer in the longer term, and for both partners in the couple, if emotional meaning can be held onto for as long as possible. My clinical experience has been that what is so crucial – even in states of cognitive loss and deterioration, as in dementia, where language is being lost and projection may increasingly replace verbal communication – is the presence of another mind to take in, to accompany. People need to be met, emotionally, by another mind and helped to make their experience thinkable.

Loss of the couple in old age

Many people in late life are no longer in couple relationships, often as a consequence of divorce or the death of their partner, and loneliness and depression are a common experience. Indeed, the incidence of loneliness in old age is an increasingly recognised problem. Perhaps the most profound loss in old age may be of a partner. How difficult to lose someone with whom you may have spent a lifetime. For some people, after such a loss, a strong internal sense of the presence of their partner may be retained. The novelist Penelope Lively (2014) writes of how her husband who has died remains a presence inside her, an inner companion: "Jack is nearly always present in my dreams. It is 12 years since he died, but at night he returns, not always recognizably himself, but a shadowy dream companion figure that I always know to be him" (p. 44). But for others, there can be an experience of feeling cut off, without inner supports, and this state of mind may be very difficult to endure, linked to depression and withdrawal in old age. I shall explore this in the following case example.

In the situation where there has been a prevalence of unresolved grief and ambivalence, and within a relationship where the projective system has been more rigid and inflexible, with the loss of the partner there may be more likelihood of experiencing profound loneliness and depression and greater difficulty in mourning and in reparative processes emerging. This would otherwise afford more of a sense of restoration of the other in the internal world, of their being experienced as an inner companion, as Lively puts it. In the following example, I shall discuss work with an individual whose husband had died a few years before she came for help and where the "ghost of the couple" was an important feature of the work with her.

Case example 3

This example of an elderly woman illustrates the situation of a psychic retreat into a state of "timelessness", which can be encountered in patients of any age, but which may become amplified as a response to facing the end of life and the limits of time remaining, signifying a retreat from the reality of loss and the vulnerabilities of the end of life and death. The work with this patient involved helping her to bear the mental pain of the limitations of time and her underlying anxiety about the state of her objects. It describes her gradual emergence out of her state of timelessness to bear more the reality of loss and guilt, becoming more in touch with her internal and external objects, and more able to face the limits of the reparation that was possible at this point in her life.

She had outlived her husband by several years. They had had a difficult marriage, and since his death she had withdrawn into a depressed state of mind. Whilst I was not doing couple therapy "beyond the grave", many will be familiar with the notion of working with the individual, but with the couple in mind. Such work with people at this point in life, where the partner has died, has particular dimensions to it, where the scope for effecting change in the actual, external relationship is gone and there can be a struggle with the question, "Is it too late?" The hope that may be part of therapeutic work with younger patients is that inner reparation leads to changes in current relationships – with an adult partner, with children. For the therapist working with older people where the partner has died, one has the "ghost of the relationship" in the room, which cannot be repaired in actuality, though, perhaps, may be in mind.

As she had encountered more and more physical difficulties, there was the sense of her feeling increasingly isolated and lonely. She said she couldn't believe what had happened to her, "… all of these things, blood pressure, pain and swelling in my feet and hands, the pain in my neck … I am a mess … everything is fragmenting". She was preoccupied with the thought that she had dementia (though psychological testing did not confirm this) and this terrified her. Her body was felt as a source of persecution and she had become, for the most part, out of contact with the people around her who could have provided some emotional companionship.

She spent a lot of time berating herself for "failing" in her marriage as well as for her ongoing failure to complete her thesis (she was currently the oldest student at the university). These thoughts dominated her mind in a repetitive way and, as I came to understand, served to disallow any real thinking about her relationship with her husband and her current situation with important people in her life. From the start of the work, I was struck by the internal pressure upon her to cut off from her vulnerabilities, particularly her physical problems, and to behave as if time had stood still, as though she was in the same body as she had been in her younger days. Despite arthritis and physical pain, she felt under pressure to be studying and writing, staying up late and restricting what she read to literature relevant to her work. The pressure of her thesis and the work that she should be doing always came before other things – her ordinary physical needs or going out to see friends and family. She would often tell me that she had planned to stay up late working, but that she had "failed" and had succumbed to exhaustion instead. This would be presented as a failure of willpower on her part – as though she could have done differently if she had only tried harder. It seemed that the self-blaming attitude replayed old themes, and she conveyed to me how she had always felt like this. These lifelong internal accusations that she was not good enough and was failing had renewed purchase now, when things were not, in reality, working anymore, when her body was "failing" her, and perhaps functioned protectively, defending against the reality of the changes in her body by converting this situation about which nothing could be done – a fact of life – into something familiar, a failing for which she was responsible and, by implication, could control. Thus, the reality of her aging body and the new situation of her diminished functioning were "changed into the past".

Keeping going the very familiar state of recrimination perpetuated the belief that everything was in her gift, and I felt this was part of her retreat, which kept her out of emotional contact with others and with her own need and vulnerability. If she left this state of retreat, she would have to face the reality that she could not control her deteriorating body that was aging and this seemed to be linked to fears of disintegration and fragmentation. This psychic withdrawal, where she "switched herself off", disabled her by keeping her out of contact with other people in her world who could have supported her. It kept her in a state where she was also cut off from internal objects that might have provided some sense of inner support to help her at this point in her life. There was the sense of her living "parallel lives" – her work as a student on the one hand and the life that she might in due course have, at some future point – when there was time – with her daughter and grandchildren. A life that was "on hold", as though it could be put down and picked up at any time, with no impact upon the family or on her.

Whilst in the sessions, I could feel I was "drifting along" with her. I also began to feel uncomfortable, that she was running out of time to see friends who were ill, to speak to her daughter, to spend time with her grandchildren. Yet, always there was a refrain that these things were distractions from the real work of shutting herself away with her thesis. I came to understand that the omnipotent expectations on her body denied the reality of how compromised her functioning was and her fears about how much worse it might become. Although she felt persecuted by accusations of failure, these had an unchanging, repetitive quality that was very familiar to her and that I came to feel offered a "psychic shelter" from other anxieties and fears. The timelessness of the internal criticism served to keep her away from facing the realities of where she was in her life: the limits of time remaining, real questions of how did she want to spend the time that was left to her.

She was often late for her sessions, acting as though nothing had happened, and in full flow at the end, as if with no awareness of the limits of time available. I found it difficult to tell her that the session was over, having to interrupt her abruptly, with the feeling that I was doing something cruel and dislocating to her. She would often give long narrative accounts of her failure with her thesis, tending to talk in an insular way, as though on her own in the room and my presence did not matter. I found myself worrying about her lack of urgency, and yet I felt that to say anything about this would be a cruel puncturing of her fragile state. What was the point in trying to enable her to face the situation, when there was so little that I could offer her to help? And often, I felt that I was manoeuvred into an experience of helplessness. I was told of other analysts she had seen a long time ago – these were famous names – leaving me feeling, "What could I do?" As time went on, I began to feel that I was in the position of being asked to carry her anxieties about the limits of time remaining, and of what could be repaired at this point in her life, and the fear that to know about this, to emerge from the comforts of the "timeless" state, would be a psychic disaster. My anxiety about how catastrophic it would be to put into words how she was self-destructively limiting the life she had now seemed to reflect the fear that it would be impossible to bear the mental pain of knowing about this.

In terms of her earliest experience, I was told that her mother, who was struggling with a husband away at war and then deeply troubled upon his return, had put her in the care of her grandmother in her earliest months of life. Her early dependency relationships had been very difficult and, as I came to understand it, her contemporary terror of falling apart, which was brought close by her physical decline and the threat of worse to come, rekindled an early infantile terror of fragmentation. I came to think of her situation in the way Winnicott describes: the feared state of impending fragmentation was something that had already happened in the past, in her earliest life, consequent on failures of containment in her relationships with her primary objects. There was a sense of a "narrowing of the gap" between the impinging realities of aging, the sense that physically and mentally she was falling apart, and these underlying fears, which perhaps had "waited in the wings" all her life. It seemed to me that this amplified the internal pressure on her to rise above her vulnerabilities and her dependency, to escape the terrors that these entailed – but at the same time, her mental and physical exhaustion made it increasingly difficult for her to sustain the harsh regime, the escape into solitary work, which she imposed on herself.

The feeling that it was "too late" was very painful, glimpsed at moments when she did allow herself to be more in touch with the realities of the marriage and how she was spending her time now, cutting herself off from people who were important in her life. Such moments tended to be fleeting, as she felt in touch with painful feelings of loss and then retreated again. She would say to me, "What is the point in coming here? You can't change any of these things." Indeed, I couldn't hold back time, could not take away the painful losses she was confronted with, nor change the past. I began to think that her preoccupation with how she was failing in her task with the thesis might be a displacement of the reparative work that she neglected, but which I felt she was perhaps becoming more conscious of, and there were hints that she was starting to think about how she was neglecting the life that she could have available to her, particularly with her daughter and grandchildren. On one occasion, she hadn't gone to a family event, a concert involving her grandchildren, because of the thesis, and yet, though she had missed it, she hadn't then managed to get much work done and felt such a failure. Her response was to speak of how she had to work harder, shouldn't waste her time reading novels. I said that I thought she had been feeling bad that there was something that she was attending to, the preoccupation with her thesis, which was stopping her from attending to the life she had – with her daughter and granddaughters – and that when she sees this she feels terrible and punishes herself by stopping herself from having anything pleasurable, going back even more forcefully into her world of the thesis. The difficulty was that she couldn't know about what she was doing without feeling tremendous pain and then returning to the persecutory state of mind again, going back into her retreat.

Gradually, she showed evidence of being aware of the significance of time lost. She started arriving on time and asked to move to twice-weekly sessions. As she began to be more in touch with the reality of the passage of time and the limits of time remaining, there was a poignant sense that each session, each gap between, could be the last. When she was ill, or caught cold, I had an acute awareness that this could be the illness that overtook her, and she expressed this feeling – how each thing she decided not to do may be her last chance to do it.

As the therapy went on, a sense of urgency became more apparent in the work, and there seemed to be an increasing pressure for her to repair things, alternating with her sense of helplessness at being able to fix herself, or her inner objects, which, as I have said, she managed by retreating back into the state of "timelessness". Yet, she conveyed to me the terror that she would run out of time and that this would happen before she had been able to sort things out in herself, before she had been able to put some order inside in relation to internal and external objects. And she brought accounts of people who had died before they were ready. As the "timeless" feeling began to be moved away from, what was faced more fully were the limits of time left for repair and, in particular, the time that had been lost for the actual repair of the relationship with her husband. She conveyed the difficulty of bearing the pain of the fact that she couldn't, in reality, make things better with him, and that the man who may have helped her to bear the pain was not any longer there. But there was more of a sense of his being felt as an available presence in her mind, and there was less persecutory guilt – though this felt much sadder and more painful. She told me that she had started tending his grave, which had been left neglected and overgrown, and there were also signs of her beginning to look after her own body more – recognising her vulnerabilities and getting help where she could, for the things which could be improved.

At that point in the therapy there was a painful quality of sadness, as the possibility of more creative reparation began to emerge. She became in touch with a more mixed picture of her relationship with her husband. She told me that she had been looking at photographs of him and was reminded of when he was younger: it was like seeing a ghost of the man who had loved her, she said – "I suppose, I can see the shadow of an earlier picture of him, and it is uncanny, sort of spooky." And she told me that she had found old pictures of her and her father holding hands, seeming happy, and one where she was with her father and her mother, a picture of the family as intact. She began putting together a photograph album for herself, integrating pictures of her husband, herself, her daughter, and her parents – and she gave one to her daughter, for her to hold onto for the future.

A little later in the work with her, she told me that she had been having very vivid dreams where she was on a journey, and she remembered that in the dream she had wondered why she had to be alone, why the others who were there couldn't come with her. She thought of *King Lear*: at the end of the play, the Duke of Kent says he must "go on a journey", which is to his death. She added, "I tend only to think of death as a release, but maybe there are anxieties about it – will I be in pain, will I suffer?" She told me that she wouldn't any longer be able to make the journey to see me in the wintertime, it would be too dark, and although there were practical ways around this, I thought that symbolically she was conveying how she wouldn't be with me at the end of her life, on her final journey. I thought that she was struggling with how to make the "final journey" with a sense of not being totally alone, how to feel accompanied – in contact with her good objects. It felt that the journey in therapy with me had been to let go of the more persecuting state – so she wasn't stuck in her retreat, not totally alone – even though I would not be there with her at the end.

In a sense, she had spent a lifetime seeking to make reparation; working therapeutically with damaged people, taking on worthy causes. But this activity perhaps had evaded a more real reconciliation which contained an acceptance of what couldn't be repaired – reconciling herself more to the husband she had had, and the partner she had been, which allowed more recovery and restoration of the man who once had loved her and whom she had loved, before the relationship had become too damaged by their mutual attacks and withdrawal from one another. It felt that there had been an importance about capturing this before she died. Perhaps what had brought her to therapy, unconsciously at least, were thoughts of the "midnight hour". During the work, there was a softening and lessening of her tormented state, more capacity to grieve and to face losses and a recovery of earlier pictures, particularly of her husband and of her father and mother, which felt to be significant in terms of her feeling that she had some inner companionship and was not totally alone in facing the end of her journey.

Conclusion

What is unique to our times is the scale upon which we are faced with the problem and the opportunity of longer lives. I have described some of the challenges that this can present. At a psychic level, living longer means more of us are exposed to age-related illness, bringing a new relationship to the body that signifies the diminution and loss of capacity and eventual death. De Masi (2004) points out that the fear of death is "irreducible" (p. 66) and working through persecutory anxieties is not going to do away with it, death being the ultimate expression of our human vulnerability. In the face of this, we all need our protections, and as Brearley (2005) says, perhaps all we can hope for "… is a balance between thick and thin skin, between destructiveness and reparation, between illusion and reality, between K and – K" (p. 1497). But there is a question of how the end of life can be "good enough", and as much restoration as can be possible achieved. I would add to this list the hope of being able to be accompanied; the struggle to keep an inner and external companionship with a good object.

The difficulty, then, is in defences that destroy good objects that are needed to help manage the challenges of this time and that can leave the person feeling abandoned with a sense of inner loneliness, whether or not they are actually alone. In couples, retreat, withdrawal, and loss of emotional contact is painful to witness, and the research indicates that the quality of our relationships at this point in life have profound material consequences linked to rates of decline in illness and even mortality. The fragmentation of physical and mental states, which is threatened by age-related conditions such as dementia, gives "corporeality" to primitive psychic phantasies of fragmentation and dissolution of the self. Unsurprisingly, in the face of these threats, people may withdraw into states of psychic retreat, depression, or psychotic decompensation. Defences that may have served well enough before may no longer hold up, and where there have been problems in dependency relationships earlier in life, failures of containment early on, there may be particular problems, and defences can become amplified or break down, leading to more destructive states of mind taking a grip.

There is often a need for help to manage the losses of this period, which may bring the fear of worse changes to come. I have tried to highlight how, for the therapist working with people in late life, there might be particular pressures felt in the countertransference. We are faced with our limits in terms of what we can offer such patients therapeutically and the challenge of knowing about these limits without giving up in despair or becoming manic in what we do. It is difficult to tolerate close emotional contact with states of psychic or physical fragmentation and diminution in functioning when we are faced with our own mortality.

This brings to mind again McDougall's (1986) words: "… in our unconscious fantasies we are all omnipotent … externally young and immortal" (p. 9). This work challenges such fantasies – and how difficult it can be, then, to allow oneself to know about this situation of late life, of the limits of time remaining, without distancing oneself. And it can be very difficult to hold onto this knowledge whilst also retaining a sense of the possibility of psychic development that may still take place.

The first case example showed a primitive constellation of anxieties and defences that appeared to have broken down in the face of the difficulties the couple encountered in old age. They struggled with powerful claustrophobic anxieties, and massive projective identification within the couple gave a sense of being hemmed in by a damaged internal object, represented in the experience of damage to somatic and psychic integrity, which each partner projected into, and recoiled from, in the other. In the second case example, the picture of the couple was one where both partners' minds had been very developed with considerable emotional maturity, but it was difficult to hold onto their capacities, which were being so challenged by the dementia. Despite the fragmentation of psychic functioning attendant upon dementia, there was evidence of this couple's struggle to manage this and to face the losses together – and at least for the moment, a sense of their trying to accompany one another through their experience. In the final case example, I focused upon more omnipotent defences: the retreat into timelessness as a reaction to the mental pain of vulnerability, loss, and fragmentation.

If couples can be helped to emerge from the psychic restriction of internal retreat or withdrawal, they may be able to mourn and recover more contact with good objects internally. And with each other, there may be less persecution and greater internal and external support for facing the "final journey". What is apparent here is the importance of containment – being helped to think, to process experience, to mourn losses – including grief for development that was not possible, life that hasn't been lived. What we might hope for is that the partners in such couples are not driven to retreat nor recoil from one another in the face of the losses and threats to psychic and somatic integrity in aging, but are equipped instead with a tolerance that allows for contact and accompaniment through the process of late life and dying. These lines from a poem of Elaine Feinstein's (2007) come to mind:

> Hold my hand, you said in the hospital
> … Hold my hand you said. I feel I won't die while you are here.
> You took my hand on our first aeroplane
> And in opera houses, or watching
> A video you wanted me to share.
> Hold my hand you said. I'll fall asleep
> And won't even notice you're not there.
>
> ("Hands", p. 12)

I think this conveys the importance of feeling accompanied in that final journey. This behooves us – at both a social level and at the level of the individual, couple, and family – to engage with the experience of aging and the end of life. Quinodoz's "window" needs to be opened – a window of thought on this area of lived experience that we all face and yet which can be so hard for us to know about.

Notes

1 A state of mind in which splitting and projection dominate, along with a lack of separateness, feeling persecuted, and persecuting in relation to the other.
2 A more integrated state in which there is greater reflexiveness, separateness, capacity to bear guilt, and to mourn. See Klein (1975) for an expanded description of both the paranoid-schizoid and depressive positions.
3 Psychic retreats (Steiner, 1993) or "pathological organisations" of the personality, refer to tightly knit defences which function both (1) to enable patients to avoid overwhelmingly persecutory and depressive anxieties by avoiding emotional contact with others and with internal and external anxiety; and (2) to provide patients with a precarious psychic equilibrium that is achieved through the pathological impairment of a more responsive emotional self. Such "retreats" are attempts to provide the patient with a new position that is at a remove from the normal fluctuations between the paranoid and depressive positions.
4 Karl Abraham in 1924 described the process of "internal reparation" in normal grief as part of the psychic reconstruction of the lost object inside the ego. The work of mourning is, therefore about the stable re-introjection of the image and memory of the loved object within one's inner world. This is the only way in which the lost object, having re-established itself in the ego, can be re-animated and experienced as alive. The internalisation of the lost object in the psychic world is a compensation for the real loss and it facilitates the working through of the pain and depressive anxieties.

References

Abraham, K. (1924). A short study of the development of the libido. *Selected papers on psychoanalysis.* London: Hogarth Press.

Bion, W. (1962). *Learning from experience.* London: Heinemann.

Brearley, M. (2005). Review of the book *Making death thinkable*. *International Journal of Psycho-Analysis*, 86: 1493–1497.

De Masi, F. (2004). *Making death thinkable* (p. 132). London: Free Association Books.

Eliot, T.S. (1944). East Coker. In *Four quartets* (p. 13). London: Faber.

Feinstein, E. (2007). Hands. In *Talking to the dead*. Manchester: Carcanet Press.

Freud, S. (1923). The ego and the id and other works. In J. Strachey (Ed. & Trans.), *The standard edition of the complete psychological works of Sigmund Freud* (Vol. 19). London: The Hogarth Press.

Ince, M. (2014). Living with dementia. *Britain in 2015: Essential research on the issues that matter.* London: ESRC.

Klein, M. (1975). *Envy and gratitude and other works, 1946–1963.* London: Hogarth Press.

Lively, P. (2014). *Ammonites and leaping fish: A life in time.* London: Penguin Books.

McDougall, J. (1986). *Theatres of the mind: Illusion and truth on the psychoanalytic stage.* London: Free Association Books.

Money-Kyrle, R. (1971). The aim of psychoanalysis. *International Journal of Psychoanalysis*, 61: 153–160.

Quinodoz, D. (2014). Film Essay: Amour. *International Journal of Psychoanalysis*, 95: 375–383.

Steiner, J. (1993). *Psychic retreats: Pathological organisations in psychotic, neurotic, and borderline patients.* London: Routledge.

Stevens, W. (1954). The plain sense of things. In *Selected poems*. New York: Alfred A. Knopf, Inc.

Waddell, M. (2007). Only connect – the links between early and later life. In R. Davenhill (Ed.), *Looking into later life. A psychoanalytic approach to depression and dementia in old age.* Tavistock Clinic Series. London: Karnac Books.

Winnicott, D.W. (1969). The mother-infant experience of mutuality. In E.J. Anthony & T. Benedek (Eds.), *Parenthood: Its psychology and psychopathology.* Boston: Little, Brown & Co.

Chapter 15

Discussion of "Growing old together in mind and body"

Leslye Russell

As we ourselves age – and particularly in my own cohort of clinicians in their 60s and 70s – a fearful symmetry occurs between our development and that of our patients. Of course, throughout our professional lives we often encounter patients who are facing similar problems to our own, but this happens more frequently in older age. Within the past few years, nearly all of my closest colleagues have dealt with caring for aging and dying parents and siblings, our own and our spouse's illnesses, anxiety over retirement, and multiple losses. While our training and experience help us contain our primitive anxieties, none of us are exempt from the ravages of age. The counter-transferential context changes and new difficulties arise as the line between our aging patients and ourselves blurs. While this blurring is problematic, it also reminds us that we are all in this together.

If we think of our professional selves as having a developmental trajectory, then we, too, are faced with regression in this context, and this in turn potentiates further growth or debilitation. The kinds of anxieties that beset us early in our careers return and, once again, we struggle with basic questions: *Can I really help this person or this couple? Do I have the right training or experience to handle these frightening issues? Would another therapist be better able to work in this arena?* And so on. Like our patients, we don't want to know what lies ahead and yet we know that turning a blind eye will impoverish our inner worlds and darken our remaining days.

Balfour poses several questions throughout the chapter, but one, in particular, seems vital and, I think, serves as the organizing principle for the argument he advances here. He writes, "The question, then, is what scope is there for development in late life...." This chapter addresses the question in a highly nuanced way. He tells us that the forces against development are formidable, yet there are possibilities for growth as we age. This orientation creates a psychological attitude that suffuses the chapter; it comforts us personally and helps us escape the medicalization and sociologese that can compromise our professional work. I'll comment on the theoretical and clinical contributions of this chapter first and later consider some theoretical musings of my own.

The theoretical center of Balfour's chapter is the Kleinian developmental model of psychological positions known by the shorthand PS-D. Klein viewed the paranoid/schizoid position as one that we outgrow on our road to maturity as we take up the depressive position. In a radical shift, the work of Bion and his followers showed us that these modes of experience are present throughout life and are the source of psychological vitality as we oscillate between them. Balfour demonstrates in his clinical material how crucial this movement between the positions is, as he reaches the potential for growth in couples many might have given up on. He points out that one position or another might be dominant for a couple at any particular time.

For aging couples, with intensified and often terrifying difficulties, he says, "The regressive pull can overwhelm depressive position functioning and reinstate the dominance of the paranoid/schizoid position." Notably, this oscillation is as dramatically visible in the aged as it is in the toddler, when, for example, a thoughtful conversation can change rapidly to petulance or rage at a perceived slight or an ordinary inconvenience. It is sometimes tempting to see these rapid oscillations as evidence of an earlier character problem, but for many older people, these are not characteristic patterns and instead speak to a new, though troubling, aspect of development: managing the dread of one's demise.

Some older couples who have found their way into treatment with me were able to call upon their depressive position functioning to articulate their reasons for seeking help. I've sometimes had the experience of wondering what they needed from me, as they could be so clear, compassionate, and seemingly wise in their initial meeting. Once in the door, however, the deep fears about their losses and their impending decline emerged quickly; then, as Balfour says, the anxieties and defenses of the paranoid/schizoid position begin to dominate. Typically, the couple fears that their anger and terror will overwhelm the strength of their bond and, in the face of rising needs, they will lose each other physically and emotionally, just when they need each other most.

One couple I've seen for a number of years – both well into their 70s, though still robust and healthy – speak of a recurring conflict: a competition between them about who is "losing it" the most. Any sign of forgetfulness or other infirmity in either of them is likely to bring forth anger from the other. The terms of the conflict are couched in the language of their younger selves, as in, "You don't listen to me," or "You just pretend to pay attention, but you don't really take in what I'm telling you," but they have come to see that these spats are designed to keep hope alive. Alas, the hope that might be sustained through their anger is illusory, while hope that is lodged in accepting aging and death is realistic. The wish contained in their anger is that their aging is not real, and their inevitable infirmity does not have to be. A realistic hope is that they will be able to accompany, support, and love each other to the end. These repeating spats reveal how frightened they are, even while still in relatively good health, of what lies ahead.

In Balfour's felicitous phrase, old age ushers in "a resurgence of the body," he writes, quoting Penelope Lively (2014), "… You have to come to terms with a different incarnation." This different incarnation is not only felt and seen in our own aging bodies, but is underscored as we are faced with the visible evidence of our partner's physical change. The body is "more silent" in young adulthood, he claims, and asserts itself again in later life.

By more silent, I think he means that it is less likely to be full of aches and pains and the infirmities of age. But, I would suggest that the young body is pretty noisy in its own way, it just asserts itself differently; it is the source of sexual and narcissistic gratification (or humiliation) and is the source of strength and vitality (or weakness). The young body, in health, is the platform for manic and omnipotent defenses as well as the healthy capacities to take on the challenges of family and work. In the different and older incarnation of pain, weakness, and vulnerability, the narcissistic blow can be devastating.

Two personal reminiscences: my mother-in-law, already in her 90s, a year or so before her death, was being weighed at her doctor's office. As she stepped onto the scale, she yelled out urgently, "Wait!" She then took off a small silk scarf and handed it to my husband who was standing nearby. My own mother religiously kept her hair appointments, even when she had to be wheeled to them in a wheelchair, later fussing that lying on her pillow flattened the back of her hair. While both of our mothers aged relatively gracefully and accepted many of the limitations aging brought, their investment in their appearance persisted until they were comatose. We have to agree with McDougall (1986) that aging itself would seem to be a narcissistic injury not only to our vanity but a blow to our sense of self as our physical and mental capacities diminish.

The heart of the matter, however, is that the changes in our bodies signal death and bring the awareness of death closer with each iteration of deterioration. Balfour writes beautifully, "Yet, how difficult it is for us … to be in a state of mind where knowledge of the fact of our death shapes our perception of time passing …" (p. 233). I worked with a couple for whom this was almost intolerable. The wife was in her early 70s and he in his 80s. As her own aging body began to compromise her formidable and successful manic defenses, she frequently would say bitterly, "I want to be alive to the end." His slowness and quiet nature, which had attracted her when younger, felt like a living death. To be fair, his introversion could slide into withdrawal and passivity. But his well-developed capacity for reverie was threatening to her and she often criticized him for not being more active in the world. She desperately wanted him to join her in a manic assault against the inevitable.

Balfour's point that "… the infant you once were, you will always be …" (p. 224) is poignantly, sometimes maddeningly underscored for the elderly. He tells us that the fears and anxieties of early life – dissolution or fragmentation of the self – reassert themselves. Where once these largely unconscious phantasies lived in early life, in our aging bodies and minds they come ever closer to reality. But, unlike the infant, we will not out grow this phase. He writes:

> unconscious anxieties of fragmentation … have always been part of the internal world. The aged, declining body is a reality. We are all gripped by destructive drives, and when the body as an object of projection really is deteriorated and damaged, then inside and outside, inner phantasy and external reality converge.
>
> (p. 226)

This convergence means a collapse of the psychological space needed for thinking and, with that, the loss of the capacity for symbol formation. Finally, in this cascading horror of deterioration, the capacity for managing all kinds of destructive impulses and emotional storms is weakened or lost.

Working clinically with older couples, we frequently see one or the other of them lapsing into the concreteness of a child. The loss of psychological functioning, alongside the loss of physical and cognitive capability, is exasperating for everyone involved, but especially for the primary caregiver. Yet, I'd like to suggest that this very concreteness contains the seed of realistic hope for growth, which I'll discuss later.

The two couples Balfour discusses so beautifully illustrate his developmental thesis and the challenges faced by the aging couple and the therapist who would help them. He points out that the regressive pulls that accompany aging have potential for despair and hope. The first couple, alas, shows us how the ravages of old age can lead to psychic collapse, while the second vignette shows us that, even in the face of dementia, the possibility of growth in the couple can be realized.

In the first couple, the destructive forces that their aging and infirmities unleashed ultimately destroyed their ability to live together, overwhelming each other as well as their psychiatric team. Though their separation seemed unavoidable, Balfour writes that this "solution" was not sustainable and we don't know what happened. Why wasn't it a workable arrangement? Was it ever on the cards that they would find a way to withdraw their projections and better contain their anxieties? Did the separation make the situation worse? Balfour's account of the second couple teaches us something profound: that even for clients with dementia, our work can be more than case management.

As Balfour helped the husband face losing his wife, whom he regarded as the most precious thing in his life, he was able to sustain a realization of the fullness of her being despite her diminishing capabilities. This, in turn, helped him restore his emotional and physical affection for her. In a touching comment, she said, "We are having a very open discussion now.... This is the antithesis of the dementia, which makes me feel so hemmed in...." (p. 233). We know that these gains will soon enough give way to the disease, yet for whatever time is left, the intensity of this couple's emotional connection will be even more meaningful. It seems extraordinary that the restoration of an emotional and physical link between the couple can actually significantly slow the depredations of dementia and restore the wife to earlier pursuits. She began reading novels again! I'm reminded of a couple where the debilitated husband demanded that his wife not allow anyone else into the house. Friends and even most family members were asked not to visit. The wife's respite was grocery shopping and trips to the pharmacy. Though devoted and loving toward her husband, this isolation took a toll on her health. As it happened, her husband died within a year and she was able to recover her own health and remember those months with a sweet melancholy. I thought that as she experienced her own capacity for devoted love, she felt herself to be a profoundly good person, and this greatly increased her chance for growth in her later years.

Meltzer wrote of the ordinary beautiful face of the mother (Meltzer & Williams, 1988). I think the ordinary beautiful face of the caregiver – often spouse – touches the soul. Yet, it is important to keep in mind that this beautiful face of the caregiver can also be problematic. How often do we meet caregivers who have exhausted themselves, or fortified themselves with moral masochism (Russell, 2011), or disguised their hatred in obsessive care? We have all recoiled against the aggression apparent in the caregiver's insistence on controlling irrelevant minutiae – "not so much salt on an egg" – or at the harsh criticism leveled at an aide for failing to put on the proper sweater for an outing, or excessive fretting about temperature, nutrition, cleanliness, and so on. I once wrote a paper, "Worry: A Mother's Revenge" (2008). At that time, it hadn't occurred to me how relevant it would be to the caregiver of the elderly. Here, we are at the interface between love and hate that Winnicott (1975) taught us. Somehow the aging couple must make room for yet another edition of what Winnicott called "objective" hatred (p. 201).

The wife who is becoming demented tells Balfour how important her husband's touch is to her; she wonders what sort of physical contact animals have with each other. This couple brings to mind Ogden's (1989) conception of the autistic-contiguous position. In this mode of experiencing, largely preverbal and based in the sensorium, of course, touch is centrally important. The concept of the autistic-contiguous position contains a theoretical space for locating realistic hope for growth in old age.

Ogden posits a time even earlier than the paranoid/schizoid period when the infant begins to organize its chaotic physical and physiological sensations into experiences. Ogden calls this rudimentary schema the "autistic contiguous position." This theoretical construct helps us account for what we often observe in elderly and demented people and, like the other positions, has a progressive as well as a regressive aspect. The autistic-contiguous position, along with the other Kleinian positions, creates a more complex theoretical map that helps clinicians manage affects and states of mind when confronted with the immutable facts of aging.

Here are examples of how the theory of the autistic/contiguous position might be applicable. Elderly people, as they become more concrete, often fixate on a particular object – an autistic object – and their daily lives may devolve into rigid rituals. A rare visit from a beloved grandchild might be ignored or met with irritation because it interrupts the ritual of an afternoon television program. Or a usually fastidious housekeeper ignores the damage that overwatering a plant is doing to a table because the regularity of watering itself is more important than the plant or the table. Or a specific pen used to write lists and notes cannot be replaced by any other pen or pencil.

This rigidity can be an obstacle to the possibility of coming to some internal, fluid acceptance of the realities of old age. Yet the autistic-contiguous position is also the site for potential growth and pleasure. Again, to refer to my mother – as her physical mobility became more restricted and her world shrank from her community to her apartment to her bedroom and finally to her bed, she spent hours "inside" a complex Chinese landscape painting she'd had for decades. Visits to her often included a virtual tour of the scene as we followed the path up the mountain, stopping at a small bridge, or noticing a hut in the distance. As her outer world shrank, the intensity of her inner world and its beauty became greater. Pain and pleasure here converge – this is not masochism or other perverse states but psychic growth at the end of her life that became possible because she had mourned many, many losses and had developed the capacity to accept the realities of death, including her own.

Perhaps it is this very shrinkage of the larger world that forces the psyche back upon the sensorium as a source of experience and meaning. The concreteness of the child, now present in old age, is the basis for something new; it is a return, a regression, and yet not a repetition. The elderly may be forced to slow down and their slowness is a sign of loss and impending death, but it is also exactly the right pace for beholding the beauty of the world.

This brings me to Meltzer's notion of the aesthetic conflict, which he discusses in *The Apprehension of Beauty* (Meltzer & Williams, 1988). He places the aesthetic conflict at the beginning of life and at the core of the emotional and psychological development of the infant. Meltzer and

Ogden's concepts are highly congruent and each enhances the other. I think of the aesthetic conflict as the motivational engine within the autistic-contiguous position.

The capacity for growth in old age rests on the Bionian concept of an emotional experience, which he regarded as the primary source for growth and development. Those of us who have lived, worked, and perhaps overvalued depressive position functioning during our adult lives will have to suffer what feels like a regression to more bodily based knowledge and the facts of increasing dependency. The irony is that this regression helps reinstate negative capability, and by going backward we will be able to go forward into the unexpected pleasures of not knowing. We will have to allow the resurgence of the body, frail though it may be, to become the site of emotional experience and meaning. Development for aging people requires a kind of reverse engineering. For children, symbol formation must make its way slowly against concreteness. But in old age, symbol formation gives way to concreteness as language gives way to the sensorium that is once again our gateway to the world.

I would suggest that the aesthetic conflict in old age is the primary source of growth and pleasure and this is directly analogous to the developmental process of the young child. To quote Meltzer:

> The ordinary beautiful devoted mother presents to her ordinary beautiful baby a complex object of overwhelming interest ... her outward beauty ... bombards him with an emotional experience of a passionate quality, the result of his being able to see these objects as "beautiful." But the meaning of his mother's behavior, of the appearance and disappearance of the breast and of the light in her eyes, of a face over which emotions pass like the shadows of clouds over the landscape, are unknown to him. He has, after all, come into a strange country where he knows neither the language nor the customary nonverbal cues and communications.
> (Meltzer & Williams, 1988, p. 22)

The strange country we must enter as we approach death is at once beautiful, frightening, and mysterious. Just as our beautiful Mother does what she can to help us mitigate fears of the unknown, she will be more effective if she, herself, has been able to mourn her losses and can wonder about the mystery of things. Similarly, we will be better able to help our patients and our family members, not to mention ourselves, if we can corral our own fears and stay open to what goes on in this strange land and, finally, accept that all this, too, shall pass. And if we are very fortunate, we might gather our courage to catch a glimpse of the beauty even in this new world. I believe Andrew Balfour's chapter is an important contribution to that end.

References

Lively, P. (2014). *Ammonites and leaping fish: A life in time*. London: Penguin Books.

McDougall, J. (1986). *Theatres of the mind: Illusion and truth on the psychoanalytic stag*. London: Free Association Books.

Meltzer, D. & Williams, M.H. (1988). *The apprehension of beauty: The role of aesthetic conflict in development, art and violence.* Strath Tay, Scotland: Clunie Press.

Ogden, T. (1989). *The primitive edge of experience.* Northvale, New Jersey/London: Jason Aronson, Inc.

Russell, L. (2008). Worry: A mother's revenge. Unpublished Paper.

Russell, L. (2011). Freud's theory and Trollope's depiction of moral masochism. *fort da*, 17(2), 25–36.

Winnicott, D.W. (1975). Hate in the countertransference. In *Through Paediatrics to Psycho-Analysis*. New York: Basic Books.

Index

abandonment 11, 56
Abraham, K. 243n4
Abse, S. 21
abuse 21
acting out 76, 86
action 102, 103, 116
activity/passivity 216–17
aesthetic conflict 251–2
aggression 11, 34, 125, 195
aging/old age 221–44, 245–53; and aesthetic conflict 251–2; and autistic-contiguous position 250–1; and the body 222–3, 247–8; and death 223–4; and dementia 228–31, 232, 241, 249; and loneliness 233–4; and loss 222, 226, 232, 233–4, 242; and return of early anxieties 15, 224–6, 248; and timelessness 234–40, 242
Alexander, M. 157
alpha-function 103
ambient trauma 161
ambivalence 10, 12, 20, 46, 69, 98, 117, 199, 205, 234
anaclitic love 36
anaclitic object choice 36
"Analysis Terminable and Interminable" (Freud) 33
analytic third 15
anger of despair 156, 198
anger of hope 156, 198
annihilation 11, 23, 225
anxieties 11, 37, 38, 49; of excess 218; infantile 16, 224–5; primal scene 22; shared 65, 118, 145
anxious attachment 199, 205

anxious-ambivalence 199, 205
Aron, L. 167
attachment 2, 4, 11, 31, 35, 156, 157, 160; alarm 158–9; anxious 199, 205; avoidant 199, 205; disorganized 160, 161, 182, 183, 184; insecure 160, 184, 198–9, 205; romantic 162–3; secure 162, 169, 198, 199, 200, 205; and sex 194–204, 213–14; theory 3, 21, 22, 160, 184, 186, 209, 219
attention 102, 103, 111n3, 116; joint 164–5
attunement 56, 74, 75, 76, 77, 78, 79, 80, 84, 86, 88, 205
autistic-contiguous position 11, 22, 250–1, 252
autonomy 31, 82
avoidance 199
avoidant attachment 199, 205

bad objects 172
Balfour, A., "Growing old together in mind and body" 221–44; L. Russell discussion of 245–53
Balint, E. 2, 113
Balint, M. 2, 39, 113
Barber, C.L. 93
Bateman, A. 159
Bateson, G. 159
Beebe, B. 157
beliefs 6, 64; religious 63, 85; *see also* unconscious beliefs
Bell, D. 129
Benioff, L. 213–20
Benjamin, J. 157, 159, 166, 172, 215, 216–18

Index

Berg, J. 22
betrayal 75, 76, 98, 105, 130, 133, 136, 137, 140, 144, 145
Bion, W. 2, 3, 24, 32–3, 73, 80, 92, 101, 102–3, 104, 111n3, 114, 115, 117, 120, 142, 146, 149, 181, 190, 246, 252; catastrophic change 22; container/contained 12–14, 15, 55, 187, 230; dynamic unconsciousness 184–5, 186; projective identification 17; psychotic/non-psychotic personalities 36, 40, 90, 95
blaming 12, 21, 58, 60, 123, 128, 165, 170, 172, 187, 189
Bloom, H. 93
body, and aging 222–3, 247–8
body language 209
Boerma, M. 22, 195
Bollinghaus, E. 65
borderline couples 21, 154, 155, 158–9
Boszormeny-Nagy, I. 167
Botella, C. and Botella, S. 103–4
boundaries 6–7, 14
Bowlby, J. 2, 156, 157, 198
Brearley, M. 241
breast, mother's: infant's relationship with 124, 125
Britton, R. 3, 15, 18, 19, 30, 31–2, 36, 50, 51, 59, 62–3, 64, 76, 84, 114, 126, 142, 143
Bromberg, P. 157

Caper, R. 33
care, ethic of 166
caregiving, tactile 208
Cartwright, D. 181
change 145; catastrophic (Bion) 22
children 52, 55; empathy in 59–60; *see also* infants
Civitarese, G. 184
claustro-agoraphobic dilemma 11, 22, 56
clinical examples: aging 226–8, 242, 249 (dementia 228–31, 232, 242, 249; timelessness 234–40); Bill and Jane 170–7, 186–90; Grant and Elizabeth 74–7, 78, 79, 86–7, 88; Mr. and Mrs. A 40–5; Mr. and Mrs. X 130–4, 143, 147, 149–52; Mr. and Mrs. Y 134–9, 140; Stephanie and Richard 71–4, 80, 84, 85
Clulow, C. 21, 22
Clulow, C, "How was it for you?: Attachment, sexuality and mirroring in couple relationships" 193–212; L. Benioff discussion of 213–20
Cocktail Party, The (Eliot) 54–5
Colman, W. 14, 22, 209
communication 6; emotional 119; and evacuation distinguished 120; non-verbal 209; projective identification as form of 17, 31, 40, 48, 82, 118–19
competition 9, 11
complex: core 11, 22, 56, 195; Oedipus 17–18, 50, 143, 196, 197, 208
conflict resolution 6
consistency in the frame 7, 14
container/containment 17, 31, 46, 168, 216, 241, 242; Bion 12–14, 15, 55, 187, 230; and dementia 228, 230–2; maternal 37; therapist 6, 7, 9
Cooke, S. 48–61
core complex 11, 22, 56, 195
countertransference 2, 6, 8, 9–10, 23, 58–9, 113, 151, 241; physiological 155; and unconscious beliefs 77–8
couple formation 10–11
couple state of mind 15, 181–2
creative couple 18–19, 51, 82, 83
curiosity 13, 60, 86, 88; absence of 20; and unconscious beliefs 78–80

Davies, J.M. 163, 170, 172
De Masi, F. 223, 224, 241
death 225; awareness of 223–4; fear of 241
defense(s) 11, 12, 32, 114, 214, 241; projective identification as form of 17; shared 64, 65
defensive relating 7, 8, 40
dementia 226, 228–33, 241, 242, 249
denial 12, 125
dependency 16, 19, 40, 51, 52, 56–7, 162, 214, 225, 241, 252
depression 223, 234, 241
depressive position 11, 12, 18, 19, 33, 37, 38, 46, 55, 83, 88, 127, 134, 140, 143, 146, 222, 225–6, 243n2, 246, 252

Descartes, R. 63
desire 195, 213; sexual *see* sex and sexuality
despair, anger of 156, 198
destructive narcissism 39, 125
devaluation 53
developmental relating 8, 40, 139–41, 148–9, 150–1, 152
Diamond, D. 207
Dicks, H. 2–3, 3–4
difference 34, 57–9, 124; apprehension of 117–18, 119; as intrusion 57; toleration of 50, 51, 52
disorganized attachment 160, 161, 182, 183, 184
dissociation 218
divorce 21
double binds 169–70
dreams 103–4, 108, 109, 184
dynamic unconsciousness 184–5, 186

Eagle, M. 195, 197
ego 221; normal and abnormal 33, 40, 46
elderly couples *see* aging/old age
Eliot, T.S. 224; *The Cocktail Party* 54–5
emotionally focused couple therapy 5, 157
empathy 59–60, 168
enactments 70, 86–8
engulfment 11, 23
envy 16, 34, 39, 40, 44, 83, 125, 214
epistemophilic instinct 80
erotic transferences 9
ethic of care 166
ethic of justice 166
evacuation 31, 120
excess 216, 217, 218, 219
exclusion 40, 50, 51, 52, 83, 145, 150
externalization 7
eye contact 73, 198, 209

Faimberg, H. 183
Fairbairn, W.E. 3, 4, 24, 156, 162
false-self couple 20
Family Discussion Bureau 2
family of origin 49
family systems theory 184
family therapy 3
fantasy 11, 24n3; *see also* phantasy

fear 108, 111n1, 195
fees 6–7
Feinstein, E. 242–3
Feldman, M. 3, 114
feminine passivity 216–17
femininity 162, 163
Ferro, A. 184, 189
fetishes 218
field theory 184, 186
Fisher, J. 20, 39, 49, 54–5, 66, 84, 146–7
Fisher, J., "The Macbeths in the consulting room" 90–112; S. Nathans discussion of 113–22
Fonagy, P. 49, 154, 157, 159, 167, 199, 206, 207
Fonteyne, F., *Une Liaison Pornographique* 200–4, 206, 217
forgiveness: depressive 140; paranoid-schizoid 140
fragmentation of the self 225, 226, 228, 236, 237, 241, 242, 248
frame 6–7, 14
Freud, S. 2, 4, 24, 111n3, 115, 208, 213, 222, 223, 224; on dreams 103, 104; on the ego 33, 40, 46, 221; on epistemophilic instinct 80; on hallucination 101, 102, 106; on libido 196; on love 36, 38, 126; pleasure principle 101; reality principle 90, 92, 98–9, 101–2; on repetition compulsion 52–3; on transference 35; on the unconscious 49, 224; "Analysis Terminable and Interminable" 33; *Interpretation of Dreams, The* 101; "Project for a Scientific Psychology" 101; "Two Principles of Mental Functioning" 101–2
Friend, J. 142–53
frustration 28; toleration of 95, 146

Gabbard, G.O. 155
gender inequality 163–4
Gerson, S. 88
Gilligan, C. 166
Gilligan, J. 163
Glasser, M. 11, 22, 56, 195
Goldman, R. 166
Goldner, V. 162, 163, 164

Goldner, V., "Romantic bonds, binds, and ruptures" 154–79; R. Peltz discussion of 180–92
good objects 241
Goodman, G. 197
Gordon, M. 59
Gosling, R. 35, 52, 53
Gottman, J. 59
gratitude 40
Greenberg, L. 166
Greenblatt, S. 91, 100
Grier, F. 22
Grier, F., "Psychotic and depressive processes in couple functioning" 123–41; J. Friend discussion of 142–53
Grossman, D. 180–1, 182, 191
group psychotherapy 2

Haley, J. 169
Hall, S. 111n1
hallucinations 101, 102, 105–11, 115
Hass, R., "Misery and Splendor" 219
hate 31, 40, 195, 250
Heidegger, M. 49
Heimann, P. 39
Hesse, E. 160, 161
Hewison, D. 22
histories 149
holding complexity 168–9
hope, anger of 156, 198

I–thou relations 157
ideals/idealization 10, 12, 53, 123–7, 143, 144–5; betrayals 140; loss of 11
identification, projective *see* projective identification
imaging-state-of-mind 103–4
inclusion 40, 51, 145
individualism 162
individuation 19
infants: anxiety states 16, 224–5; relationship to mother's breast 124, 125; *see also* mother – infant/child relationship; parent – child/infant relationship
inhibitions 11
insecure attachment 160, 184, 198–9, 205
insight 86

internal couples 67
internal objects 67
interpretation 118; of projections 119–20; transference 73–4, 85–6
Interpretation of Dreams, The (Freud) 101
intersubjective theory 23
intersubjectivity 157, 159, 193
intimacy 10, 12, 19, 32, 36, 49, 117, 181, 197, 198, 208, 214; fear of 65, 69
introjection 37
Isaacs, S. 64

Jaques, E. 128–9
Johnson, S. 157, 161
joint attention 164–5
Jones, E. 111n1
Joseph, B. 3, 40, 114
judgment 102, 104, 116
Jung, C.G. 2
justice, ethic of 166

Kernberg, O. 11
Klein, M. 3, 11, 22, 24, 36–7, 39, 65, 114, 124, 125, 146, 225; developmental positions 222, 246 (*see also* depressive position; paranoid-schizoid position); epistemophilic instinct 80; Oedipal complex 17–18, 143, 197; projective identification 16; transference 35
Kuhn, T. 84

Laing, R.D. 159, 169
Laplanche, J. 207, 215–16, 217
Lasch, C. 191
Laschinger, B. 198
Le Doux, J. 211
Levenson, E. 87, 169
Liaison Pornographique, Une (Fonteyne) 200–4, 206, 217
libido 162, 196
Lichtenberg, J. 207
linking 102, 104, 116
listening 77
Lively, P. 222–3, 234, 247
Living Together with Dementia project 229, 232
Lombardi, R. 146, 149
loneliness, and aging 233–4

loss 2, 12, 18, 83, 214; and aging 222, 226, 232, 233–4, 242
love 22, 31, 156, 195, 250; anaclitic 36; falling in 10, 35, 126; narcissistic type of 36, 38; and sexual desire, split between 196–7
Lyons-Ruth, K. 158
Lyth, I.M. 2

Macbeth (Shakespeare) 66, 90, 91–101, 105–11, 117, 120–1
McDougall, J. 225, 242, 248
Main, M. 160, 161
marital triangle 15, 51
masculinity 163
masturbation 218
maternal reverie 13, 37
Matisse, H. 222
mature object relating, vs. narcissistic object relating 36–8
Meins, E. 169
Meltzer, D. 3, 11, 22, 24, 114, 250, 251–2
memory/notation 102, 103, 116
mentalization 3, 154, 157, 159, 167–8, 199–200, 226
merger 22, 58
Mikulincer, M. 197, 199
mirroring 194, 195; and sexuality 204–8; therapist role in 208–9, 210
"Misery and Splendor" (Hass) 219
Mitchell, S. 162, 163, 214, 217
Money-Kyrle, R. 128, 224, 225
moral third 166
Mordecai, E. 161
Morgan, M. 15, 16–17, 18–19, 20, 39, 50, 51, 114, 115, 126, 143, 151, 181–2
Morgan, M., "Unconscious beliefs about being a couple" 62–81; M. Schaefer discussion of 82–9
mortality 221, 223–4
mother – infant/child relationship 13, 17, 37, 50, 124, 125, 161; adult couple relationship as 68–9, 85; and infant sensuality/sexuality 197, 198–9, 205–6, 207–8, 215–16
mourning 12, 80, 83, 88, 225, 234, 242, 243n4

multipartiality 167
mystification 169

narcissistic relating 12, 16, 19–20, 33, 39, 45, 48, 53, 57, 58, 125; chronic vs. acute 38–40; vs. mature object relating 36–8, 46, 48
nascent third 166
Nathans, S. 1–29, 66, 113–22
negation 167–8
neuropsychology 184, 186
"no-sex" couples 22
non-verbal communication 209
notation/memory 102, 103, 116

object choice, anaclitic 36
object relations 3, 4, 23, 31, 114; narcissistic *see* narcissistic relating; primitive 37, 39, 40
objects: bad 172; good 241; internal 67; part- 22, 189, 215, 217
Oedipus/Oedipal: complex/conflict 17–18, 50, 143, 196, 197, 208; myth 142, 196; transferences 8; triangle 194, 207; triumph 135, 147
Ogden, T. 11, 15, 22, 88, 184, 250, 252
old age *see* aging/old age
one-person psychoanalysis 23
open-endedness of treatment 7
otherness/Other 52, 57, 168
oxytocin 195

paranoid-schizoid position 11, 12, 16, 19, 33, 37–8, 39, 45, 46, 55, 58, 59, 69, 124, 127, 129, 134, 140, 144, 222, 243n1, 246
parent – child/infant relationship 5, 13–14, 160; *see also* mother – infant/child relationship
parenting 52
Parsons, M. 218
part-objects 22, 189, 215, 217
partner choice 7–8; unconscious 32, 82, 114, 145
passion 190, 191
passivity 216–17
Péloquin, K. 208
Peltz, R. 180–92

Penn, P. 164
perversion 21, 218
phantasy 10, 24n3, 37, 101, 103; *see also* fantasy; unconscious phantasies
Phillips, A. 194, 195
"Plain Sense of Things, The" (Stevens) 224
pleasure principle 99, 101
Pontalis, J.B. 215–16
post-depressive position 19
power 22
pre-Oedipal transferences 8
pre-paranoid-schizoid position 22–3
predictability 7
pretend functioning 199, 200
primal scene anxieties 22
primitive object relations 37, 39, 40
"Project for a Scientific Psychology" (Freud) 101
projection(s) 9, 10–11, 12, 35, 37, 52, 114, 115; interpretation of 119–20
projective gridlock 17, 20, 39, 53–6, 82–3
projective identification 7, 10, 12, 16–17, 37–8, 48, 54–5, 82, 83, 91–2, 115, 242; case example 42–5; as communication 17, 31, 40, 48, 82, 118–19; as evacuation 31, 120
proleptic imagination 20, 66–7, 71, 84, 101, 115–17, 146–7; in *Macbeth* 90, 91–101, 105–11, 117, 120–1; negative 105–11; shared 98–101, 108, 116, 117, 120–1
psychic apparatus 184
psychic determinism 5
psychic equivalence 167–8, 169, 199, 200
psychic retreat 38, 223–4, 234, 241, 243n3
psycho-sexual development 196–7, 205–6, 207–8
psychoanalytic couple therapy, core principles of 5–23
psychotic states of mind 36, 40, 56, 90, 95, 123, 124, 134

Quinodoz, D. 229, 243

reality principle 90, 92, 98–9, 101–5

reality-testing 99, 117
reality-testing ego functions 102–3
reality-testing-state-of-mind 104–5, 108
relational psychoanalysis 23, 87
relational (small "t") trauma 156, 159–61
relational unconscious 6
religious beliefs 63, 85
repetition compulsion 4, 7, 52, 113, 115, 182
representations 5, 144, 210, 216; *see also* self-representations
reverie, maternal 13, 37
Rey, H. 11, 56
rivalry 9, 34
Rosenfeld, H. 3, 39, 56, 125
Russell, L. 245–53
Ruszczynski, S. 15, 16, 20, 65, 114, 126, 143, 145, 152
Ruszczynski, S., "Couples on the couch: working psychoanalytically with couple relationships" 30–47; R. Cooke discussion of 48–61

Sabbadini, A. 204
sadomasochistic relating 21, 34, 140, 148
safety 185; relational 162–3, 214
Schaefer, M. 82–9
scheduling 6–7
Schore, A.N. 157, 158
Schore, J.N. 157, 158
secure attachment 162, 169, 198, 199, 200, 205
Segal, H. 39, 92
Sehgal, A. 22
self: differentiation of 34; fragmentation of 225, 226, 228, 236, 237, 241, 242, 248
self-interest 31
self-reflection 19, 51
self-representations, projected 10–11
Seligman, S. 172
separateness 16, 37, 40, 124, 150, 218; capacity for/toleration of 19, 33, 50, 51, 217; denial of 16, 34, 214; narcissistic relating and refusal of 39, 52, 124
separation 2, 11, 12, 20, 22, 56, 82
separation (marital) 21

sex and sexuality 21–3, 193–212, 213–20; and attachment 194–204, 213–14; and love, split between 196–7; and mirroring 204–8; and mother–infant/child relationship 197, 198–9, 205–6, 207–8, 215–16
sexuality of despair 198
sexuality of hope 198
Shakespeare, W.: *Macbeth see Macbeth*
shame 208
shared defense 64, 65
shared proleptic imagination 98–101, 108, 116, 117, 120–1
shared unconscious 5–6, 8, 10–11, 55, 114
shared unconscious phantasies 6, 32, 64, 65, 114, 210
Shaver, P. 199
Sheinberg, M. 164
Shnueli, A. 21
Siegel, J.P. 10
Slade, A. 158
Smith, H. 87
Snyder, R. 163
Solomon, M. 158
Spark, G.M. 167
Spillius, E.B. 2, 113
Spitz, R.A. 92
splitting 12, 16, 17, 37, 38, 40, 125; case example 40–5
states of mind 11–12
Stein, R. 214, 216, 217
Steiner, J. 3, 38, 87, 114, 243n3
Stern, D. 158, 205
Stevens, W., "The Plain Sense of Things" 224
Stuss, D. 157
superego 125, 140, 143
systems theory 5, 159

tactile caregiving 208
tantalizing object 156
Target, M. 199, 206, 207
Tarsh, H. 65
Tatkin, S. 158
Tavistock Centre for Couple Relationships (TCCR) 1–3, 24
Tavistock Clinic 1

Tavistock couple psychotherapy model 23, 24; theoretical origins of 3–4
Tavistock Institute of Human Relations 1
tenderness 190
testosterone 195
theory of mind 12–13
therapeutic alliance 210
therapist: aging of 245; containing function of 14; countertransference *see* countertransference; mirroring role 208–9, 210; unconscious beliefs 70
thinking feelingly 101–5, 117
third position 15, 18, 51, 73, 79, 86, 88–9, 126, 143
the third 15, 19, 51, 181
thought 102, 103
time, experience of 127–9, 143, 146–9
timelessness, and aging 234–40, 242
Tithonus myth 221
Tomasello, M. 164
transference 2, 7, 8–9, 31–2, 35, 36, 49, 113, 115, 210; erotic 9; interpretations 73–4, 85–6; mutual 5; parental/therapist 9
transference-repetition 53, 58
trauma: ambient 161; relational (small "t") 156, 159–61
triangular space 50, 51
triangulation 9, 18
"Two Principles of Mental Functioning" (Freud) 101–2
two-person theory 23

unconscious 2, 9, 24, 32, 35–6, 49, 52, 224; dynamic 184–5, 186; relational 6; shared 5–6, 8, 10–11, 55, 114
unconscious beliefs 62–81, 82–9, 144–5; awareness of 69–70, 77; case examples 71–7, 78, 79, 80, 84, 85, 86–7, 88; countertransference experiences indicative of 77–8; and curiosity 78–80; interpretation of 78; listening technique 77; mother – baby couples 68–9, 85; mourning of 80, 88; of therapist 70
unconscious partner choice 32, 82, 114, 145
unconscious phantasies 62, 64–5, 66, 114, 187–8; shared 6, 32, 64, 65, 114, 210

vasopressin 195
Vincent, C. 21

Waddell, M. 231
war victims 2
Winnicott, D.W. 3, 13, 14, 24, 53, 88, 114, 207, 225, 250; false self 20; mirroring 194, 195, 205, 206, 208–9

Wright, K. 200

Yeoman, F. 207

Zinner, J. 77

Taylor & Francis eBooks

Helping you to choose the right eBooks for your Library

Add Routledge titles to your library's digital collection today. Taylor and Francis ebooks contains over 50,000 titles in the Humanities, Social Sciences, Behavioural Sciences, Built Environment and Law.

Choose from a range of subject packages or create your own!

Benefits for you
- Free MARC records
- COUNTER-compliant usage statistics
- Flexible purchase and pricing options
- All titles DRM-free.

Benefits for your user
- Off-site, anytime access via Athens or referring URL
- Print or copy pages or chapters
- Full content search
- Bookmark, highlight and annotate text
- Access to thousands of pages of quality research at the click of a button.

REQUEST YOUR FREE INSTITUTIONAL TRIAL TODAY

Free Trials Available
We offer free trials to qualifying academic, corporate and government customers.

eCollections – Choose from over 30 subject eCollections, including:

Archaeology	Language Learning
Architecture	Law
Asian Studies	Literature
Business & Management	Media & Communication
Classical Studies	Middle East Studies
Construction	Music
Creative & Media Arts	Philosophy
Criminology & Criminal Justice	Planning
Economics	Politics
Education	Psychology & Mental Health
Energy	Religion
Engineering	Security
English Language & Linguistics	Social Work
Environment & Sustainability	Sociology
Geography	Sport
Health Studies	Theatre & Performance
History	Tourism, Hospitality & Events

For more information, pricing enquiries or to order a free trial, please contact your local sales team:
www.tandfebooks.com/page/sales

Routledge
Taylor & Francis Group

The home of Routledge books

www.tandfebooks.com